T0302488

Religion and the Public Conscience

Ecumenical Civil Rights Work in Seattle 1940-1960

Randi Jones Walker

Circle Books

Winchester, UK
Washington, USA

First published by Circle Books, 2012
Circle Books is an imprint of John Hunt Publishing Ltd., Laurel House, Station Approach,
Alresford, Hants, SO24 9JH, UK
office1@o-books.net
www.o-books.com

For distributor details and how to order please visit the 'Ordering' section on our website.

Text copyright: Randi Jones Walker 2010

ISBN: 978 1 78099 081 1

All rights reserved. Except for brief quotations in critical articles or reviews, no part of this book may be reproduced in any manner without prior written permission from the publishers.

The rights of Randi Jones Walker as author have been asserted in accordance with the Copyright, Designs and Patents Act 1988.

A CIP catalogue record for this book is available from the British Library.

Design: Stuart Davies

Printed in the USA by Edwards Brothers Malloy

We operate a distinctive and ethical publishing philosophy in all areas of our business, from our global network of authors to production and worldwide distribution.

CONTENTS

Preface

This book grows out of a long struggle with the question of why the mainline Protestant churches in the United States have such a long history of stated commitment to racial justice and yet find it so hard to influence public opinion and policy in support of that commitment. I have struggled especially with how this history unfolds in the urban areas of the American West. I chose to work with the city of Seattle, not because it has somehow a better record, or because it is unique in some way, but because there was a particularly interesting group of people, the Christian Friends for Racial Equality, mostly lay people, and mostly women who managed to become a well known organization in their community and whose story illuminates some of the characteristics of the civil rights struggle in their era. They openly proposed to shape a public conscience in the city of Seattle toward racial equality. They struck me with the boldness of this proposal and the confidence with which they undertook to shape their community's conscience. Whether they succeeded or not, I very much wanted to find that they had.

Thus, this book is not about a successful crusade for racial equality, nor about a city with a well-developed public conscience about racial justice. I am still on the lookout for such a city with such a conscience and for the story of a completely successful crusade for racial equality. This is rather the local and particular story of a racially-mixed, religiously and culturally diverse group of people who once again attempted, according to their wisdom, to apply the Christian gospel to one of the most difficult problems of our society and respond to the cry for racial equality, and who did manage to achieve some success despite all the structural barriers in their way. This is the story of what people with an engaged spirituality can do over two decades of sustained, patient and persistent effort to change a local community.

Their success is ambiguous. These ambiguities make the story important. If we are to understand the civil rights movement in the United States over the long haul and if we are to understand the role of Christian churches in that movement, we need to look at those local groups who achieved partial success. What they left undone others have to finish. I also want to speak as a white woman and as an insider, a member of a Protestant Christian denomination that is proud of its record on racial justice, but troubled by how little difference it sometimes seems to have made. My hope is that by telling this story, we and others like and unlike us, may come to understand why this is so. The story is also important because the struggle for racial justice is one that every generation must inherit unfinished from another. The Christian Friends for Racial Equality set the stage for the generation of the 1960s. My thesis is that the public conscience they tried to achieve, though not as strong as they had hoped, helped that younger generation to achieve what they did in Seattle.

Many people assisted and encouraged me in the work on this project. I am grateful for my many diverse friends from my youth until the present day who helped me understand the difference among people's experience in this country as structures and systems based on race color our lives in the world and our dealings with one another. I am particularly grateful for colleagues who listened to me as I explained what I was doing and thought this project was worth pursuing. They include Graduate Theological Union Colleagues Eldon Ernst, and Archie Smith Jr. who both grew up in Seattle during the period I am considering and gave me valuable insight into their experience of that environment; other Pacific School of Religion colleagues Boyung Lee, Fumitaka Matsuoka, Del Brown, Mary Donovan Turner Mary Tolbert, and Marquita Chamblee; and colleagues from around the country, especially Laurie Maffley-Kipp, Joanne Braxton, Sharon Thornton, Rudy Busto, Barbara Brown Zikmund and Larry Murphy, and Rev. Gayle Dickson. Many of them read parts or all of the manuscript or an earlier paper on the subject and helped me to understand many things.

I am particularly grateful for the conversations with my publisher, Timothy Staveteig, of Circle Books, whose knowledge of what makes a book readable has been indispensible to me.

The librarians and archivists of many libraries have helped me in this project. The staff at the University of Washington Library, Special Collections department showed the way to several important pieces of information; the librarians at the Seattle Room of the Seattle Public Library were equally helpful. I am also grateful to the staff of the Presbyterian Historical Society where the Federal Council of Churches archives are located, my friend Peggy Bendroth at the Congregational Library, the Hoover Institute Library at Stanford University and the reference librarians at my home library at the Graduate Theological Union, particularly Kris Veldheer and Lucinda Glen. I thank the Congregational Library for a travel stipend to visit their collection and Pacific School of Religion for a sabbatical year in 2005-2006 in which I did most of the research, and a writing leave in the spring of 2010 in which I could complete most of the manuscript. Pacific School of Religion has been exceedingly generous with its support of faculty research and writing. Finally, I want to thank Suzanne Jones and Tim Malone for their hospitality and, as always, Jerry my friend and spouse.

Seattle is a complicated city and the issue of race relations is a complicated one. Despite the wise help of all these fine people, I will not claim that I understand either Seattle or its race relations enough to have created a flawless story. The mistakes that turn up in this work are my own.

Introduction

> Rev. Paul Fong, Chinese Baptist Church announced an interracial dinner at the Chinese Baptist Church at 6:30 P. M. June 26th [1942]. This to be a potluck dinner to which all present invited. The Chinese will furnish the tea and the Filipinos the dessert.[1]

With this announcement, Rev. Paul Fong invited the members of the Seattle Council of Churches to one of the first of the Christian Friends for Racial Equality interracial dinners. The setting was the Chinese Baptist Church social hall. The church is located in the Jackson Street neighborhood, one of the most diverse communities in Seattle. While the size of the group gathered that evening is not known, we know that a month before, seventeen people had gathered to officially form the organization after informal conversations and meetings starting as early as 1939. It was a diverse group representing at least four racial or cultural groups, Chinese, Black, White, and Filipino. Conspicuously absent were the Japanese who had been part of the initial conversations leading to the formation of this ecumenical civil rights organization.[2] The meeting was advertized by such announcements as Rev Fong made to the Council of Churches and by articles in local newspapers and the group eventually claimed seven hundred members. One can imagine the variety of food people from more than four ethnic groups might have brought to such a gathering. Drinking Chinese tea would have been novel for many people. Perhaps the Filipino dessert was sweet rice with ginger or coconut, or flan, or fried bananas with brown sugar. At this potluck, there was no particular entertainment. In years to come there would be folk dancing, sing-along sessions, lectures, or international music. Through the end of the 1950s, the CFRE social gatherings, teas, dinners, concerts and picnics were a regular and popular feature of their civil rights work. They believed that acquaintance led to relationships and fostered racial equality and justice.[3]

In May 1942, the group of seventeen church people mentioned above, representing four races, gathered in the Seattle home of Mrs. Edith Steinmetz because they were disturbed by the lack of coherence between the ideals of equality and freedom proclaimed by their church and country and the actual experience of people of color they knew. They decided that they, as church people, should be doing something about it. Over the next twenty years, they embarked upon a project of creating a public conscience in the city of Seattle. They called themselves the Christian Friends for Racial Equality.

They took a two-pronged approach. Fundamentally, they believed that society could achieve lasting justice only when people were acquainted with each other as human beings, so they organized well-attended social events, concerts, international dinners, picnics, and teas. However, it was in getting to know each other that they discovered the specific circumstances that caused their neighbors to suffer. They could not wait for relationships alone to create changes in these circumstances, so they also began to address the issues that came to their attention. In both ways, they strove to create both a just social structure in Seattle and the personal acquaintance across racial lines that would make it last.

In the same period, the Seattle Council of Churches and Christian Education formed a Race Relations Department, following the model of the Federal Council of Churches. This representative body of member churches in the Seattle area undertook a similar project of creating a public conscience in the city that would feel distinctly uncomfortable in the presence of racial injustice. Their approach also had two main directions, one through lines of communication with the city government to influence public policy decisions and the other through the churches to foster educational efforts and cooperative action in certain cases. The celebration of Race Relations Sunday in the winter of every year was one example. There was significant overlapping in membership between the two groups, especially among the clergy.

The members of both of these groups worked as religious people in one of the most secularized regions in the United States, one facing rapid social change as a result of the impending Second World War and rapidly adopting Jim Crow social practices imported from other parts of the country. Many of the members of the CFRE began their work as retired people. The Progressive Republican political movements of the early twentieth century and the Social Gospel movement as well as liberal religious and political trends that emerged before the First World War and the Great Depression had influenced them. In turn, they severely challenged these same movements. In contrast to the other civil rights organizations in Seattle, they were primarily women; most of their leadership was female and they were mostly lay people in their churches. While the CFRE had clergy members, and these mostly male, the members of the Seattle Council of Churches were primarily clergy, and except for the Christian Education department, they were mostly male. The Council of Churches represented an international ecumenical movement, and fostered in the local congregations of Seattle patterns of Christian life and thought developed in national and international settings. The Federal Council of Churches exercised its influence in society through the work of local councils of churches with their member congregations. The CFRE, on the other hand, developed its programs on the ground in Seattle. Like the CFRE, the generation of people who had begun their working careers at the turn of the century and were often identified with what later historians term the Progressive Republican political tradition and the Social Gospel branch of liberal theology significantly influenced the Council of Churches during this period.

In the Sixties, though some began to regard the methods of both groups as simplistic, even quaint, it would be a mistake to underestimate them. They pioneered in addressing almost every major concern of their time, though other groups may have carried more weight. If one looks only at the Christian Friends for Racial Equality, they proved to be of little significance in the end and they came to an ambiguous end, as many of the aging major players in the CFRE could no longer participate. The church representatives to the Council of Churches changed from time to time and thus altered the agenda of the larger group. If one considers the fact that almost all of the members in both groups were also active in other civil rights organizations, their significance becomes clearer. Precisely because they were concerned to form relationships across racial lines, especially in the CFRE, they served as a networking nodal point within Seattle. They did not naively think that friendships alone would address structural injustices. Nevertheless, they found relationships with each other to be fruitful and sustaining. They pursued projects of economic, political and social justice through CORE, the Urban League, the Civic Unity Committee, the YMCA and YWCA, the NAACP, various ethnic advocacy organizations, and political parties.

In particular, they exhibited an engaged Christian spirituality. Their methods were deeply rooted in their reading of the Christian scriptures and the Hebrew prophets. They were painfully aware of the inability of most American Christians to apply their faith to the problem of racial injustice. They sought to reframe the general understanding of Christianity to emphasize the potential within the Christian religion to support justice. The goal of their engaged Christian spirituality was to create in human society the "Beloved Community"[4] that they considered to be that community which fosters the well-being of all its members. Similarly, in Christian tradition, the "Kingdom of God" was a more common term in this period. The means by which an engaged spirituality fosters the Beloved Community is through the development of a public conscience. Where Christianity is present, but is not the majority tradition, Christians may cooperate with people of other religious traditions in a shared effort to shape a public conscience, not founded on specific Christian theological principles, but on more widely shared moral teachings.

I. Religion and Public Conscience in a Secular Society

Fifty years ago most historians would not have felt the need to argue that religion plays an important role in shaping public conscience in society whether that historian thought such a role was helpful or not. Nonetheless, there was evidence even then that what passed for a religious conscience was not always as effective as its rhetoric might suggest. In 1965 Ralph Moellering, a professor of oriental languages at the University of California in Berkeley noted that religious people picket Woolworths in Berkeley where it did not practice segregation because of its practice of segregation in other places, but then attend segregated churches in Berkeley on Sunday morning.[5] Since then, the experience of rapid global social change has shifted the public understanding of both religion and conscience and the task of the historian becomes more complicated. Across the world, modernity has called into question traditional ways of life and thought and the accompanying social and economic developments affect almost all human beings. In particular modern people question religions of all kinds, though seldom their own, and have diverse understandings of what religion is or should be.

People in the twenty-first century continue to hold conflicting opinions about the continued relevance of religion for public life. Since the Enlightenment, the conflict between human reason and religious revelation or experience has grown. Human reason has proved to be highly effective in solving practical problems.

Human societies increasingly have considered traditional religious terms less helpful in describing the nature and grounding of truth about nature. Religious claims have not entirely disappeared. Instead, they remain important in conversations about the meaning of human life and the way we should live together across lines of difference. The Pacific Northwest regional culture is arguably the most clearly divided about the relevance of religion for deciding matters of social and public policy. The black churches were heavily engaged in efforts to change policies that discriminated against racial minorities, whereas the other mainline churches were inclined to separate religious and public life, though a few were know for their work for social justice. The region is historically the least religiously affiliated population in the United States. On the other hand, the religiously affiliated people in the area are more likely to be deeply committed to religious organizations, beliefs and to participate in public life out of those religious commitments.[6] This is particularly true of the mainline Protestants, Roman Catholics, and Reformed and Conservative Jews. Patricia O'Connor Killen argues that if we can identify a religious establishment at all in the Pacific Northwest, this cluster of groups would be it. "They have been most influential when able to offer a compelling vision of the public good characterized by tolerance, fair play, and social responsibility toward the less fortunate that resonated with the general population."[7] In other words, they have participated successfully in shaping a public conscience.

Many people these days dismiss religion all together as being important in public life. They may recognize some forms of it are hurtful; they may regard it as irrelevant; or they do not know enough about it to make it a factor in their thinking about the world. Others stake their understanding of the world and themselves on religious ground; sometimes they are willing to engage a more secular view in conversation. Sometimes they see such secular arguments as false, even sacrilegious, to be denied or avoided. Many hold much more ambiguous views and spend little time worrying about the implicit contradictions in their thought. They still live out what they fundamentally believe to be true, even if they avoid recognizing the role of their beliefs in the consequences of their lives.

Particular societies sort out these competing claims as their members work consciously or unconsciously to shape life collectively to their advantage. Reason and religion are often, but not necessarily at odds. Many aspects of community life shape conscience and, in Chapter 2, we will expand on these. Strong molding forces shape it through unconscious means rooted in family life and early experiences of the community outside ones home, which may include religious teaching, and experience. This book seeks to explore the relationship of community, conscience, and social practice and to understand what role religion, more specifically Christianity, plays in this relationship, by means of a study of some particular people in a specific context of place and time.

A. Religion in American Society in the 21st century

Sometimes considering two specific cases is helpful in order to see the broader picture more clearly. I propose to look at an example from American society, from the northwestern United States, from the city of Seattle. These cases, the Christian Friends for Racial Equality and the Seattle Council of Churches, illustrate several important things about the continued relationship between religion and public life, despite the ambiguous place religion already held in Seattle society before World War II and the understandably limited understanding of these two organizations. They do not stand for American religion and society in general, but by looking at these particular cases, we have a window into the larger society. I have deliberately chosen to focus on the larger context of the Pacific Northwest as the "None

Zone"[8] because the religious effort to shape the public conscience stands out in greater relief. Before further introducing the cases and the underlying story, I would like to clarify some terms and concepts that historians of religions use to talk about their interests and which I use in this account.

I. Religion and/or Spirituality

People have innumerable ways to define religion, but in order to be clear about what I am talking about here, I mean generally systems of belief and practice, sets of symbols and ritual interaction within which a community understands itself meaningfully within the world, tries to make sense of life and death and encourages particular ways of life for its individual members, and which leads the community to flourish. Religion may also seek the flourishing of the world. A religion often bases its practice in a belief about divine or transcendent tangible reality, a concept of deity, but not necessarily. A religion usually has both individual aspects and communal or institutional expressions. In this work, I primarily discuss Christianity. In Seattle, many other religions were present, formed the primary frames of reference for many people, and are thus part of the story. For instance, there were at least 14,000 Jews, at least 200 Japanese Buddhists and around 45 Baha'is in Seattle by the end of the 1930s compared to around 85,000 Christians.[9] Since there were almost 400,000 people in Seattle by this period, we see that a large number of them did not report affiliation with any organized religious body. Already in this period, many people in Seattle did not regard any religion as a primary frame of reference. Instead, they lived without active participation in a religious community and often without any religious belief, though they found life meaningful and had a moral sense. Many of these unaffiliated people would say, to use a widely current phrase in the early 21st century, they were "spiritual but not religious."[10] There were in addition groups related to social movements such as that of

Marcus Garvey which had religious beliefs and ethics.

Not only were there multiple religious options in Seattle in the period of the twentieth century, but they changed over the course of the twentieth century. Spirituality is not a term the people of Seattle would have used in the 1940s; they would have associated it with the National Spiritual Association, a small spiritualist congregation of about a hundred people, or perhaps an even smaller group of Progressive Spiritualists, both on the margins of Seattle religious life. As the population grew in the 1940s and 50s population shifted and several religious organizations moved from one location to another following their members' movements. Their spirituality shifted too, as the options for daily life changed with the introduction of radio, telephones, automobiles and television. Radio and television were particularly popular media for making religious expression widely available at any time of the day or night. In fact, many clergy worried that these innovations, along with the automobile, which allowed people to travel cheaply and easily for the weekend, would make people stop attending church on Sunday. It gave them more options, and churches increasingly had to compete for people's attention with other attractive social venues. The Seattle World's Fair in the 1960s brought Seattle to the world's attention and served as a motivation for another influx of new people, often interested in the natural environment, but perhaps less aware of the historically layered human environment around them. These cultural shifts would inevitably reshape the spirituality of many people.

Many of those who study spirituality as a religious phenomenon define spirituality as does Joseph Driskill, a scholar specializing in the study of Protestant spiritual life. "Spirituality is concerned with the lived experience of faith, the communities which shape it, the practices which sustain it, and the moral life which embodies it. Such spirituality works to discern the action of God's transforming love in the intra-psychic, interpersonal, structural and environmental realms of life."[11] Spirituality is a practice or set of practices rather than a theology or an institution, but the institutions, beliefs, including rituals and symbolic representations of interpersonal relationships social organizations and communities, of a particular religion foster spirituality, as does the larger environment in which those communities exist. By this definition, few people could be spiritual without also in some sense being religious. Spirituality then, for those who use the common phrase "spiritual but not religious", may be something that can be separable from what they mean by religion, or individual symbols, practices, or rituals separated from the larger context that produced them and used for another purpose. In contrast, they could mean some inner individual experience they interpret as religious without reference to any specific religion. By "spirituality," historian Mark Shibley argues that they mean "direct, personal experience with the sacred," in contrast to "religion" or "mediated, institutionalized experience with the sacred."[12] Religion, in this more common view, seems to connote organization, institution, and probably an enforced orthodoxy. Spirituality, in this view, is more private, spontaneous and open to the individual's interpretation or creative insight. Seattle had and has many people who have spirituality, but have deliberately disconnected themselves from any particular religion.[13] Certainly spirituality exists within organized religion as well, and those connections often enhance it. The CFRE and the Council of Churches attracted people who thought organized religion was important and that was their means of expressing their spirituality. In addition, they wanted their spiritual practice to have an influence in the world for the good. Though spirituality is a more recent term scholars use to look at religion in a particular way, it is useful for our consideration here, because I believe what the CFRE and the Council of Churches promoted was an engaged spirituality, a spirituality that concerns itself with the relationship of religion and social structures in society.

The concept of religion is also constrained by community; the individual religious adherent belongs to the community and therefore conforms to its practice and beliefs. Spirituality, as practiced by those who may choose not to be religious, thus can be free from institutional responsibilities, though the practitioner might share these practices or beliefs with friends or with members of an organized religion in an informal way. In exploring the case of these particular groups of Christians in Seattle as an influence in developing a public conscience, I will treat Christianity as a religion made up of organized communities and institutions growing out of particular beliefs and practices. This is also spirituality in both senses I have discussed it here, as the lived expression of the Christian faith, but also as the inspiration for individual practice regardless of the person's formal relationship with any organized Christian community or church.

2. The Persistence of Religion in a Spiritual "None Zone"

The number of religiously affiliated people in Seattle is difficult to compare from one decade to another because the data available was not consistently gathered. From the 1930s to 1960, religious affiliation was about 30% of the total population, slightly less than average for the United States during that period. From 1960 to the present, the percentage of religiously affiliated people has declined sharply.[14] In spite of the increasing secularization of Seattle society in the late twentieth century, and its location in one of the areas where people are least affiliated with organized religion, a wide variety of churches, synagogues, temples, and other religious institutions persist and many thrive. They persist because besides providing a place for worship and contemplation, they preserve tradition, help people nurture meaningful ways of understanding their lives and foster their spiritual growth, serve people in need, advocate for justice, and build networks and communities of people with similar beliefs and concerns. Very few other institutions in society do these things as well.[15] Religious institutions in the region also tend to maintain a strong religious identity. In a highly secular society, religious participation is much more of a conscious choice than something everyone does and therefore society supports by norms or laws, for instance by closing stores on Sundays. Those who do choose religious affiliation tend to have high commitment to those religious communities.[16] Despite the secularizing trends in American society in the modern period, religious congregations or communities continue to dot the Seattle landscape and influence public life.

Most of the members of the Christian Friends for Racial Equality were also active members of ecumenically minded mainline congregations in the city. Both of the largest African American congregations in Seattle during the 1940s, Mt. Zion Baptist Church and the First African Methodist Episcopal Church, their denominations and the white mainline congregations and denominations were long time members of the Federal Council of Churches and the local Council of Churches. In addition, the mainline Chinese and Japanese Christian congregations, also part of the ecumenical bodies, were part of ethnic networks such as the Japanese American Citizens' League. Work addressing race relations lent itself to collective effort. We will consider the extent of their collaboration in Chapter 3 below.

Christianity in particular encourages the expression of spirituality in community. For the Christian, individual spiritual experience leads in the direction of community, if not in the direction of a traditional denomination. This is because Christianity is a religion founded on the ideal of fostering love of one's neighbors. "You shall love the lord your God with all your heart and with all your soul and with all your mind. . . .You shall love your neighbor as yourself." Jesus is said to have summarized the Jewish teachings in these two principles (found for instance in the Gospel of Matthew 22:37-39 Revised Standard Version).[17]

This principle has fostered a long tradition of attention by the church to the needs of its neighbors. Many urban churches, especially the black churches, had a variety of significant social services for their members and their community.

This ideal of love for neighbor is not always what people experience from Christians, and black Christians were often skeptical about white Christian's ability or commitment to actually live out this spirituality in their dealings with all their neighbors. One of the young people who grew up in the Mt.Zion Baptist Church in Seattle went on to be a seminary professor. He teaches the practice of pastoral ministry of the church in relationship to the social structures that affect the lives of church members. He frames the skepticism in this way:

> My parents were from Mississippi, and my father was a follower of Marcus Garvey, who believed that black people would never be accepted as social equals in this society. The experience of growing up as a black male during the early part of this century confirmed his belief that blacks, as a people, would remain marginal to society. There was, in my father's awareness and experience of racial and class oppression, an existential interest in emancipation, but he could not foresee emancipation emerging for black people within a country that practiced genocide, interned and enslaved people of color.[18]

Those who regard themselves as "spiritual but not religious" often keep a sense of Christian spirituality in experiencing love of God and neighbor, but become disillusioned by the failure of churches or seek to avoid the responsibilities of membership in a community. Sometimes they are unaware of the social work and social justice work of many churches or they want to understand spirituality as something private and personal unrelated to the larger world. Though they were in the minority, Seattle in the mid-twentieth century had a large number of professed Christians, many churches, and the basically Christian ethos of American society. The cases I want to consider, represent efforts by religious people to shape public conscience that would not allow discrimination in housing, employment, schools, health care or any other venue of human interaction. It came out of this mid-twentieth century American ethos shaped deeply by Christianity. From the perspective of a half a century later, after the tumultuous decade of the 1960s in which the CFRE disappeared, the question of their success has bearing on a larger question of the role of religion in modern globalized society.

3. Quest for meaning in a secular society

One of the most persistently valuable things religions at their best offer the world is a structure of meaning within which individuals find a healthy relationship to the world and the community. Religions are not the only social structures that offer meaning and they persistently fall short of their goal. Nonetheless, throughout the history of human societies, religion has given people a way to understand their lives in connection to others, to repair damaged relationships, and thus to foster the flourishing of the community and provided hope in the face of suffering and death. Whether or not a particular religion relies on a divine or transcendent foundation, religion allows the individual to find a meaning for and beyond his or her daily life. In situations of rapid social change, such as in Seattle in the Forties and Fifties, organized religions, like individuals, often succumb to efforts to preserve tradition and social status at the expense of their moral teachings. Wherever Christianity has become an influential or official religious tradition in a particular culture or nation, efforts to preserve theological purity or orthodox practice have contradicted the teachings of the faith about love of neighbor. Defense of the faith has served to justify a number of political and economic projects of expansion and exploitation in history, notably the Crusades of the eleventh and twelfth centuries, the many regulations and expulsions of the Jews, and the European conquest of the Americas.

Christianity has remained a popular religion since its founding because it has several distinctive characteristics (though they are not unique to Christianity). It provides people with a sense of identity within a community that loves them and knows their names. Its theology of incarnation, that the divine became human, allows people both to have a practical understanding of the divine as active in the world, but also to give a sense of holiness to their own lives when they practice the Christian life. The Christian belief in the power of forgiveness and in resurrection following sacrifice on behalf of others, signaled by the death and resurrection of Jesus, has lent enormous courage to individuals seeking to make the world a more just and loving and holy place.[19] Christianity offers conversion from self-centeredness, the teaching of a way of life that creates community, and a body of tradition that helps to preserve the key features of the religion transmitted from generation to generation and culture to culture. That Christians, as individuals and in their institutions, express the meaning they find for their individual and community lives in an effort to shape society according to Christian belief in a variety of ways—this is only part of an age-old pattern. Modernity has presented significant new challenges to the popularity and survival of Christianity as well as to other religions.

Some Christians have responded defensively disallowing any modern challenge to their beliefs. Fundamentalism is one result of this effort. A literalist reading of scripture is also necessary for support of racial inequality or slavery and therefore fundamentalist approaches to Christianity often supported segregationist efforts which otherwise contradict the major teachings of both Judaism and Christianity. Some Christians responded to modernity by losing their faith entirely. Some reframed

Christianity in scientific language if not scientific method, such as the Christian Science movements or the Spiritualists. Both of these traditions in Seattle were tiny minorities. The truth claims of science and the ineffectiveness of the churches to produce the justice, peace, or beloved community they promised, made being Christian untenable in the modern world. Most of the mainline Christianity in the United States, including mainstream Roman Catholicism made an effort to consider the modern challenges to Christian belief and practice. The churches often adopted practices of modern culture, including the use of electronic media, acceptance of scientific medicine, and appropriation of the governance forms of representative democracy. Theologians, in more liberal branches of Christianity, have also considerably reframed traditional Christian theologies, which are rooted in the philosophical traditions of late antiquity. All but the most fundamentalist Christians in Seattle participated to some degree in the CFRE and the Council of Churches.

The question of the role of Christianity in the culture of the United States at present mirrors the question of the role of religion in current societies across the world. Secularization exists as an alternative religion, without a god, or an anti-religion, and serves the global economy in many ways with certain beliefs, rituals, and ideas about the meaning and purpose of human life. In particular, secularization fosters an individualism that assists in the exploitation of labor and fosters the individual mobility needed to sustain economic growth. Economic realities make it more and more difficult for individuals to participate fully in traditional religions. In addition, science continues to press a worldview critical, if not at odds with, religious worldviews. Ordinary people, whether religious, spiritual, or secular, do not often have access to the discourse among scientists, philosophers and theologians about the nature of truth and the social implications of worldviews or belief or unbelief in some transcendent reality. At the popular level, the rhetoric of competing ideologies drastically oversimplifies the questions. Often religious commitment and ideology look much the same. People blur the distinction between religious commitment and consumer choice. Spirituality easily becomes a commodity bought and sold; churches, synagogues, or temples become corporations, purveyors of religious services. Because spirituality as well as religion connects in this way to the global economic system, the moral position of religious or spiritual people may be corrupted.[20]

If only because religiously committed people still have considerable influence in American public life and in public life across the world, understanding what religious people may be trying to do and why is worthwhile. Anyone who thinks religious commitment is a viable option, may be interested in whether they participate in any advantage by being "religious" in addition to "spiritual." Those who see connections between the teachings and practice of religion to difficult social issues such as racial justice, poverty, or the deterioration of the environment may well be interested in how religious people have approached these issues in the past and with what results. Despite its difficulty and ambiguous results, I will argue that the project of creating a public conscience is a viable one. I hope that this Seattle story can offer wisdom and companionship for those still attempting to create a more just world, and a reminder that it is not easy or simple, and no generation has entirely succeeded.

B. Public Conscience as a Religious Phenomenon

The primary phenomenon under consideration in this book is that of a public conscience. In the Chapter 1, I will give a more complex and critical discussion of the concept. Christian participation in efforts to achieve racial justice in the pre- World War II period were shaped by an assumption that the public could be said to have a conscience and that religious institutions were the primary means of shaping that conscience. Regardless of what one thinks about the appropriate relationship of church and state, Christian people in the United States tend to assume they and their religious tradition had a role to play in shaping the way society as a whole understands right-wrong and what is good. For people to believe and even preach that racial injustice is wrong is one thing. For them to recognize it when they see it and act according to their belief is quite another. The CFRE wanted to move the conscience of people from acknowledgment of wrong to active work toward justice.

The United States was a religiously diverse country even at this period, and the West Coast region was even more religiously diverse than other areas. Within this growing diversity, the majority of the population remained Christian. Though the culture of the country reflected a long steeping in Protestantism thought, by the twentieth century, the largest single group in much of the United States was the Roman Catholic Church.[21] A loose collection of moral teachings (e. g. tell the truth, respect your neighbor, and do not murder), derived explicitly from Christianity and Judaism and which were also familiar in most religious traditions, formed a basic common denominator of ethical principles taught in public school and voiced by public officials.[22] Students of American civil religion have pointed out the role of public schools in addition to religious organizations in conveying these principles to the American public. Charles Long, an African American scholar who has considered the problem of civil religion pointed out that the tendency to frame the United States heroically serves to make people of color invisible, and allows white Americans to forget the disparity between actual American behavior toward racial minorities, particularly African Americans, and the religious aura surrounding the ideal of equality and freedom.[23] In Seattle, as we will see, there were controversies over who could authentically represent the heroes of American history and who was an appropriate worker for a particular job. Black soldiers might be fighting in World War II, but the U. S. Army kept them separate from their white compatriots. In Seattle, they had to go to a separate beach to enjoy the scenery of Puget Sound. The disparity of belief and behavior was the issue at stake in the founding of the Christian Friends for Racial Equality.

1. Judeo/Christian Senses of Public Conscience

The Judeo Christian religious traditions understand the public conscience as more than knowing, as individuals, what ought to be right and wrong. Individual conscience recognizes right and wrong. Parents teach their children to recognize what they believe or wish to believe to be right and wrong. This sense, developed by thought and practice, becomes an internal sense of right and wrong that asserts itself, even subconsciously, to urge us in the direction of what we think is the right and good. It troubles us when we move in the direction of what we were taught is wrong. In some Judeo-Christian theologies, this conscience or sense is not understood to be something a person achieves alone, but is an aspect of divine activity within the individual of faith; so with the public conscience. A whole community may have a sense of what it commonly believes to be right and wrong, developed by individual and collective effort, and passed on generation to generation by tradition and social structure. This is particularly true of the black churches and other black civil rights movements. It arouses a public reaction of opposition, often strong enough to prevent or overrule the action when the community moves in a direction the public conscience considers the wrong way. Religious people of some traditions may argue that this is also something the community cannot achieve without divine activity. No matter how one understands conscience to be related to the divine, in those moments in history that exhibit the working of a public conscience, sadly many of them are manifestations of community regret after something has already happened that violates this public conscience, for instance the expressions of community regret and promises of change in the aftermath of the civil unrest of 1967, which though it touched Seattle somewhat more lightly than other cities in the United States, nonetheless suddenly illuminated unjust patterns of economic and social life that had caused frustration in the black community for a long time.[24]

The Judeo-Christian tradition (by far the most influential in the United States) makes provision for a public conscience. Jewish histories, contained in the Hebrew Scriptures, describe the relationship of the Hebrew people with their God as a covenant. The covenant between God and the people was a public commitment of the whole people by virtue of their birth, not that of a collection of individuals who happen to have made the same choices. Fundamental principles of justice, relationships among family members and within the community, and more relevant to our story, relationships with strangers, outsiders, and the poor, were spelled out in the covenant relationship between God and the Hebrew people.

These two religions took different directions after the Romans destroyed the Jewish temple in Jerusalem in the early years of the Common Era. The destruction of the central focus of Jewish worship required a radical change in the expression of the covenant. Synagogue-based Judaism retained most of the traditional covenant requirements that did not directly relate to temple sacrifices. Christianity tended to be less specific about the details of covenant requirements, but emphasized two of them; regarding love for ones neighbor, and treating others as you would like to be treated yourself as most essential for keeping the covenant with God. Christianity also made it much easier for those outside the Jewish community to enter into the covenant. The Christian community, like the Jewish community is a body of people who believe God called them together or, depending on their specific theological tradition, may believe they have themselves chosen a particular faith. Consequently, regardless of how an individual comes to convert to one of these religions, it is often through incorporation into a community. The collective expression of individual religious conscience contributes to the formation of a public conscience within the larger community. The Christian and Jewish understandings of the public conscience both influence American society. This understanding shows the influence of Puritan forbears, who developed some of their political forms from the idea of covenant between deity and people earlier developed within Judaism.[25] The Puritans in particular considered the obligation to act justly as central to the enjoyment of liberty.[26] The history of the Puritan effort to establish their particular interpretation of Christianity in the British colonies reveals their sense of the role of the church as an organized religious institution which fosters both the effort to shape social practice and the closely related temptation to use religious influence to solidify the social status of its own faith.

The conscience of the minority Christian communities, particularly those that suffer from racism, deals with the historical memory, framed as a community of memory and relationship with ancestors gone before, what Archie Smith Jr. calls "a sense of *anamnestic solidarity*." He defines this as "a conscious identification with the cause of freedom forged by the innocent and oppressed victims of past injustices who have been destroyed by their oppressors, but who are nevertheless remembered in the praxis of the survivors in the community of the oppressed."[27] The black community as well as the Jewish, Chinese, Filipino and Japanese communities in Seattle participated in this solidarity of memory with those in their communities who had gone before them. The white people might occasionally enter this solidarity if they were willing not to forget what had happened to others.

In Seattle, another form of conscience was in play in public life stemming from the religious traditions of Asian and Pacific Islander immigrants. In these cases, conscience closely links with the practice of religion, including living according to a moral code with roots in that religious tradition. The ability of organized forms of Christianity, the congregation (First Presbyterian Church or Mt. Zion Baptist Church) or ecumenical collaboration (the Council of Churches, The National Conference of Christians and Jews, or the CFRE) to influence social practice in the city is clear, whether or not we regard their efforts to create a particular public conscience over the long term to be successful.

C. Public Conscience and "Engaged Spirituality"

The development of this kind of public conscience is an example of an "engaged spirituality."[28] My colleague Joseph Driskill argues that understanding this is necessary for understanding the nature of Christian life. This is not the spirituality of private prayer or even public worship, but rather the expression of Christian belief by one's manner of life or action in the world. The Christian person's engagement with the complex problems of society while attempting to follow the way of life outlined in the Christian Gospels is not always easy to trace and will differ widely depending on the denomination, culture, and the complicated web of social relationships to which the person belongs. Sometimes people focus such engagement on a single social problem. Historical examples include the Christian Anti-Slavery movements, the conscientious objector to wartime military service, or the efforts of the late twentieth-century Christian Right to influence laws regarding abortion. In Seattle, examples include the Council of Churches opposition to the Japanese Internment and their support of the Fair Employment Practices Act and the Open Housing movement. More often conscience is subtly located in a person's general approach to life rather than conspicuous advocacy of a particular cause, and the question of how such personal conscience comes to be articulated so as to influence public and social policies is something with which the CFRE and the social justice advocates in the Council of Churches struggled.

Both the Seattle Council of Churches and the Christian Friends for Racial Equality were practicing an engaged spirituality, as it was generally understood in American mainline Protestant Christianity. Their personal conscience, their sense of right and wrong, related to their spirituality through certain theological ideas or symbolic understandings of Christianity: the Kingdom of God, the Good Samaritan, or the portrayal in the Prophets of a just society. The members of both organizations understood their practice of Christianity to require certain kinds of public practice. *The Racial Equality Bulletin* aimed to shape a public conscience out of the engaged spirituality of the individual members of the CFRE. The CFRE pointed to the "Golden Rule," "Do unto others as you would have them do unto you,"[29] as one requiring the effort to shape a more racially inclusive and just society. *The Racial Equality Bulletin* regularly reprinted this rule of life in terms of several religious traditions.

> From Confucius: "What you do not want done to yourself, do not do it to others."
> From the Hindu: "Men gifted with intelligence . . . should always treat others as they themselves wish to be treated."
> From Zoroastrianism: "Do as you would be done by."
> From Islam: "No one of you is a believer until he loves for his brother what he loves for himself."
> From Christianity: "All things whatsoever ye would that we should do to you, do even so unto them."
> From Judaism: "Whatever you do not wish your neighbor to do to you, do not do unto him."[30]

The problem was that not many people, particular people of privilege, recognized the person of another race as a neighbor. Most people had heard of "the Golden Rule," in church or in school as well as in their families, that their treatment of people unlike themselves whether understood as good manners or business policy, or understood religiously in terms of what is necessary for salvation, was something good for society. Too many young people did not see their elders practice it; it was an ideal but not a practical reality. The CFRE articulated this rule as their basis of action, proposing that society actually live by it.

The Seattle Council of Churches understood itself as having a responsibility to provide a public Christian voice on the issues facing the people of Seattle.[31] Among other things; this entailed an engagement with issues of racial justice. The Council of Churches and the CFRE did not speak for all the Christians of Seattle. Certain churches were notably absent from both organizations, the Russian Orthodox, the Latter Day Saints and some independent Protestant churches were not inclined to participate in ecumenical activities or were excluded from them. Some Pentecostal congregations such as the Church of God in Christ, more conservative or fundamentalist churches and some mainline Protestant congregations often believed that the church should refrain from comment on political issues even if the majority of their members might be supportive of the issue at stake. Occasionally the Church of God in Christ, an African American Pentecostal denomination, and a congregation of the Reorganized Latter Day Saints participated in CFRE activities.

1. Relationship of Engaged Spirituality to Economy

The relationship of Christian spirituality to community life could thus be controversial in itself. One reason for the controversy was that such engaged spirituality was often effective. To the degree that most Americans practiced the "worship" of more than one thing of importance to them, if one object of worship called into question another equally important to them, an explicitly engaged spiritual practice would be difficult to manage.

The difficult moments in the efforts of the CFRE to encourage the integration of public accommodations and housing in Seattle will illustrate such conflicts of engaged spiritualities. Segregation often expressly gave worth to (or worshiped) a middle-class lifestyle for which high real estate values necessary. Integration expressly gave worth to racial equality, or, to put it religiously, worshiped a deity who regards all people equally. Where a person conscientiously tried to hold both values of middle class lifestyle and racial equality, to express both forms of worth giving at the same time, the contradiction in values was often painful.[32]

2. Twentieth Century Struggle for Racial Justice as Engaged Spirituality

Believing they should foster the Beloved Community, Christians and Jews, Buddhists, Confucians and Muslims, and many who did not affiliate with any particular religious tradition, have generally regarded justice as a value. The ongoing difference between the articulated value of justice and the entrenched nature of racial segregation and injustice is a problem for all of these traditions. Though many religious traditions contained accounts of the divisions of the human race in their sacred histories, and many cultures regarded themselves as a race favored by deity or by fortune, most also taught that ideally justice was an important practice for human society to flourish. The modern development of concepts of race and the prejudices that developed in each culture over time often acted against these ideals of justice. Religious self-perceptions of divine favor and disfavor supported these prejudices. In Seattle, as in the rest of the nation, the outcome of a long period of modern development left white people with privilege, power and wealth by virtue of their racial identity, which many interpreted as signs of God's favor, and this created enormous differences in economic and educational opportunity between those available to white people and those available to people of color.

Integration as a solution to the problem of social injustice was almost always an ambiguous case because the possibility of social interchange leading to intermarriage and family-making was still, in the mid-twentieth century, the most difficult aspect of integration for most people to accept. Hence, the kind of racial justice advocated by the Christian Friends for Racial Equality and by the Council of Churches, which involved direct social interaction among people of different races, was difficult to achieve. From a post-sixties perspective it seems that their emphasis on social equality was not getting to the structural heart of the problems faced by racial minority communities, but from their perspective, social injustice was the root of the problem and they believed social equality was necessary to produce structural change.

For those Christians and other religious people who engaged in this practice of social equality, it was an expression of their spirituality, and engaged living out of what they understood to be the central teachings of their faith. This engaged spirituality was not just lip service, but attempting to put their bodies where they said their beliefs were. Along with other civil rights organizations in Seattle, the CFRE and the Council of Churches formed a network of relationships from which they were able to begin to engage the political and economic structures that prevented racial equality from being a reality. The specific shape and working of this network is the subject of Chapter 3. Those who engage in this kind of spirituality have always been up against great odds. This pre-war generation found the structures to be too strong for them to accomplish all they intended. Even the following generations through the 1960s and 70s and beyond have not been able to dismantle and rebuild these social and economic structures into a more equitable framework. These generational struggles and differences are the subject of Chapter 4. The sense of a religious cause lingers around present efforts to achieve racial justice. I argue that this religious aura has its origins in the engaged spirituality of our forbears in the struggle.

3. Explicitly Christian examples of this effort framed as spiritual practice

Christianity is not the only religious tradition engaged in the quest for racial justice, but is the one represented most strongly in these case studies. Through the twentieth century, religious aspects of the civil rights movement garnered from Christianity are some of its most familiar characteristics: the processions, marches on Washington, pilgrimages to Selma and Sacramento; the practice of non-violent resistance in sit-ins, vigils, and other acts of civil disobedience to laws that supported racial injustice; and the conversion experiences people had in the presence of prophetic preaching from the saints of the movements sometimes speaking, like the apostle Paul, from prison.

The Seattle Council of Churches understood itself as acting in a long line of ecumenical councils in the history of Christianity to speak to the churches and to the greater society with a united Christian voice for what they argued God required. The Christian Friends for Racial Equality developed their projects based on their understanding of a particular way of life taught in the Christian Gospels. Eating together with people of different backgrounds, races, and cultures was a hallmark of early Christianity. Christian community grew from the commitment to be friends with strangers and to eat with those society had marginalized. The CFRE followed a biblical method in their engagement with political and economic structures where racial discrimination was present as outlined in the Christian scriptures in the Gospel of Matthew 18:15-17.[33] They first engaged in direct conversation with people concerned, and if that did not work, they made the problem public and they were not afraid to create embarrassment if it would lead to a change of heart and more importantly a change of policy. This book explores this practice of engaged spirituality in the project of shaping a public conscience in the city of Seattle. In the end it should illuminate the role religion did and does play in the effort to build racial justice in a diverse community. The particular spirituality I see at work in these two ecumenical religious organizations is one that understands the relationship between God and an individual person to be experienced primarily in the effort to love ones neighbor or to treat one's neighbor as one wants to be treated. The rituals involved are rituals of relationship, eating together, working together, and creating friendship across racial lines in a society suspicious of such inter-racial friendship and fellowship. This spirituality is engaged with the neighbor and does not exist without that engagement. For the members of the Christian Friends for Racial Equality, God was present where such engagement was present. They were not inclined to advocate a purely private practice of religious sensibility, finding a private relationship with God that did not require a relationship with the neighbor to be a misunderstanding of the Judeo-Christian faith.

II. Attention to Religion in the History of Civil Rights

Religion plays a prominent role in the history of Civil Rights movements in the United States. Many of the main characters in the story were religious leaders; most acted out of some kind of religious commitment. Historians sometimes regard religion as a problem. Accounts of the life and work of A. Phillip Randolph are a case in point.[34] Many historians have assumed that, since he was critical of the role of the churches in the civil rights movements of the early twentieth century that he himself was not religious or was even anti-religious. In fact he had religious commitments and the historian Cynthia Taylor maintains that he acted out of an engaged spirituality from which he challenged the world and also his own faith tradition. White mainline Protestant churches come in for their fair share of critique in the history of the civil Rights movements, and their shortcomings are prominent in the work of major civil rights advocates.[35] This study is an effort to see more clearly the nature of religious, particularly Protestant Christian engagement with racial justice issues, to look beyond the official denominational statements of policy to what ordinary people in the churches were doing. Denominations often made policy pronouncements in favor of racial justice, but the difference between official policy and local practice could be enormous. On the other hand the radical inclusiveness or advocacy activity of some local congregations directly challenged more conservative denominational practice.[36] In some cases, such as the Pacific Coast examples of Rev. Fred Shorter of the People's Church in Seattle and Rev. Howard Thurman of the Church of all Peoples in San Francisco, individual pastors, discouraged with the reluctance of their denomination to work toward their own ideals, left and started their own churches independent of denominational ties.

A. Memory (history) and its Relationship to Conscience

The generation that formed the CFRE and that was active in the Council of Churches in Seattle is now largely a memory. Most of the people involved in these organizations in the 1940s and 50s were in the later years of their careers or retired. Few remain and those who do were very young in these years, seldom playing leading roles.

Historians are just recently beginning to study the 1960s as a historical period. It was an era of worldwide rapid social and economic change. There was enormous optimism about what people could achieve if only they decided to do the right thing. It was also an era of great anxiety about all that seemed to be falling apart.[37] The 1940s and 1950s were a period of outward consensus against a background of international tension and domestic economic and social disparity. The Sixties merely made explicit frustrations that had existed for a long time among racial minorities, women and colonized people around the world.

The 1960s form the background from which this study of the just earlier period emerges. This was a period of rapid social change. A number of important social movements began within a short decade all at the same time, the civil rights movement, the women's movement, movements to end the persecution of gay and lesbian people, movements to end the war in Vietnam, to end hunger and poverty, to preserve the natural environment all converged together. In the backdrop of the Cold War, these movements competed for attention with concerns about education, science, technology, military power, and increasingly complex international systems of global capitalism. The strong sense of conscience which motivated public life in the 1960s, whether one was a liberal or a conservative, whether one was concerned about the Vietnam War, nuclear energy, women's rights or race relations, integrity of conscience was important to people. Though people were leaving organized religion in droves, religion shaped much of the content of their conscience, notably, but not exclusively, by Protestant Christianity. The hero stories[38] of the "long sixties," the period from Brown vs. the Board of Education in the late 1950s to the end of the Vietnam War in 1972, judged people by their character, their ability to be true to their conscience. This sense of integrity of conscience was an integral part of the engaged spirituality practiced by the CFRE. These local Seattle hero stories will emerge in the following chapters.

These memories in turn shaped the conscience of the next generation and provided inspiration. The heroes of the Sixties acted out of a conscience that shaped by the history of their parents. Telling their stories, keeping such memories alive, is important in giving present-day people a continued reason to struggle for racial justice.[39] The process of creating such a conscience through story and memory is not as simple as it seems. The experiences of racial minority people have been excessively painful. The decision to tell one's story to someone of the dominant white race required (and still requires) a spiritual act of forgiveness not always appreciated by white people.[40] Deborah Lee, in her essay "Faith Practices for Racial Healing and

Reconciliation," notes that the seemingly simplistic strategy of building friendship across racial lines and openly telling and listening to each other's stories requires a deep commitment to an engaged spirituality. Lee argues that if one is Christian, one has to let go of social and economic security, or of hatred and anger, in order to reclaim one's belonging to the Beloved Community.[41] By "talking story," we have some hope of coming to know each other and of healing the torn fabric of community.[42]

B. Seattle Memories: Council of Churches and Christian Friends

Late in the 1960s, Seattle people pointed to their memories of efforts by organizations such as the Christian Friends for Racial Equality to explain why Seattle was not as torn by racial violence as other cities.[43] The particularly ecumenical effort of the Christian Friends for Racial Equality and the Seattle Council of Churches Race Relations Department to shape public conscience in Seattle in the pre 1960s era, on the surface, appears hugely successful.

1. What really happened?

This is of course a rhetorical question. Importantly, what the CFRE's own mythology says about the organization differs from its actual influence. Seattle did not experience the same level of violence that tore many other cities in this period. In 1968, the Kerner Commission charged by the President of the United States, to account for why there was so much urban disorder in the spring and summer of 1967, reported that there were eight cities that experienced major disorder (many fires, intensive looting, sniping, violence lasting more than two days and use of national guard), thirty-three that experienced serious disorders (some fires, isolated looting, rock throwing, violence lasting one or two days and use of state police), and over a hundred that experienced some kind of minor disorder (a few fires, broken windows, only a small number of people involved, lasting a day or less, and used only local police). Seattle was among the cities experiencing minor disorders. The city appears only in two footnotes, one placing it with the group of urban areas experiencing minor disorders and the other noting that there were no deaths in the city related to this uprising.[44] The Kerner Commission did not specify what aspects of Seattle's civic life contributed to this, but presumably the entire network of civil rights organizations, including the CFRE, had some influence on the situation. Religious people, particularly Protestant Christians were working early in the century to counter the development of a segregated, prejudiced society. People claiming religious affiliations were and still are a minority in the city of Seattle. In spite of this, evidence of the operation of some kind of conscience about the rightness of racial justice in Seattle is discernable. This study seeks to investigate the relationship of groups such as the CFRE and the Council of Churches who had as their main purpose the creation of such a conscience, and its development and influence in the larger population by means of a difficult calling to interracial community. They worked primarily through a complex network of other civil rights organizations and engaged individuals. Writing about the network has proved to be akin to writing about a tangle of thread or a maze, but the dense overlapping sets of relationships operating in Seattle provided the net under which these activists worked. In the 1980s, the U. S. Commission on Civil Rights issues a report on "The Benefits of Racial and Ethnic Diversity in Elementary and Secondary Education." In this report, they discussed the city of Seattle among other U. S. cities. They found Seattle to be among the least racially isolated cities in the country. This meant that people of all racial groups were more in contact with each other than was the case in other cities. If this high level of inter-racial relationship is an indicator of past work on the problem, then surely the CFRE and the work of the Council of Churches contributed to this success.

2. Saving community

Civil rights work and efforts to achieve racial justice in society are fundamentally efforts to build a particular kind of community.[45] In the United States; such efforts to shape community have often depended upon principles derived from Christianity, whether explicitly or implicitly. The Seattle Council of Churches and the Christian Friends for Racial Equality represent two organized efforts to build such a community based explicitly on Christian ideals. For Christians this project of building community was part of a larger concern for "salvation."

For those modern Christians who draw a closer connection between the individual and society, society or community is an important venue within which the individual can experience salvation. In the mid-twentieth century, mainline Protestant Christianity followed the Reformation and inherited the reformers confidence in the individual's capacity for choice. The Social Gospel, developing from nineteenth century post-Enlightenment theology and philosophy, broadened the concept of salvation from something that manifested itself only in the afterlife to something that included the state of people's lives in the present. We might compare the Social Gospel sense of the Kingdom of God with the salvation of society with the more ancient view represented in the Hebrew Scriptures that salvation has to do with the whole people, as Israel experienced collective blessing or disaster according to their faithfulness to their covenant with God. The Social Gospel theologians read the Prophets and brought this view back into the mainstream of Protestant thought.

In most of its manifestations, Christianity connected the salvation of souls to the salvation of society, not simply in religious or spiritual terms, but in terms of the alleviation of suffering caused by injustice, in other words, by other people's sin. The premier example of such a theology in the Seattle context was the Presbyterian pastor Mark Matthews, pastor of the First Presbyterian Church in Seattle. He arrived in the city in 1902 and remained until he died in 1940. Though he was fundamentalist in his theology, he was a socialist in his economic philosophy, had a broad social concept of salvation that made him connect the Christian gospel with the labor movements, with the moral life of the city, and with efforts to improve education.[46] For Matthews, not only should Christians, out of love for their neighbors, seek to eliminate poverty; those who had access to the economic structure, elected officials and owners of business, should shape that structure so that all people had meaningful work to do and the ability to support themselves and their families. Matthews sought to shape a public conscience in Seattle that would save not only individual souls but also save society from the evils resulting from poverty. Just so, a generation later, the Christian Friends for Racial Equality sought to shape the public conscience in order to save Seattle from the evils of racial injustice. Within their American democratic context, this required an act of decision on the part of individuals in order to create the means of community decision.

3. Relationship of this memory to understanding the Sixties: Ideal and Reality

Looking back through the lens of the 1960s, clearly they found barriers they did not expect in their quest to save society. One problem they faced, but did not recognize, was that understandings of racial identity changed over the course of the twentieth century. What the CFRE and the Council of Churches thought of the nature of race was only part of a complex social construction they were able to address at some levels but not at others.

The second problem was that integration also changed its

meaning and significance. In the 1940s and 1950s, integration of all the races in the venues of social interchange appeared to be the solution to the problem of racial inequality. Knowledge of each other was the key to justice. The assumptions lying behind the integration effort contained an unspoken acceptance of white middle-class life as a norm, a lifestyle that would benefit everyone. The deeper economic structures, shaped in many ways by racial discrimination, worked against the project from the beginning. The CFRE and the Council of Churches focused less attention on the class divisions within the races and more on the class divisions between the races. In addition, integration eroded the cultural aspects of racial identity, losing languages, forgetting customs, and reshaping family relationships. Neither the Council of Churches nor the CFRE recognized this cultural resistance to integration even as both made specific cultural celebrations an important part of their effort to acquaint people of different races with each other.

Finally, there was the problem of Christianity itself. Both of these organizations were active at a time when Christianity was on the wane. By the 1960s, churches lost a great deal of their former social influence. In Seattle and the Pacific Northwest region of the United States, this decline was particularly noticeable. Mainline Protestantism did not cope well with the deluge of post-World War II social and cultural change. Having become the American cultural religion, Protestant churches (the clergy in particular) did not know how to be critical of society and also keep members of that society in their pews. Both the Council of Churches and the CFRE still assumed that Christianity had an influence that it no longer had. On the specific issue of racial justice, Christianity had a mixed record. While the ranks of people working for racial justice always included some Christian people, some churches, as institutions, were too often silent or worse, helped to support racial inequality through the proclamation of supporting theological constructions. Both the CFRE and the Council of Churches failed to attract members from many of the congregations largely attended by racial minorities in Seattle.

Briefly, we can compare the CFRE and the Council of Churches in two ways. First, their rhetoric was much the same. Members of both groups, regardless of race, tended to be Protestant Christians strongly influenced by liberal theology, the ecumenical movement and the social gospel. Many were also aware of the weaknesses in all of these movements. They expressed optimism about the possibility of applying Christian principles to shape society and believed that committed Christian people had a responsibility to do so. While a few of them understood the systemic nature of racism, something the liberal theologians and social gospel movements had not fully comprehended, they believed that nothing could change within the structures until the whole community recognized the need. Both the CFRE and the Council of Churches thus focused on the need for people to know each other. Their emerging work for structural social change emerged from their relationships. Integration was not the end, but the means to attack structural inequalities. Through their meetings, and particularly through the CFRE's *Racial Equality Bulletin*, they put forward the Christian case for racial equality, for integration of society, and for the churches to be the site shaping public conscience by preaching and by friendship. Later, the next generation, exemplified by Rev. Samuel McKinney and the Black Panther Party, developed more direct action strategies to change systemic inequalities. Theirs was a different project, and the CFRE recognized that it needed to step aside to allow the next generation to work in its own way.

III. Outline of the Book

The story will have this shape. First, I will look at Seattle as the setting, the stage, upon which the story unfolded. Chapter 2 will expand on the idea of the Public Conscience and will create groundwork for understanding what the CFRE and the Council of Churches thought they were doing and why it was important to them. Chapter 3 will focus on the people involved, and build up a picture of the network of individuals and organizations that actually participated in the effort to shape a public conscience and to reframe social structures in the interests of racial equality. It will also present a closer look at the preaching, writing, speaking, and rhetorical strategies employed by the Christian Friends for Racial Equality and the Council of Churches to try to persuade Seattle people to make changes in their customary thinking and ways of life. The Chapter 4 will look at the record of success and analyze the work of both groups through lenses of gender and generation. It will conclude with a discussion of the discernable legacy of these groups to those who continue to try to find ways forward in building a racially just community.

Chapter 1

Setting the Stage: The Ideal and the Reality in Seattle and the Problem of Integration

"He made it clear that something very serious was very wrong ; just what did we mean, we missionaries and teachers, going to the Philippines with the open Bible and the Constitution of the United States, teaching the principles of democracy? His people coming to our country met with conditions and difficulties which, as he related them to me, were a most unhappy revelation."[1]

1. The Characters: The Seattle Council of Churches Race Relations Department and the Christian Friends for Racial Equality

We have briefly introduced two ecumenical organizations in Seattle within which people engaged in an effort to improve race relations in the city. These two organizations serve as the characters of the story in this book. Now we will sketch the history of each organization and then describe the larger social context in which they worked. Expanded details about each organization will emerge as the story evolves. The ecumenical organizations become the central characters in the story because, when religious people came together across lines of denomination, race, nationality or religion, they, particularly the white people, became more aware that something was "very wrong." The situation touched their consciences. The Christian Friends for Racial Equality and the Council of Churches were not the first and certainly not the only civil rights organizations in Seattle, but these two groups were active and well known to a degree unusual for religious bodies in Washington public life. We could have discussed some other religious groups, for instance, the Jewish Anti-Defamation League and the Roman Catholic Church's Interracial Council, certain Protestant congregations, and the entire phenomenon of the black church. In addition, Seattle had, and still has, large secular civil rights organizations: the Civic Unity Committee, the NAACP (National Association for the Advancement of Colored People), the Urban League, the Black Panther Party and CORE (Congress of Racial Equality). The city also had smaller organizations watching out for the civil rights of particular groups such as the Japanese American Citizens League and the Chinese Chong Wah Benevolent Association. The CFRE and the Council of Churches were also not the only ecumenical organizations. The YWCA (Young Women's Christian Association) and YMCA (Young Men's Christian Association) were also active in civil rights work by the middle of the century. Between them, the CFRE and the Council of Churches managed to create a network of almost all of the religious bodies in the city and the individuals in them interested in civil rights activism and to connect this network of religious people to the larger secular organizations. If indeed they set out to create a public conscience, they had the structural means to attempt it in this network of related organizations.

A. The Christian Friends for Racial Equality

The Christian Friends for Racial Equality began as we have seen, with a conversation between the Filipino immigrant Victor Carreon and the former Baptist missionary to the Philippines, Edith Steinmetz. It took the two of them two years to gather a core group of people interested enough to begin meeting once a month. In May 1942, they formally organized the Christian Friends for Racial Equality. Accounts differ on the details of the founding. Edith Steinmetz, who was the president of the organization for many years, gives the credit to Victor Carreon,[2] although in most accounts Steinmetz herself appears as the founder.[3] The founding group was remarkably diverse; four Chinese, two Filipino, six African Americans, three Euro-Americans and one Native American. Three of the founders were pastors (Two American Baptists, Chinese and African-American; one was Episcopalian) and the rest were lay people. Half of the original group was female. Bertha Pitts Campbell, one of the founding women members remembered that they had a hard time finding a place for their office because of the inter-racial character of their membership and the lack of office space in the Central Area where people of all races could comfortably come together.[4] By the end of the 1940s, the group regularly had seven hundred people attending some of its interracial concerts and international potluck dinners. The circulation of the *Racial Equality Bulletin* spread nation-wide.

In their efforts to strengthen the bonds between people of different races, they relied on a regular cycle of social events that brought people together to eat, listen to music and lectures, and talk together about what they had in common and how they experienced life in Seattle differently. From this social conversation, the CFRE derived its sense of which issues needed more direct action. The CFRE events were public and open to anyone. The social events took place once a month in addition to a monthly business meeting that was open to anyone who wanted to be a member. Joining the group was not difficult or expensive. In the early years, the CFRE did not have membership dues, and when they instituted dues in an effort to know more accurately who wished to be an active part of the group, the amount was minimal, one dollar per year, though some people contributed more. The volunteer effort made the organization possible; though later in their history, they employed a part time executive secretary, Mary Lund, for a time. The primary focus of their interest was on integration. The issues they addressed almost all had integration at the heart. The CFRE developed a wide range of projects over the twenty-five years of their active existence as a group, and were most prominently active in the period of the Second World War and the immediate post-war years.

The Christian Friends for Racial Equality was most at home tackling discrimination and advocating for integration. As we will see, the most active members were women of a particular generation who were uncomfortable with the street demonstrations and other more confrontational methods of CORE and other newer, younger groups. By the end of the 1950s, it was becoming clear that their organization was in decline. In the mid 1960s, the *Racial Equality Bulletin* contained articles that pressed this problem more urgently. Edith Steinmetz had moved to Atlanta in 1960 and the loss of her leadership took some of the energy out of the remaining group. More importantly, what had been in the 1940s a pioneering effort to create social integration in Seattle was no longer a cutting-edge issue in civil rights. The CFRE did not reframe its methods as society changed.[5] They observed in the *Racial Equality Bulletin* that other organizations now did the work they had set out to do more effectively than they did. In 1966, they noted that they had achieved one of their main goals; to get the churches more involved in working for racial justice.[6] This is one of the last pieces of information available about the group. It seems to have faded away as the civil rights movements of the Sixties gained strength.

B. The Seattle Council of Churches Race Relations Department

In 1942, when the CFRE organized, the primary ecumenical bodies in Seattle, representing a majority of the churches, had recently merged into one body called the Seattle Council of Churches and Christian Education. The Washington Northern-Idaho Council of Christian Education focused on cooperative religious education projects and the Seattle Federation of Churches, associated with the Federal Council of Churches, brought the churches together on a broad range of projects of mutual interest. The stated purpose of the combined body was "to promote and extend the Christian religion in Seattle through cooperative action on behalf of the member bodies in such fields of effort as Christian Education, evangelism, temperance, comity, and public affairs."[7] The Council of Churches focused their attention on the churches, and understood itself to exist primarily to provide resources to the congregations of Seattle and to serve as a point of interaction between the churches and the city.[8] In the 1930s and 1940s, the Council of Churches gave increasing attention to race relations, first through its International Affairs Committee which watched the Japanese situation carefully and provided important ministry to the Japanese community after the attack on Pearl Harbor, through the internment, and in helping the Japanese to resettle after the war.

In 1939, this newly combined body formed a Race Relations Department. The main emphases of the department focused on an integration model of addressing race relations problems. They proposed round table study groups to look into specific situations in Seattle; planned a joint interracial Christmas service, and promoted the observance of Race Relations Sunday in churches. The Federal Council of Churches designed Race Relations Sunday to encourage churches to consider the problems of race relations, to foster moments of integration such as pulpit and choir exchanges and other activities to bring members of white churches and black churches together. In Seattle, the integration effort expanded to include Japanese, Chinese, Filipino churches as well. Several members of the Race Relations Department of the Council of Churches were also involved in the CFRE, most notably Mrs. Bertha Campbell, of the African Methodist Episcopal Church, Mrs. Walter Hiltner of Plymouth Congregational Church, and her pastor John Gibson, and Rev. Paul Fong of the Chinese Baptist Church. The close relationship between the two organizations appears in the only extensive history of the Council of Churches in the author's assumption that the CFRE was a branch of the Council of Churches.[9]

The Seattle Council of Churches and Religious Education represented congregations and regional jurisdictions of denominations that, through their representatives, chose to act together on the concerns they had about their city. During the early part of the twentieth century, the concerns focused on gambling, prostitution, prohibition, and the ethics of city government. After the Depression and the beginning of World War II, they began to attend to issues of racial prejudice and discrimination, and the attending inequities in social and economic well being of minority communities. The Council of Churches was the local expression of a national body, the Federal Council of Churches of Christ made up, not of separate congregations, but of denominations in the United States. Through the Federal Council of Churches Race Relations Department, both the Seattle Council of Churches and the Federal Council of Churches addressed issues of racial justice with greater seriousness and appointed committees to keep such work in the forefront of the organization's agenda.

Both the CFRE and the Council of Churches understood that discriminatory policies lay behind the experiences of injustice suffered by people of color in Seattle. Both understood that beyond affecting personal relationships and countering manifestations of personal prejudice, it was necessary to change laws and business policies. Neither group seems to have grappled with the long term effects of such inequities on the economic and social life of Seattle even after the enactment of civil rights legislation. The typical member of the CFRE and the Council of Churches worked as part of more than one organization and were often engaged in more radical strategies in one group than in another. To judge the aims of the people involved in these two organizations simply based on their stated policies is unwise. Johanna Phillips is careful to note the involvement of key CFRE members in CORE and the Urban League. At least one CFRE member, Rev. Samuel McKinney, was active in the CORE sit-ins protesting segregated housing in 1963, active in the Central Area Civil Rights Council, and in sympathy with the Black Panther Party in the Sixties.[10] Judson Jeffries and Jeffrey Zane, historians of the Black Panther party, note that in Seattle there was a remarkable for having a united front on the part of civil rights organizations, including the Council of Churches, in its support of open housing.[11]

II. The Time and Place: A Social History of Seattle

A. A Social History of Seattle

1. A Society Shaped by Race[12]

Seattle is characteristic of the cities in the American West, made up of immigrants from across the world who found themselves classified by a complex scheme of racial identities. Seattle grew up at the end of United States expansion over the mid North American continent, and thrived in the twentieth century as the capitalist economic system and European cultures spread across the Pacific. These racial categories organized the population's access to jobs, goods and services, education, and political power and privilege. White American expansionists moved in on the Native Americans in the Puget Sound area and created new economic enterprises and patterns. The initial twenty or so created a small village in 1851 and made a living supplying timber to San Francisco. A handful of African Americans lived in the town before the railroad arrived in the 1880s. With the arrival of the railroads, Seattle was a small city by 1890 with a growing population of Chinese and African Americans in addition to the substantial Native American population surviving in the area. The white population was already the majority and consisted of large numbers of new immigrants from Europe, Ireland, Scandinavia, and Eastern Europe. In 1897, Seattle's economy turned to serving the Alaskan gold rush, in addition to exploiting timber and fishing resources. Seattle became a city, as San

Francisco had before it for the California Gold Rush, a center of supply and financing for miners headed to the gold fields in Alaska. A few African Americans were present from the beginning, some engaged in lucrative commercial enterprises; George Washington Bush in real estate, Horace R. Cayton the publisher of *The Seattle Republican*, Conrad Rideout an attorney who also ran for public office are good examples.[13]

In 1940, Seattle was still a relatively new city, remaining a small town until the end of the 1880s when it suddenly became the fourth largest city on the Pacific Coast. The majority of the population was still European American, but the displaced Native American population was still present. Native Americans moved to the urban area of Seattle, displaced from their lands by changing government policies. The city itself encroached on remaining Native American living spaces. Immigrants from Asia, mainly Chinese working on the railroads and in mining, Filipinos and Japanese working in agriculture and later opening small businesses, formed the lion's share of the racial and cultural diversity. Until the 1940s African Americans were a small group compared to the Japanese and other immigrants from across the Pacific.

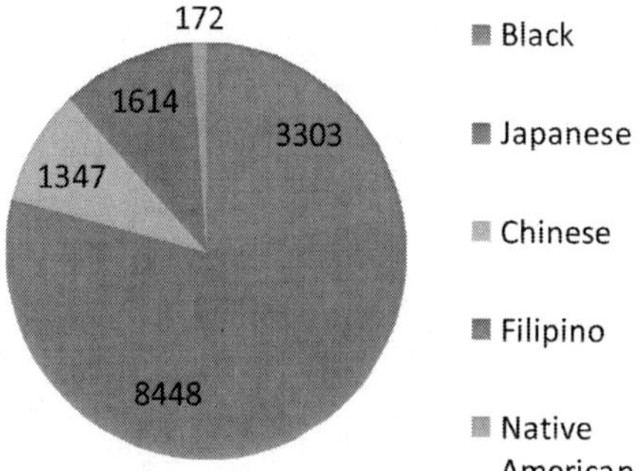

Figure 1 Seattle Minority Population 1930

After the Alaska Gold Rush boom, the city settled down to a moderate rate of growth, still fueled by commerce and extractive industries. Another population explosion was underway in 1940 to make airplanes and ships for the war effort. Joining them, were people from all over the world who came to take advantage of the economic opportunities these enterprises offered. After the war, commercial aviation continued to make Boeing a major employer joined by newer technology industries such as Microsoft which designed computer software. The opportunities still drew people to the city, but some found the opportunities limited by their assigned racial identification.

2. Prevailing Ideas about Race and the Development of Seattle Society

By the mid-twentieth century the typical system of racially and religiously restrictive real estate covenants rooted in the more explicit systematic segregation in the American South known as Jim Crow, as well as the simple desire of people to live among familiar faces, familiar languages, and familiar customs had created culturally and therefore racially segregated neighborhoods, and thus segregated schools and religious institutions. In addition, the prevailing constructions of racial identity and their meanings created segregated institutions and a host of other social mechanisms for keeping racial groups separated from one another. Inter-marriage was a primary fear lying behind this segregation.[14]

Seattle matured as a city during a period in the twentieth century dominated by concepts of race derived from Social Darwinism. This primarily biological understanding of race, following a misreading of Charles Darwin's theory of evolution, categorized race by physical characteristics and ranked the races as biologically more or less "fit" by reference to their relative economic and political development and power. Those following this theory regarded less "fit" or less "evolved" races as permanently flawed.[15] The mixture of less fit with more fit races, these theorists believed, would produce hybrid races, presumably with characteristics somewhere in between the more and less evolved groups, thus diluting the advantages of the so-called more advanced race. This theory, developed by European and white American sociologists, supported racial segregation and strengthened objections to intermarriage. Social Darwinist theories of race overlay an earlier theological theory that held that God had created the races as they were, and discouraged changes in the divinely created social order. Both Jim Crow legal structures in the South and movements for Asian exclusion in the West rested upon these theories, one secular and the other religious.[16]

People who took a particular critical approach to the Social Darwinism of the earlier generation dominated the Christian Friends for Racial Equality and the Seattle Council of Churches during the 1940s and 1950s. They tended to frame race as ethnicity.[17] Particularly on the West Coast, a more complex meeting place of races, the ethnicity frame was common in explaining the presence and social dynamics of race. The ethnicity category allowed for consideration of differences within races, such as between Japanese and Chinese or Irish and Scandinavian or African Americans born in Seattle and those coming from the rural culture of the American South. Some who took this view overtly valued racial pluralism; others looked toward the end of an assimilation process in which all the races would blend into a standard American ethnicity, usually assumed to be like that of English-speaking white people. Tensions arose in the conflict of this assimilationist ideal and the still powerful belief that the races should not marry and blend biologically.

During the late nineteenth century, the process of extending English-speaking empires and hegemony over the American West and the Pacific region complicated patterns of racial stereotyping. In this early industrial globalization, people applied these stereotypes rhetorically to identify other people's place in the economic hierarchy. Often they transferred a set of stereotypes from one group to another as that group replaced the earlier one in the economic niche. For instance, in the American West, by the end of the 1850s Chinese labor filled labor shortages in the mining, railroad, and later agricultural economies. When agitation from white workers and others who believed the increasing Chinese population to be dangerous to American society succeeded in bringing about the legal exclusion of the Chinese from the United States, it was not long before railroads, mines, and agribusinesses sought Japanese and Filipino labor to fill the gap. The vocabulary of racial stereotyping moved from the Chinese to the Japanese and Filipinos. The stereotype had a specific shape linking dark skin color, savagery, and childlikeness or feminized demeanor, images sure to signal within American cultural norms that the object of such a description was not fit to be a citizen. The equation of Asians with women to serve this purpose suggests that the issues of gender and race relate closely together.[18] Those who put forward this rhetoric understood these characteristics as innate, not something subject to development. They ignored the fact that society had assigned people these characteristics to fit a particular political need.

Eventually many applied these stereotypes to almost anyone from Asia. The sense of a single Asian "race" of yellow color was the result of this racialization process.[19] This racial identification by stereotype was not an exclusively American concept.[20] Internationally, most imperial powers used the rhetoric in an effort to assert European hegemony.[21] By 1907 Seattle had a chapter of the Asian Exclusion League and communities nearby, including Vancouver, British Columbia, experienced considerable unrest over efforts to exclude the Chinese. Increasingly during this turn of the century period, it became difficult to disentangle concepts of racial and national identity. The resulting tensions in the Pacific Coast states, where multiple racial groups met, persisted throughout the twentieth century.

In Seattle, a city with a large European immigrant population, the assumption of immigrant assimilation was widespread and affected people's views of Asian, Pacific Islander, and African American newcomers. The prevailing public understanding of racial identities in Seattle during the early twentieth century derived from a still prevalent form of social Darwinism connected in part with identities imposed by colonialism. This theory likened races to the species Darwin discussed in his book of a century earlier, *The Origin of the Species*. The willingness to understand people of different races as somehow different species predates Darwin by three hundred years or more. The Spanish colonial powers had to decide this basic question in the sixteenth century. The willingness to entertain such a degree of difference among different human beings also lay behind the belief that it was not wise for different races to intermarry. Although not in effect in Washington, misogyny laws were still in the books in most Western states. Washington and Kansas are the only two states west of the Mississippi that did not have anti-miscegenation laws in the twentieth century. Most states repealed them in the 1950s, but Utah, Wyoming, and Arizona did not repeal theirs until the 1960s.[22] These laws aimed to prevent the genetic mixing of races, and people, largely of European decent and the majority population in these states, supported them. White women were among the most restricted by these laws. The legal system often overlooked a white man marrying a woman of another race, but they would arrest and prosecute a white woman along with her spouse. In Native American and African American communities, there was some sympathy for discouraging mixed race marriages because low birth rates and population decline threatened the survival of their cultures. The understanding of race as something genetic or biological, something inherited and inherent in a person was widespread. Growing segregation in cities such as Seattle during the twentieth century pointed to a desire to keep young people from mixing with each other and forming illicit relationships against their racial interests.[23]

One important proponent of the assimilation model was the Chicago sociologist Robert Park. He was the director of the Survey of Race Relations on the Pacific Coast, undertaken in 1924-1927. In 1926, he noted in the initial findings of the survey, "The race relations cycle - contact, competition, accommodation and eventual assimilation - is apparently progressive and irreversible."[24] Omi and Winant point out that he failed to note his own assumption that the white race, specifically its Anglo Saxon branch, was the norm to which all others must assimilate. Park's theory left the problem of racism based on skin color in place.[25] Examples of this problem can be found in the data from the Survey itself. Among the interviews and documents related to Seattle are two examples of Japanese young people taking part in ordinary schoolroom patriotic exercises and causing a furor among white parents. Tadeo Kimura, valedictorian of the Franklin High School graduating class of 1924, gave an address on the power of education in a free society. *The Star*, a conservative Seattle newspaper of the time, criticized the high school officials for allowing a student its editors did not regard as American to give such an address.[26] In another incident, a Japanese elementary school student was selected to portray George Washington in a school play which his class presented to the entire student body in celebration of Washington's Birthday. Again, *The Star* reported the incident and was highly critical of the teacher who allowed a non-white student to portray one of the country's founders.[27] In both cases, the ability of the student to speak, write and act like any white American public school student was not enough. The Japanese immigrant students simply did not look American in the way that a second-generation Scandinavian immigrant child did.

Also based in evolutionary thinking, the dominant European American view of cultures was one of evolutionary development from "primitive" societies surviving by hunting and gathering and living migratory lives, through more settled societies based in agriculture and dependence on biological forms of energy, to the more sophisticated merchant societies and finally technologically advanced societies made possible by the application of fossil fuels to the problems of energy provision.[28] Attached to this evolutionary scheme based in the descriptions of economic organization, were cultural and religious associations with Protestant Christianity, advanced technological industries, and the global expansion. American global hegemony was rapidly supplanting the British Empire and European Americans had come to assume that their form of economic life was the result of a superior culture and a superior ethic. The often-cited Protestant work ethic[29] regarded work as a vocation, a calling from God, and certain Protestant preachers regarded the practices of hard work, thrift, and temperance as sure roads to prosperity, a divine reward for hard work. In this scheme, the worldly prosperity of various cultures was a measure of their evolution of an advanced ethic. Max Weber understood that the development of this ethic related directly to changes in the economy, but those changes affected people of different races and cultures differently. Race, understood as culture, was something more malleable than skin color. One could adopt a different cultural value and practice, and move, theoretically, into a different cultural sphere and perhaps therefore into another race. This was the foundation of the assimilation dream. Often the dream of upward mobility failed to come true for people of color.

In the mid twentieth-century, the most powerful and pervasive way of defining and categorizing people by race was that of skin color. Skin color became, in the social Darwinist sense, an immutable marker of race, and remains a highly subjective criterion, having nothing to do with inheritance, ethics, or culture, nor is it associated in any provable way with intelligence or moral quality. The ultimate decision about one's race rests with the outside community, often with the Government. Individuals are and were whoever their neighbors determined them to be.[30]

The privileges the greater society assigned to light skin were many and deeply ingrained in the expectations and assumptions of people of all colors. In fact, because skin color is difficult to assess, some people's skin color changed depending on who was looking at them. In several celebrated cases, a U. S. law court changed an individual's racial identity.[31] Awareness of the fluid nature of one's racial identity based on skin color rarely surfaced to consciousness among the light-skinned folks, despite their belief in and work for racial equality. In addition, society had ensured the enforcement of discrimination and privilege by enacting sanctions against those who treated others with equality. The fear of these sanctions worked against all efforts at integration. For instance, homeowners could lose their property rights if they violated racially restrictive covenants governing the sales of their homes. Though Seattle was a relatively new city, its citizens brought with them from their places of birth, the same prejudices about race as pertained in other parts of the country. Being a new city, Seattle society had not had the same time to work out the full complex of sanctions to protect light-skin privilege, though discrimination was certainly evident in most sectors of Seattle social and economic life.

It seemed intuitively clear to the members of the CFRE and others like them, that in a world where the injustice of racism seemed to be expressed by a policy (formal or informal) of segregation based on prejudice, that the solution would be a systematic effort to integrate the races and allow for people to know each other across racial lines in order to break down prejudice. It was only later in the 60s and 70s that it became clearer that this was too simple.

B. American Religious Ideologies and Assumptions about Race

So far, we have discussed ways of categorizing people by race that are based largely in secular thinking, often backed by particular interpretations of scientific theory. Theological paradigms played a part in explaining and identifying race, as we have already seen.[32] Religious people of all races developed theological or symbolic explanations and critiques of the race relations they observed in their society. Though ordinary American Protestants and Catholics did not read or even hear from their pulpits a great deal of sophisticated theological discourse, churchgoers did absorb theologically based understandings of race in the course of sermons, missionary writings, and Sunday school classes. In the nineteenth century, Protestants expressed these ideas about race by reference to biblical materials.

1. White Religious Paradigms

For white Christians the most familiar of these paradigms came from particular interpretations of Genesis 9:18-26 where the writer assigned Noah's sons as the progenitors of the major peoples of the world. Because, in the story, Noah's son Ham had the misfortune to stumble upon and see his father's naked body, he received a curse making him the slave of his brothers. In Genesis, the early characters often represent whole nations, therefore the curse of Ham and his descendants fell upon those nations where his descendants were thought to live, Egypt, Cush, Put in Africa, and Canaan. Christian imperial discourse often symbolized colonized people of whatever geography as the Canaanites. Some American Christians concluded that since in this biblical account, God assigned the descendants of Ham to a subservient position with regard to the others, that this position was divinely ordained for all time. Scholars of American history have pointed out the application of this biblical passage to the justification of African slavery, and subsequently to the permanent subordination of black people to Europeans or whites. Use of this religious rhetoric had a clear role in shaping secular white people's beliefs in the inferiority of people with dark skin.

The Bible does not present a uniform picture of humanity. Because Genesis begins by picturing all human beings as descendants of the original human beings created by God, one might conclude that all people are related. In other parts of the Bible, writers divide human beings into those whom God favors and those God does not favor. The careful reader of biblical texts will note historical shifts and discrepancies in these identifications as the literature that makes up the Bible developed over centuries. Particularly in Christianity, previous distinctions may disappear in the minds of biblical writers, as when the apostle Paul wrote in Galatians (3:28), "There is neither Jew nor Greek, there is neither slave nor free, there is neither male nor female; for you are all one in Christ Jesus." This suggests a significant stream of Christian thought that makes all baptized believers equal.

2. Alternative Religious Paradigms of Racial Identity

African Americans and Native Americans felt the constraints of the white religious paradigms closely because those paradigms developed in large part to define their places in a society whites wished to shape for their own advantages. Early in the nineteenth century, African American alternative paradigms appeared and became part of the discourse of the black churches. Common elements of these alternative constructions of racial identity focused first on the liberative aspects of the biblical narratives, the Exodus of the Hebrew people from slavery in Egypt and the Gospel promises of the salvation of the soul regardless of a person's position in society. A second paradigm came out of the study of the history of Christianity and the realization among African American historians of how influential the North African churches had been in the early centuries of Christianity, and the persistent traditions of Christianity in the Nile valley and Ethiopia. The historical realization of the connection of Africa with the Eastern Orthodox traditions of Christianity and the simultaneous growth of African American Masonic traditions in the nineteenth century which also used Egyptian motifs, offered African American historians a way to present the full participation of African people in the history of civilization.[33]

African American thinkers later in the nineteenth century directly countered the social Darwinists and their essentialist views of the evolution of race and culture and the theories of those who argued that the different human races were actually different species. African American writers pointed out the diversity and antiquity of African civilizations, particularly Egypt, and some posited that Jesus was black.[34] W. E. B. DuBois in *The Souls of Black Folk*, argued that the characteristics white people attributed to black people as the effects of evolutionary difference were in fact the result of white efforts to form a segregated society. Du Bois also noted the alternative reading of biblical texts toward a critique of this segregation effort, namely, what he thought of as the essentially egalitarian character of the Christian Gospels.[35]

Asian American Christians have also sought to challenge these white paradigms of race by using alternative biblical interpretations. Tat-Siong Benny Liew, New Testament scholar who explores the problem of culture and race in biblical interpretation, points out the paradoxes inherent in this project because of the origins and history of the Bible and its interpretation. In considering the question of the usefulness of the Bible for Asian Americans, he uses a yin-yang view of the texts. On the one hand, he keeps in mind that no biblical text is unambiguously on the side of liberation. On the other hand, he notes the powerful possibilities in the ambiguous language used by biblical writers, in the stories that offer alternative views of community and the open-endedness of the constant need to interpret and reinterpret the biblical text.[36] Earlier Asian American thinkers such as Paul Nagano, who negotiated as a young person the difficult history of Japanese Americans during World War II and the internment experience, using Christian interpretations of these events, also took this stance. Nagano shared with the African American interpreters the use of Moses and the Exodus stories as a location of meaning for the Japanese experience. With the yin-yang eye that Liew pointed out, Nagano locates Moses as both a member of the elite and as a relative of the Hebrew slaves. The ambiguity of his position and role in society forced him to make choices that determined his own sense of identity but also determined the identity that those in power assigned to him.[37] In all of these examples and the many others available, the Bible serves an ambiguous purpose because it contains such a complex set of texts, translated from ancient languages into modern ones, covering such a wide range of historical contexts, peoples, and human dilemmas.

C. American Theological Views of Non-Christian Religions

A second aspect of the theological rhetoric had to do with the assessment of non-Christian religions and the cultures that grew out of them. With the diversity of people present on the Pacific Coast of North America, religion and ideas about race connect. White American Protestants tended to regard themselves as being at a peak of religious development from more primitive paganism, through the almost Christian Greek Philosophers and great Jewish Prophets, to the earliest Christian communities, the splendid but corrupt Roman Catholic and Orthodox traditions, to the pure rarified air of the Protestant traditions that had distilled the essence of the Gospel and could apply it to modern society. By the early twentieth century, especially among the liberal Protestant traditions, this developmental view was combined freely with evolutionary ideas from the world of science; even the more conservative traditions, reluctant to grant admission of

Darwin into their theological consideration, were eager to allow for religious and therefore cultural progress resulting from conversion to Christianity. The possibility that any human being could become a Christian by a change of heart and decision to join the church and that such a change would also ensure a better material future undergirded the optimism of Christian missions from the nineteenth century to World War II. African American missionaries in Africa shared this view and converts to Protestant Christianity around the world adopted it as well.[38] American people unaffiliated with specific Christian churches retained the idea long after they or their parents had heard such constructions presented from a pulpit. This innate belief in the changeability of human beings, and therefore the possibility of their improvement, made many Protestant Christians disinclined to adopt explicitly the more essentialist paradigms of racial identity that located racial identity in genetic structures or in indelible characteristics conveyed by upbringing in certain environments. Unconsciously these optimistic Protestants continued to hold essential assumptions about race as an innate characteristic, since the actual experience of people of color indicates that this essentialist position still governed their lives.

The historian Jennifer Snow argues that the Protestant missionaries, though a minority voice in public debates about race, nonetheless were disproportionately influential. Their ideas about racial identity and the relationship of immigrants of other races to white America changed over time. She argues that, even when they adopted the prevailing view of immigrant assimilation, they focused on a cultural assimilation that they thought any immigrant regardless of race could accomplish. This, however, was not the general experience of immigrants from Asia who worked hard to assimilate only to find out that their skin color made it impossible to enter fully into American society.

Early in the twentieth century, Protestant leaders began to

argue in favor of an American society of multiple cultures.[39] The expanding Christian worldview after the 1910 Edinburgh International Missionary Conference and the developing ecumenical movement among the Christians of the world shaped the Protestant change of view. The year following the Edinburgh meeting, many of the same Christian leaders were in London for a meeting remembered as the Universal Races Conference. Many associated with the missionary projects of European and North American churches began to realize how racism affected their message, and concluded that often missionary-rhetoric undermined its own effort to appeal to the "singleness of the spiritual kingdom."[40] This more egalitarian and inclusive view was also shaped by their direct experience of people of other religions, and experience that tended to dissolve the stereotypes of those religions that missionary bodies encouraged among U. S. Protestants in order to galvanize support for the mission enterprise.

Finally, there was a sense that there should be some integrity between the teachings of Christianity and the practice of people who called themselves Christian, especially among American Protestants who had some experience of the missionary fields of the world, or an interest in the appeal of Christianity to others. Even conservative white Christians could not rid themselves of the Christian belief that every soul is equal before God. This belief had always troubled any Christians who sought to justify oppression, slavery, or discriminatory treatment of people of other races on biblical grounds. The missionaries, in wanting to show the practical benefits of conversion to Christianity, portrayed the United States as a place where Christian ideals prevailed in both private and public life. How could the United States continue to think of itself as Christian when these ideals turned out not to be prevalent after all?[41] The conversation between Carreon and Steinmetz, cited above, began in this very contradiction. Seattle in the 1940s and 1950s was a society shaped by conflicting undercurrents of thought about race, which were rarely uncovered and debated. Thus, they caught people by surprise in sometimes-painful ways.

III. Demographic Picture of Seattle in the 1940s and 1950s

In order to understand the reasons both the CFRE and the Church Council of Greater Seattle framed their civil rights goals in terms of integration during the 1940s and 1950s, a brief demographic history of the city up to that point will be helpful, as will an exploration of the cultural assumptions held by various constituencies of the population about the importance of racial and cultural identity for participation in employment, social life, and politics. As we have noted, from the beginning, Seattle was never a highly religious town. Only a minority participated in institutionalized forms of religion. For the most part, people in these religious groups went along with the segregated nature of their society. Before the founding of the CFRE, Seattle was a relatively open city for racial and ethnic minority people in the sense that it was better than most places.[42]

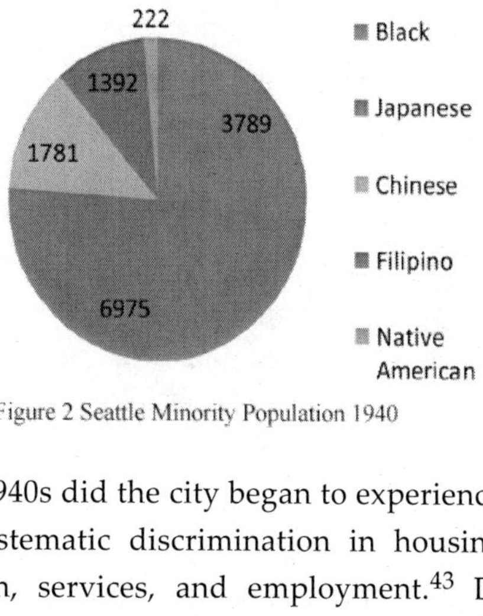

Figure 2 Seattle Minority Population 1940

Not until the 1940s did the city began to experience a significant increase in systematic discrimination in housing and public accommodation, services, and employment.[43] Discrimination was present from the beginning of this diverse community. The

Council of Churches established a race relations department in 1939. Japanese, Chinese, Filipino and other racial minorities were beginning to feel the change in social attitudes.[44] This discrimination arrived with the influx of migration to the city during the Second World War, including both European and African Americans, some of whom brought with them the segregated assumptions, practices and ideologies of their home regions. By the end of the war, the city was still relatively tolerant of multiple races, in some respects because it retained a very large white majority.

A. Race Relations Attitudes in the 1940s

In November 1948, The Seattle Urban League conducted a survey of racial attitudes in the Broadview District of the city, at the request of the local neighborhood Civic Committee. The catalyst for this survey came when a mixed race couple moved into the neighborhood of four hundred houses. The people of the neighborhood were white, middle class Christians, strongly church going compared to the rest of Seattle. 34 percent were college-educated, but they had little experience with minority groups. The survey included all four hundred houses. Predictably, a majority (63 percent) said they "did not favor Negroes living in the neighborhood." The realtors' association claimed 90 percent would sign a petition for the family to leave, but only 8 percent of those surveyed said they would do so. Nineteen percent said they would sign a petition to protect the couple's rights. Interestingly, half of the people in the neighborhood said their property values had increased since the family moved in. The report concluded, "This intolerant minority . . . is balanced by a minority who feel strongly that democracy can be practiced in daily life . . . [that] can be a strong force for influencing the people who feel less strongly about democratic principles, to implement the democracy they say they believe in."[45] We do not have a comparative survey of a non-church going neighborhood in order to discern the extent of religious influence on what is clearly a public conscience resisting unjust racial discrimination.

The same year, Stuart Dodd and others at the University of Washington conducted a second survey of neighborhood race relations in the Duwamish Bend Homes, a wartime public housing project of about a thousand families. The project, integrated from the beginning, had about one-third black residents. The reason for the survey lay in tensions developing at the site. A strike at Boeing affected about one third of the residents regardless of race. There had been some stabbings, rapes and "emotional talk." The resulting survey of about half the residents found, unsurprisingly, that whites were the least tolerant of other racial groups. The survey also found that both whites and blacks in the neighborhood were more socially tolerant than the average American population. Only 25 percent of the people desired segregation.[46] Both surveys affirm the perception that people experienced less discrimination in Seattle than they did in much of the country, but it was still far from ideal. These surveys, done in two different kinds of Seattle neighborhoods just after the end of World War II, reflect both the increasing racial tensions in Seattle (during the rapid social change from the time just before the war period through its aftermath) as well as an unusual level of tolerance in Seattle society (dating from its earlier history).

B. Seattle Race Relations in the Pacific Region Context

It was during this period of wartime change that the former Baptist missionary to the Philippines Edith Steinmetz and the Filipino immigrant Victor Carreon, the founders of the CFRE, met in 1939. The context of their meeting becomes more significant when we realize that the Filipino community in the United States was in the midst of a crisis precipitated by the changed relationship of the Philippines to the United States in 1934. Congress in 1934 passed the Tydings-McDuffie Act, which in giving independence to the Philippines; this law also changed the status of Filipinos who had, as residents of an American-held territory, not been affected by Asian exclusion acts.[47] The Tydings-McDuffie Act reclassified the residents of the newly independent country as "aliens." Suddenly Filipinos faced the same restrictions on immigration, landholding, and employment faced by other immigrants from Asia and the Pacific region.[48] In 1937, Washington State passed an Anti-Alien Land Law barring Filipinos, now classified as aliens, from owning or leasing land.[49] Filipinos also faced anti-miscegenation laws in neighboring states, and restrictions on the employment opportunities available to them. Washington State expelled Filipinos from Toppenish, a prime agricultural area in the Yakima Valley because Euro-American workers perceived them as unfair competition. The displaced Filipino workers often ended up in Seattle looking for jobs.

The kinds of economic, educational, social, religious, and demographic arrangements that emerged from the application of these racial ideologies to people's lives can be illustrated by looking at the situation of Victor Carreon in this context. Carreon had been a teacher in the Philippines and immigrated to Seattle in 1930 to go to college. He then found his race barred him from jobs that would pay enough to finance his studies. Both Carreon and Steinmetz were deeply part of the Pacific world and shaped by its religious, economic and political complexities. The United States took over the Philippines in 1898 after the Spanish American War, claiming to be liberating the people from Spain, but subjecting the people of the islands to the project of maintaining the balance of power in East Asia. The process actually removed the people from enjoyment of American ideals and standards of liberty and equality.[50] Steinmetz and Carreon were thus players on a stage set by others, organized according to views about race rooted in concepts of "scientific racism," and these views stood in counterpoint to Christian beliefs about the unity of humanity.

In the Baptist churches, the white congregations paid little attention to the circumstances of the Filipino congregations, though they celebrated their presence as evidence of the success of missionary work. Though he was one of the founders of the CFRE, Carreon eventually had to drop out of active participation because his job required him to work at night.[51] The cultural circumstances of Seattle favored Edith Steinmetz, a retired white woman, with the leisure to participate in a voluntary civil rights effort. Carreon, the Filipino, did not have that privilege and few Filipinos were active in the organization after the first few years, though Carreon's name remained on the letterhead as a sponsor for many years indicating he continued to have at least and advisory role in the group. At one meeting of the CFRE, Carreon and Grandino Baaoa described the difficulties of the Filipino community. They pointed out that Filipino young men come to the United States educated to be engineers, business administrators, pharmacists, and teachers, but the only jobs open to them are bus boy, dishwasher, and domestic work.[52]

In this period, Asian immigrants made up the majority of the non-white population in Seattle. The African American community was present and in a period of transition as the CFRE began its work. Black members of the CFRE were especially prominent and important in many aspects of civil rights work in Seattle. The earliest African American citizens of Seattle were primarily workers in the service sectors of the economy, though some found the city open to their entrepreneurial projects. While Seattle had segregated racial and cultural areas within the neighborhoods, in economic life, and in many social venues, these boundaries blurred until the 1940s; they became more sharply drawn and enforced as the African American population increased in the late 1930s and throughout the 1940s. The segregation showed most clearly in the public schools.[53] Until the 1940s, African Americans made up one of the smaller minority groups. Most of the non-white people in the city were Asian or Pacific Islander immigrants. By 1940 that changed rapidly, and increasingly African Americans were the largest racial minority group in the city. The Japanese, who had held that majority position until 1942, left the city suddenly and involuntarily during the Internment and the wartime industries pulled in an increasingly large number of African Americans. Other Asian groups did not increase because of severe immigration restrictions still in place until the 1960s.

The Seattle Central Area, where most of the African American population lived along with a significant number of the Asian immigrants, was a thriving community until the end of the 1930s. As racial restrictive covenants became more common and the population of color increased, the Central District experienced severe strains on its resources as property values declined, loans were hard to obtain and the area became increasingly run down. Employment opportunities for people of color became more restricted to the service and manual labor sectors and so incomes declined. The earlier African American population, people who prided themselves on their economic success and status, found themselves in a downwardly mobile cycle even as they found their numbers increasing in comparison to other minority groups.[54]

The black community in Seattle had its own class divisions, as did the other racial and ethnic communities. Class divisions shaped religious and social life. Economic class also shaped approaches to civil rights work. The degree to which these intergroup class divisions existed primarily because of racial prejudice might be debated in its finer points, but the fact remains that more and more of the employment opportunities were controlled by white people and the higher paying jobs were more and more reserved for people of their own race.

Regardless of the racial group, non-white people in Seattle shared in the increasing patterns of exclusion from jobs, public

Figure 3 Seattle Minority Populations 1950[i]

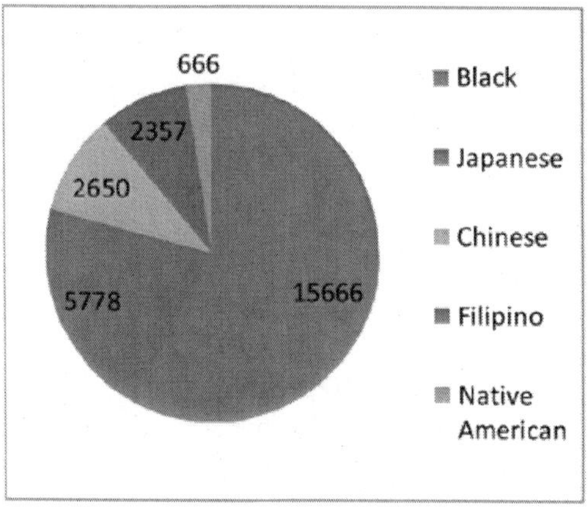

[i] Figures from Appendix 4 in Quintard Taylor, *The Forging of a Black Community: Seattle's Central District from 1870 through the Civil Rights Era* (Seattle: University of Washington Press, 1994) 245. Taylor used the data from census records and data from the Seattle Chamber of Commerce.

accommodation, housing, and education found in all the U. S. cities on the Pacific Coast. Though the patterns of segregation increased with the influx of white people who held these patterns to be proper, they took hold quickly in Seattle, with the consequence of limiting racial minorities severely in their prospects for comfort and prosperity, not to mention public influence. The overwhelming white majority of Seattle persisted into the 1960s and 1970s and well beyond the time period belonging to this study.

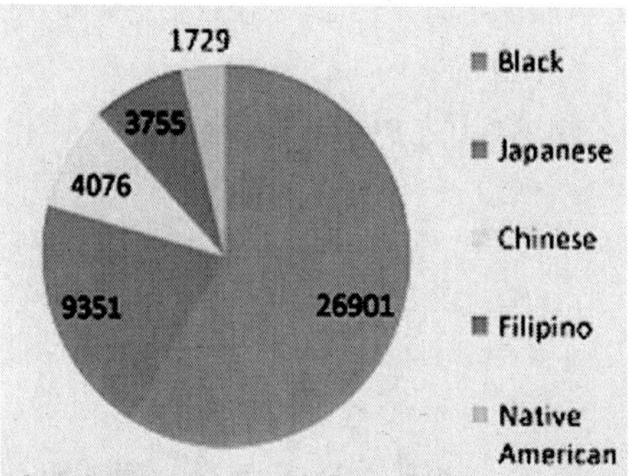

Seattle Minority Population 1960

C. Church Demographics

As in other parts of the country, patterns of segregation characterized religious bodies in Seattle. Immigrants found their way in their new society through the services of ethnic Christian churches and other community organizations sharing their language. Language differences explain much of the initial segregation of religious congregations. Many joined American congregations as part of their effort to become at home in their new country. Baptists, Congregationalists, Methodists, Roman Catholics and other Christian denominations were multi-cultural or multi-racial on a national scale, but particular congregations were almost always single race or a single ethnicity. Sometimes this was so because of language differences, but often it was due to the reluctance of individuals to worship outside their own particular cultural or racial enclave and customary cultural and racial divisions that discouraged social mixing. Immigrants from Asian nations also brought their own religious traditions; Buddhism was the most common of these. Immigrants of all cultural and racial groups, especially Europeans and European Americans, simply left behind organized practice of their religions. Some established new or hybrid religious communities.

Victor Carreon experienced exclusion from the church based on his race and this was not an uncommon experience. Another contemporary Filipino, Mariano Angeles reported the same kind of experience. As was Carreon, Angeles was attracted to the United States because of contact with American Protestant missionaries in the Philippines who painted a picture of America as a Christian society, where all are equal under the law, and all have freedom to pursue their own lives as they choose. However, when they arrived it was different. What gnawed at him was the discrimination he had encountered: entering a Methodist Church in Seattle and being told that the Filipino Christian Fellowship Group would meet in the basement, not among the main assembly of parishioners.[55]

Racial discrimination in Seattle was present in the work place where good jobs were denied to them, not because they were not qualified, but because they were Filipino. It was present in places for recreation—"They call it equality when they put you somewhere (in a separate balcony in the theater); they don't serve you [when] you go to a restaurant").[56] It was even present in the military. Such discrimination should not have been present in the church, if Christians were practicing their faith. Angeles was disillusioned as were Carreon and a host of other Asian and Pacific Islander Christian immigrants.

D. Religious Opposition to Segregation

The imposition of patterns of segregation and discrimination by whites over people of color was not unopposed. Some churches, both as denominations and congregations, actively opposed legislation of discriminatory practices. The Seattle Council of Churches in its relationship with the Washington State Council of Churches was the primary body through which Christian churches organized their lobbying efforts on behalf of racial equality. Other, religiously unaffiliated people, worked equally hard within groups such as the NAACP and Urban League to change the environment and laws of the city. Perhaps the most vocal Seattle congregations at the time were black churches; the Mt. Olive Baptist Church, the People's Institutional Baptist Church, the First AME Church, and Grace Presbyterian Church. The mainline Protestants tended to work through the Council of Churches though some such as The People's Church and Plymouth Congregational Church actively worked on their own as well. The Japanese Congregational Church, Chinese Baptist Church, Filipino Community Church (Methodist), and the synagogues Temple de Hirsch and Heral Congregation were also important in the religious effort to shape society.

The Church Council of Greater Seattle, made up of most of the mainline churches in the Seattle area, followed the precepts of the Federal Council of Churches with regard to its social principles and stances on racism.[57] The Federal Council in the 1940s officially adopted a statement of social principles and embarked upon a campaign to create a "nonsegregated church in a non segregated society."[58] The Federal Council of Churches Race Relations Department noted that "The pattern of racial segregation in America is given moral sanction by the fact that churches and church institutions, as a result of social pressure, have so largely accepted the pattern of racial segregation in their own life and practice."[59] They noted that Negro membership was less than 1 percent in predominantly white churches. The pattern of segregation was more prevalent in church than public school and was especially prevalent in hospitals; Negro doctors, Negro nurses, church-controlled hospitals largely excluded Negro patients. Church schools tended to be less segregated than hospitals, but theological seminaries frequently discriminated against minority people. The Church Council proposed integration at all levels - especially opening white churches to minority groups. Notably, they pointed out, one seldom finds notice of racial minority churches being closed to white people.

By far the largest racial-ethnic group in Seattle during this entire period were the European-Americans, many of whom were also recent immigrants, but from across a different ocean. Scandinavian, Italian, and Irish immigrants joined those born the United States in forming one of the whitest populations in the country. The European immigrants provide a good example of the limitations of the ethnicity paradigm of racial identity identified by Omi and Winant's study. As relatively recent immigrants, Seattle society did not always admit Irish and Italians to the ranks of white citizens when these groups retained their native languages or spoke accented English. Irish and Italian children received the benefits of identification as white people, and quickly were able to join the ranks of the middle class. Many of these immigrants, including many from northern

Europe, initially came to Seattle, as did those from Asia, to fill gaps in the labor market, but unlike their neighbors of color, they went on to enjoy the upward mobility white middle class Americans had come to expect by mid-century. The population of Seattle remained mostly white throughout this period. The neighborhoods were largely white neighborhoods with the exception of the Central Area and the International District that were racially diverse. The Central Area became more African American even after the practice of racially restrictive real estate covenants began to decline. Some who lived in the city before the influx of skilled and unskilled labor during the World War II years lamented the loss of a degree of comfort in inter-racial relationships. Whether this comfort was a nostalgic memory or an actual experience of a more open and egalitarian society is hard to tell.[60] In oral history interviews collected by the University of Washington Seattle Civil Rights and Labor History Project, the experience of segregation permeated the memories of many people, the inability to stay in a hotel, find a job, or buy a house.[61] All the immigrants to Seattle faced the problem of leaving customary ways behind and entering into a new society. The large majority of white American and European immigrants found it much easier to shape the new society to match customs with which they were familiar. While Chinese, Japanese, Filipino, and African Americans found less overt hostility in Seattle, by the end of the fifties, racial barriers in housing, employment, and educational opportunity hemmed them in nevertheless.

European immigrants were primarily Christian, both Protestant and Catholic, when they retained a religious affiliation after moving to Seattle. Some later became interested in Asian religious traditions, especially Zen Buddhism. Jews were present in Seattle from its beginning in small numbers. American Jews existed in a complex network of cultural, religious and racial identities. On the one hand, they participated in the privileges society gave to citizens of European descent, holding property, running prosperous businesses, and having the freedom to life as they chose more or less. On the other hand, they were not quite white to the eyes of many American Christians.[62] Jews faced segregation in particular aspects of their lives, most notably in being barred from participation in certain prestigious social clubs and organizations and being restricted from buying houses in certain neighborhoods. From the beginning, the Christian Friends for Racial Equality included Jewish members and from time to time met in Temple Hirsch in downtown Seattle. This in itself indicates that definitions of race were part of the Seattle Jewish identity.

E. Religion, Race and Demographic Patterns

A portrait of Seattle population in 1930 shows a society that was overwhelmingly European-American with a diversity of racial minorities, the majority of whom were Asian, and a majority of the Asian population was Japanese. By the time the CFRE faded from the scene in the 1960s, the white majority was only slightly less that it had been in the 1930s, but the make-up of the minority had changed substantially. The forced removal of the Japanese to internment camps in 1942 was an important factor in this change. By 1960, the largest racial minority group in Seattle was African American.

The shift in population changed the character of Seattle, especially downtown in the Central Area. The rapid increase in population during the Second World War pulled Seattle into the more general mold of racially segregated American urban society. The effect of racially restricted real estate covenants on the property values in the Central District changed the character of everything from the businesses to the schools. The decline in prosperity of the Central District ran counter to the general growth of the city as a whole. During the active life of the CFRE, Seattle was in the process of rapid social change. The project of

Figure 5 Seattle Minority and White Population Compared

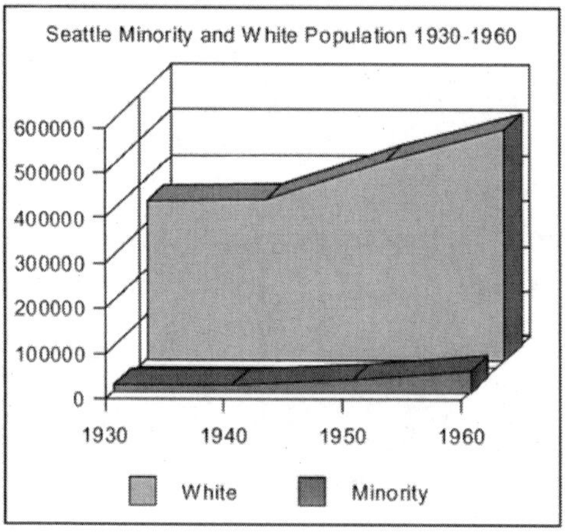

the CFRE, focused on the creation of a public conscience and a desire for racial justice based on the sure foundation of personal relationships among people of different races, was like a salmon swimming upstream. Powerful forces arrayed themselves against its success. Yet the CFRE, as we will see, was able to intervene for the good in several points in this process of social change, resulting in a society more open and just toward racial minorities than was ordinarily the case in urban America.

IV. Religious Support for and Opposition to this Segregated Society.

The concern the CFRE expressed about the segregation of the churches themselves, urges a consideration of the role of religion in shaping patterns of segregation. Due to racial divisions among Christian churches in the United States, many have called Sunday morning worship the most segregated hour in the country.[63] The church both followed the pattern of society and helped to shape it in complex ways. Certainly Christian people sometimes deliberately created policies that reinforced segregation even as many decried those policies on Christian grounds.

Early in the history of race relations in this country, the formation of the African Methodist Episcopal Church (1793) in Philadelphia was a reaction to the segregation of black church members to a less desirable area of the sanctuary during worship in a Methodist Church. This was not simply a Methodist pattern, but was common in otherwise mixed-race churches in the eighteenth century. During the twentieth century, the advocacy of segregation grew out of concern about inter-marriage between the races.[64]

The question of Christian influence on public conscience has several aspects. The church is one site of moral formation in society. The linguistic philosopher Noam Chomsky has argued that we learn our ethics like we learn our first language, steeped in a society and community. Unless the church makes an effort to counter the folk ethics of the surrounding community, children will learn racism along with their language.[65] Christian influence is hampered by the divisions among the churches in the United States; by the lack of an established or state church and hence the voluntary and fluid nature of church membership; by the nature of American theological education both for clergy and laity; and finally by outside pressures for the churches to conform to patterns beneficial to those with money and power. If Christianity is to bear some accountability for the establishment of a racist or a segregated society, we need to explore the options Christians and churches thought they had in doing what they did.

A. The Diversity and Disunity within Christianity

Christianity in the United States is not a uniform or united religious body. It may be a religion among several large and influential religious traditions of the world, but Christians themselves rarely understand Christianity as encompassing the whole range of those one with an outside view might define as Christians. Christianity arrived in the Americas already fragmented by the Reformations of European Christendom and more ancient fissures among churches rooted in the Latin West, the Greek Speaking Eastern Mediterranean, and churches found further East. The fragmentation had a number of causes. It was in many ways internal to Christianity, caused by differences in theology, practice, and understanding of the nature of the institutional forms of the faith. The fracture lines followed boundaries between nations, empires, languages and cultures. The rapid development of the nation states in Europe after the breakdown of the feudal economy in the Early Modern period also shaped the sense of modern fragmentation. As the Reformation progressed, European rulers protected various branches of the reform in their attempt to unite citizens in a common national religious expression.

In the American British colonies, Christians of diverse sects and former state churches[66] found themselves living next door to each other rather than at arm's length across national borders. The British actively exiled their religious dissidents to the American colonies. Thus, some of the smallest Christian sects in Europe became prominent denominations in the United States. The Baptists are an important example of this. In addition, growing numbers of American churches were born from innovations on American soil rather than having roots in European Christianity. These political divisions in Anglo American Christianity meant that it could speak with a unified voice about very few things. The few denominations that took an early stand against slavery were the smaller, less influential ones such as the Quakers. The larger churches eventually took strong stands, but paid a price in further divisions. The major white Seattle churches came from denominations that had an ambivalent history with regard to race relations.

As the United States developed its Constitution and basic approach to nationhood, the sheer variety of kinds of Christianity made it impossible to argue for the establishment of any one of them as a state church. They wrote disestablishment into the Constitution. This does not mean that Christianity had no influence, but that influence had a generic quality, perhaps a diluted one in the eyes of many of the faithful. The divisions have continued, caused by theological disagreements, moral differences, organizational preferences, geography, and (important for our discussion) race. The fragmentation made it impossible to find an American Christian consensus, particularly not on moral issues that divided the population as strongly as did the question of the meaning of race in shaping social structures.

The voluntary nature of church membership and support also affected the ability of religious bodies to shape public conscience. Denominations and their clergy were and are often reluctant to make explicit moral claims that go against the congregation's popular opinion. Their livelihood depends upon people staying in their church and supporting it. The classical curriculum of theological education for white pastors has seldom educated them to address issues of race, and even when it has, often a wide gap exists between what the clergy know and what they teach to their parishioners.[67] Finally, the influence of people with power and money can act in many ways to shape the influence of religious organizations on the public conscience.

B. The Relationship of Religion to Public Life

The lack of an established or state church shaped the voluntary and fluid nature of church membership in the United States. Christianity as a religion consists of a way of life and a set of beliefs based in the traditions of Judaism from which it arose and as its founder Jesus and his followers further developed them. Institutional forms of Christianity consist of these beliefs and ways of life, but also structures of power, buildings and other property, and customary ways of worship and practicing the faith. The church focused on not only the teaching and practice of the faith but also on the maintenance of the institution, which sustains this practice. In a situation where participation in the activities, benefits, and life of the institution is voluntary, the means to sustain the institution is also dependent on voluntary support. This puts a certain conservative pressure on institutional forms of religion so that change will not result in a decline of membership or means. This is not to say that Christian institutions cannot change or even challenge a popular status quo; but only to say that the tendency is conservative, that they are reluctant to do things that might put their means of support at risk. This institutional aspect of Christian presence in the United States affected the way individual congregations and denominations responded to the challenges of race relations. In Seattle, as in most areas of the American West, a less religiously affiliated population can put even more pressure on clergy or congregations to be silent on matters that might be controversial. It can also cause less pressure, since those who affiliate with churches in more secularized areas are more committed members in the first place, less likely to be discouraged by challenge and controversy.[68]

Depending on the way a Christian denomination or congregation structured its power relationships and authorized its leadership, clergy and lay leaders were more or less able to work for social change in Seattle. One pastor, Fred Shorter, an early supporter of the CFRE, had been dismissed from his pulpit in the Pilgrim Congregational Church because his support for labor organizing, particularly his effort to free Eugene Barrett, a Wobbly organizer, from prison. Barrett suffered imprisonment following a general strike. Even though the Federal Council of Churches was also involved in the effort to free Barrett, Shorter's actions offended the business people who made up the majority of his congregation.[69] Shorter subsequently started an independent congregation the Church of the People, dedicated to worker's rights and other social justice causes. Shorter was one of many activists in Seattle during the twentieth century whose work for racial equality grew from his support for labor.[70] His reading of the Christian Gospel would not allow him to ignore its teachings about the way society should treat the poor.[71] While the Congregational Churches nation-wide contained many people who shared his view,[72] the polity of the denomination gave every congregation the freedom to decide such matters. Earlier in Seattle history, Rev. Mark Matthews of First Presbyterian Church had succeeded in keeping his position in a church filled with influential people while he challenged their understanding of Christian responsibility for worker justice.

The example of Pilgrim Congregational Church dismissing its outspoken pastor does not mean that the white churches of Seattle were completely silent on the matter of racial justice. Clergy and congregations had two lines of accountability. Besides their accountability in faith to their God, they were accountable to the people of the church who paid their salaries and supported their church budgets and the denominations of which they were a part. Congregations expected their clergy to represent them regardless of the pastors' specific personal views, and this could make acting against the popular will difficult. The most common way for Christians to take stands and work for racial justice in this era was to join together in Councils of Churches, ministers associations, or lay-run para-church organizations such as the YWCA or the CFRE. The Seattle Council of Churches and Religious Education was such a group, related to the national Federal Council of Churches and sharing many of its commitments.

The Federal Council of Churches formed its Race Relations Department in the 1920s and had a specific list of policies that served as guides and standards for denominations and congregations that wished to pursue the task of racial justice more locally. The FCC 1946 policy statement, "The Church and Race Relations," emphasized integration at all levels of society, especially the integration of white churches.[73] In particular the pamphlet noted, "The pattern of racial segregation in America is given moral sanction by the fact that churches and church institutions, as a result of social pressure, have so largely accepted the pattern of racial segregation in their own life and practice."[74] These ecumenical groups could issue radical statements on social justice issues because they did so as a whole group, not as individuals who could separately suffer retaliation by those who disagreed. There was safety in numbers.

At the same time, ecumenical groups were apt to pull their punches at critical moments, because the radical statements they made represented smaller groups of passionate individuals representing larger bodies of people, and those larger bodies did not, as a whole, completely agree to radical policies. Hence in testimony before the Senate committee considering the Fair Employment Practices Act in 1947, Dr. Beverley Boyd, Episcopal clergyman and Executive Secretary of the FCC Department of Christian Social Relations, made an impassioned argument for integrating the work place, citing an official pronouncement of the FCC on the matter, but had to admit that only four of the twenty-five member denominations whose representatives created the statement had actually confirmed their support for it by an official denominational action.[75] The director had to be careful not to jeopardize the support for the FCC from these denominations by going too far in his claim about what the group stood for, despite the fact that the FCC statement did represent the views of the FCC itself.

C. The Background of Theological Education

The third obstacle preventing Christian people from overcoming the contradiction between their support for a discriminatory society and their claim to believe and follow the Christian Gospel had to do with the nature of American theological education both for clergy and for laity. Until the middle of the twentieth century, the education of most Christian ministers built upon a general liberal arts education followed by study of philosophy and theology, biblical studies, acquiring skill in public speaking, and gaining an understanding of the specific faith commitments and practices of the person's denomination. The field of psychology and the study of other social sciences were only beginning to be important in the minister's professional work.[76]

The theological education of the average church member usually depended upon the efforts of the clergy to teach what they knew to their congregations. While in the nineteenth century the pulpit was an important venue for the dissemination of the latest in theological thought, by the beginning of the twentieth century, conflicts within denominations over the appropriate theological response to the findings of science and modernity in general had made the pulpit less safe as a means of conveying new theological thinking. Most pastors focused instead on individual spiritual needs and general treatments of right and wrong. They kept to the familiar words of the Bible and did not lead their congregations into the complexities of biblical exegesis and critical historical methods of reading these sacred texts. In addition, the century long effort to make sure church membership kept up with the westward expanding population movement resulted in a simplified version of Protestant Christianity that could be used in a generic way to gather congregations of people who otherwise would prefer different denominations. This generic Protestantism tended to be simplistically literal in its approach to the Bible, and to focus on widely agreed upon theological principles such as the divinity of Christ, the need for a person to convert and claim salvation, and live by a set of moral practices that avoided drinking, smoking, dancing, gambling, and working on Sunday.[77] This generic Protestantism did not lend itself to a sophisticated analysis of race relations nor did it encourage the kind of critical theological thinking that would be required to address the problem of racial justice adequately. Worse, it contributed to the fear of pastors that, if they strayed too far from this generic, commonly held set of acceptable pulpit topics, they would lose their jobs or worse their ordination credentials.

D. Outside Pressures of Money and Power.

The economic and social pressure from the larger society upon religious institutions was enormous. In parts of the country where the Ku Klux Klan was organized, the consequences of challenging discriminatory structures could be deadly. Seattle was one of the places where such activity was not prevalent yet social conventions and economic prosperity, structured in racially stratified terms, made it difficult for people to press for change. The fear of being poor or powerless was and is a powerful factor in prejudice. People perceived the loss of property value in integrated neighborhoods, the loss of prestige in jobs open to women or people of minority races, the depression of wages in situations where immigrant labor is plentiful to be the results of fair employment practices and fair housing laws.

In Washington State the insecurities of an extractive economy, subject to booms and busts in mining, timber industry, agriculture, and fishing probably increased the propensity to discriminate based on long developed, ingrained racial and cultural prejudices.[78] Seattle's economy grew up during a particularly changeable time in US economic history. The rapid development of industrialization in the late nineteenth century, and the application of industrial methods to extractive enterprises such as mining, lumber, and agriculture changed more localized and customary ways of working. The downward pressure on wages, as machinery became more refined and population continued to increase, made worker's futures uncertain at best. Periodic economic depressions further increased the anxiety of working people. In addition, the global chaos of two world wars in the first half of the century shaped Seattle's economic life in uncontrollable ways. One of the most important effects of this rapid economic change in Seattle was the influx of people seeking employment during the 1940s creating a larger pool of people supporting the majority American attitudes toward race relations. During this period, segregated social structures became more common in the city.

V. Ecumenical and Liberal Political Rhetoric Supporting Racial Justice

A. Ecumenical or Mainline American Protestantism

The rhetoric of American mainline Protestant Christianity about racial justice focused on commitment to the unity of humanity and the infinite worth of the human soul before God. These two principles were rooted in the biblical tradition. Protestant and Roman Catholic Christians alike had made the fundamental theological decision that regardless of culture, class, race, or religion, all human beings had souls.[79] Early in the sixteenth century, when first faced with knowledge of the people of the Americas, the Pacific Islands, and other regions left out of the traditional accounts of the diversity of humanity, both Catholics and Protestants debated the question. While some, in the interest of justifying chattel slavery, attempted to argue that certain of these were not actually human in the same way as they were, theirs was not the prevailing view. Christian missionaries from Europe, Catholic, and then Protestant traveled throughout the world from the sixteenth century onward in an attempt to save all these souls. Missionaries, being both religious people and citizens of their respective nations did not always separate the religious intentions of their missions from other national projects. Nor were their estimates of the possibilities for their converts' sharing fully in the benefits of their national culture always high. Individual Christians and nations made up largely of people who thought of themselves as Christian did not always give credence to this theological principle when their interest was also economic or political gain. Nonetheless, representatives of Christianity continued to argue for racial justice and they did so based on a theological position holding that all human beings were equal before God.

B. Integration and American Progressive Ideals of Equality and Freedom

Within an ecumenical organization containing the diversity of Christian denominations represented in the Federal Council of Churches, or the Church Council of Greater Seattle, there was a wide and sometimes conflicting range of Christian ethical beliefs and commitments. In the first half of the twentieth century, such ecumenical organizations appealed to unifying principles derived from American political ideals. The ideal of equal rights rested in the founding documents of the Republic even if those documents did not explicitly address the racial diversity with which Christians grappled in later eras. Confident that their Christian ideals had shaped the national commitment to liberty and equality, some twentieth-century Protestants found this appeal to civic virtue useful in promoting ideals of equality that were not always popular among the members of their respective churches.

The Progressive political movement of the turn of the century focused most specifically on economic concerns common to working class people and people of middle income. Liberal Christian theology and ethics tended to mirror Progressive social ideals, limits on the workday and workweek, protections for workers from dangerous conditions, protection of consumers from dangerous products, recognizing the right of workers to collective activity in unions, and desire to reform political processes so that they are responsive to more of the population. These Progressive political ideas often seemed congenial to mainline Protestants who held liberal theological views. Liberal theology put traditional Christianity in dialogue with modernity.

Its outlines developed over several centuries from the Reformation to the twentieth century, but blossomed after the Enlightenment. Liberal theologies commonly tried to hold a middle position between strictly traditional or fundamentalist approaches to Christianity and the skepticism or even atheism of the rationalists.[80] Emphasizing principles of Christian life rather than the necessity of particular orthodox belief, the liberal theological position advocated an engaged spirituality and supported Progressive political and economic reforms. Chapter 4 will further discuss the various ways in which the Christian Friends for Racial Equality and the Seattle Council of Churches exhibit Progressive characteristics and influence.

C. The Social Gospel

The Social Gospel was one particular branch of this liberal and Progressive influence in American Christianity. Developed by several theologians whose ministry centered in the newly industrialized cities, the Social Gospel considered Christian teaching from the point of view of the working poor. Perceiving that direct individual behaviors such as alcoholism, laziness or ignorance were not sufficient to explain the development of industrial urban poverty, they began to delineate how the industrial structures created poverty in themselves by the ways in which labor became a commodity to be bought and sold, to be needed or discarded when not needed. Many of the Social Gospel theologians embraced Christian socialism as an alternative to the industrial capitalism, which they viewed as inherently based in greed and unconcerned for human welfare. The Social Gospel shared several core interests with liberal theology and Progressive political projects. All three movements were optimistic about the ability of education to better society and that teaching the principles of Christianity to the young would naturally develop a Christian society. All three believed that a just and humane treatment of labor was not only right, but also necessary for a stable society. All three had an understanding of the common good that transcended the narrow interests of business growth. The Seattle Presbyterian pastor Mark Matthews and the Congregationalist Fred Shorter, provide clear examples of the Social Gospel in Seattle.

The Progressives did not achieve all of their goals; in fact, some historians of the movement argue that the business interests co-opted it early in its history.[81] The enthusiasm of mainline Protestant Christianity for such social projects was much more evident in ecumenical settings, in single congregations or in the social concerns committees of denominations. The mainline Protestant clergy were more likely to hold liberal theological ideals or Progressive political views than the people were in the pews. The Great War ended their collective optimism about the solutions to social problems. The subsequent Great Depression and the rise of Fascism dealt another blow as developments in Europe began to make clear that people who thought of themselves as Christian were capable of great evil.

Some denominations of Christianity were more engaged in liberal, Progressive, or Social Gospel concerns than others did. However, for most denominations it was a minority of their membership who engaged in these approaches to social problems. Individual clergy or specific congregations took their stands with these movements. Sometimes denominations had particular official offices assigned to address economic or racial justice concerns. Others maintained a non-dogmatic traditionalism, or advocated a strict orthodoxy, discouraging overt social justice work not aimed at saving souls. Thus it was sometimes more useful for congregations and clergy with such interests to join together ecumenically to achieve their purpose without having to persuade everyone in their denomination to join them. The CFRE is one such local ecumenical effort developed by the grass roots; the Church Council of Greater Seattle is another developed along more officially representative lines. The effort for Christian unity in the twentieth century became associated with these ecumenical Progressive and Social Gospel programs to increase economic and social justice. By mid-century, a gap appeared between the leadership of congregations and denominations and the laity based in theological controversies over the appropriate theological response to the findings of science and in ethical controversies over the appropriate Christian response to economic changes rooted in industrialization.[82] Often a denomination fragmented before it realized what was happening. The work for social justice moved to the side, out of the pulpit, and became an optional work undertaken by some clergy and laity in their spare time or through a special branch of denominational work, and not always as official representatives of their churches.

Some congregations, often called "institutional" churches, undertook to connect their Christian theology with the people around them. They worked together with labor union organizers, with social workers, and with local community political efforts to improve the physical lot of the people as well as their spiritual well-being. In Seattle, First Presbyterian Church, The Church of the People, The People's Institutional Baptist Church and First Baptist Church were examples of this kind. Para-church organizations were also involved in this effort. The YMCA and YWCA, the Catholic Workers, the settlement houses, and other local efforts all allowed committed Christian people to work for the society they believed was possible without having to confront or seek approval from the majority in their denomination. Many of the denominations divided and continue to divide along lines where theological differences met political differences. Many clergy and laity worked outside the denominational frameworks, in ecumenical or para-church organizations, to be more effective in addressing issues of social justice.

Protestants were not the only religious groups in the country sharing these political, social, and theological ideals. Roman Catholic struggles about whether or not to support the labor union movements were indications of the hierarchy's sometimes perceived distance from the largely working class parishes they served, as well as Catholic struggles with modernity. The Catholic position on economic issues focused on economic structures that fostered good Catholic family life, the dignity of labor, and the necessity of a living wage. As a worldwide Christian Church, the Roman Catholics had a long history of ministry to a wide diversity of cultures. European American clergy shaped the American Catholic Church, and the church often assigned them regardless of the race or culture of the parish. Many of the same issues about race and culture found among the Protestant churches were present in the Catholic parishes as well. The Maryknoll parish in Seattle served the immigrant communities from Japan and the Philippines; it was the Maryknoll communities in Latin America who first developed liberation theologies to address the Christian faith to the situation of the poor.

Jews had their own versions of the liberal or modernist controversy with fundamentalism. The emergence in this period of Reformed Judaism in the American context, more moderate Conservative Judaism, and the continued strength of Orthodox Judaism signaled similar divisions of thought and practice.[83] Though the divisions originated in debates within the Jewish communities about what it meant to be a Jew in American society, they were also about the appropriateness of addressing modern social problems using Progressive political ideals as well as theological principles. In Seattle, the Anti-Defamation League cooperated with many of the wider civil rights efforts, especially with the open housing movements. Jews suffered along with Asian Americans and African Americans from racially restrictive real estate covenants. Jewish support for labor has always been strong. In the 1960s, Jews were deeply involved in the civil rights movements of the time. Strong connections existed between major synagogues in the Pacific coast cities, such as San Francisco and Seattle, and African American civil rights leaders.[84]

American Buddhists, depending upon whether they were among the majority, working class Asian immigrants or whether they were among the growing number of middle or upper class European Americans who became interested in and sometimes converted to Buddhism, shared an interest in social matters. The Buddhist community is diverse like the Christian community. Various sects of Buddhism developed in different nations and also experience variations within cultural groups. Buddhists have no single approach to issues of civil rights any more than one can point to a single Christian approach. Buddhist thought emphasizes compassion and support of the flourishing of all life and so supports racial equality. Buddhism, while mostly a religious tradition of Asian and Asian Americans, has also attracted many European Americans and African Americans to its teachings. Taigen Dan Leighton, an important American Zen teacher, observed that Buddhism contains a history of social activism, but has also tended to use its concept of karma to explain social inequality thus tending to accept things the way they are.[85]

VI. Comparison of the Ecumenical Efforts of the CFRE and Council of Churches

During this period, roughly the 1940s and 1950s, both of the ecumenical groups we are considering, the CFRE and the Council of Churches, were concerned about issues of racial justice and both tended, as was common at the time among advocates for racial equality, to see integration as the root solution to the problem. Many of the church people in Seattle who were active in the cause of racial justice belonged to both groups. The two groups differed considerably in their sense of primary purpose and in their approach to the question of how to achieve an integrated society in Seattle.

A. The Seattle Council of Churches and Christian Education

The Council of Churches concentrated their efforts on addressing race relations within and among the churches as their primary effort and addressed public policy issues in a secondary way. Nonetheless, they more so than the CFRE, were the body addressed by the community when the community needed some word from the churches about certain issues. For instance, in 1939, the Seattle branch of the NAACP addressed a letter to the Public Affairs Committee of the council expressing concern about the pending pardon of two police officers who had been convicted of killing a black civilian in a confrontation, and whose conviction The Supreme Court upheld. The letter asked specifically for "your action in the form of a protest to Governor Martin, against complete exoneration by pardon."[86] As an official representative of the churches, the Council's voice had considerable weight. For the same reason, the Council was careful about the issues it chose to speak about in such a way because it was representative and most people would assume its views were widely shared by Seattle's church people.

B. The Council of Churches and the Japanese in Seattle in 1941-1942.

Occasionally, the Public Affairs Department's concerns, representing widely shared views among the churches, would conflict with the goals of the Race Relations Department. In 1939, the President of the Council of Churches received a letter from the Christian Endeavor Society of the Japanese Congregational Church.

> The Christian Endeavor Society of the Japanese Congregational Church which is composed of American born young Christians wishes to express regret at the Resolution recently passed by the Council of Churches, which has for its

> purpose the stopping of the shipment of war material to Japan by the United States Government.[87]

Often the controversy among the churches would have focused on the question of Christian support for war, but here, the young people were concerned about the effect of this letter in the Japanese community, the largest racial minority community in Seattle at the time. They regarded it as an anti-Japanese expression though they suspected that this was not the intent of the Council, and worried about how it would affect the Christian minority in that community. Political and perhaps generational differences of opinion among the Christian communities in Seattle could easily take on racial overtones especially for those used to discrimination. The racialized nature of issues was rarely expressly at the forefront of the discussion of such public policy issues in the work of the Council of Churches.

The Council of Churches was itself multi-racial and multicultural. Most of the mainline Protestant Churches of Seattle were members. The Council was sensitive to particular public policy issues affecting any of the churches or their members. Throughout the year 1941 when anti-Japanese feeling was building up in the state, the Council of Churches paid attention to the problems of Japanese citizens, especially Christian ones. They were aware of and contributed to the efforts of the Federal Council of Churches to address the rising tensions. They were particularly concerned about the second generation or American born Nisei since these were American citizens. In October 1941, they passed a resolution, which they published widely in the Pacific Northwest as "A Message to the Japanese in the Pacific Northwest."

> We wish to congratulate you on the good record the Japanese in the United States have for being a law-abiding people. Both the first generation and the American born, second gener-

ation, are above average in the matter of good citizenship and observance of the best social usages. We feel that you have nothing to fear from the American government or the American people as long as you continue such conduct.

We wish to assure you of the sympathy and cooperation of the Churches. We urge you to take any problem that may arise because of the international situation, or because of any local matter, to any Christians with whom you may be acquainted. Please do not hesitate to confer with any Christian Church pastor relative to any problem that may arise.[88]

They had not yet imagined what kind of problem might arise for the Japanese community in Seattle.

In November, the Council worked closely with the city redevelopment agency finding new homes for people displaced for the construction of the Yesler Terrace low-income housing project. A number of these were Japanese families who had owned homes in the condemned area and had a particularly difficult time finding a new place to live because of the anti-Japanese tensions. In a matter of a few weeks, the situation changed drastically for the worse.

On December 8, 1941, the day after the bombing of Pearl Harbor, the Council reissued their earlier statement and again published it widely in the region. In the week that followed, they also addressed the churches in this manner.

> It would be most unfortunate if our Christian people would, by their attitude and actions, add to the difficulties and trials of the Japanese-Americans who now become victims of unfortunate circumstances because of the present situation. . . . .In this crisis we would remind all that this is no hour to forget the traditions and principles of our great nation, to remain Christian in all of our attitudes and actions and not to yield to hatred, and finally to seek Divine guidance for ourselves and

our nation in this dark hour.[89]

In addition the Council worked with other organizations such as Traveler's Aid to provide relief to the Japanese who, suddenly prohibited from accepting money, were caught without sufficient food or unable to pay rent. Many lost their jobs on the Monday following the bombing. The Council also later went on record opposing the methods used by the military in the general evacuation of the Japanese from the Pacific Coast.[90]

The Seattle Council of Churches, representing the churches to the larger public of Seattle and working closely with other community organizations and city government arguably had a greater concern for the way race relations issues affected civic life than did the CFRE, which focused more on individual relationships and actions, or social life. One example was the problem of recreation for African American soldiers stationed at Ft. Lewis. Along with the black contingent was a group of soldiers from the American South who strongly objected to sharing recreational facilities with their African American comrades. In Seattle, soldiers on leave found that the usual places in which to enjoy their time were segregated. This included the YMCA, the USO, which had planned to provide additional facilities for the African Americans but did not do so, and a number of other entertainment venues, hotels and restaurants. The areas available for African American soldiers' recreation were limited to some nightspots and restaurants in the Central Area and a segregated beach. The CFRE noted and protested the segregated beach, but the Council of Churches undertook to address the whole problem because they were concerned about the "unwholesomeness" of the options available to the African Americans and their concern about growing racial tension and conflict in the city.

Mrs. Nella Carter outlined these concerns in a report to the Interracial Committee of the Church Council. Carter was a social worker in Seattle, and she shared the same concern for the youth of the city as the Council did for the soldiers. The influx of people into the Puget Sound area because of the growth of the military bases upset the longstanding relationships among the races in the city. The Council of Churches asked that the city use funds from the community to equip the YMCA building in the East Madison district to provide housing and recreational facilities for the African American soldiers and youth.[91] The Council of Churches, representing several thousand Seattle residents, felt entitled to suggest this expenditure on behalf of the whole community whereas the CFRE would not have done so, though they might have sent a representative to talk with the Mayor. The Jackson Street Community Council had a junior council made up of teenagers and young adults in the neighborhood and took their concerns seriously. They created a Friday night program for youth at the Neighborhood House and sought to provide healthy recreation opportunities for racial minority young people often turned away from public venues.[92]

In September 1945, the Council of Churches carried out an Interracial Clinic focused on housing and job concerns among racial minority citizens as the war ended. In this clinic, the Council collaborated with the Urban League and Federal Council of Churches. At the end of the meeting, they proposed several public policy changes: make restrictive covenants illegal; seek a permanent fair employment practice law; help the Japanese relocate; educate across racial lines; grant equal access to labor unions and social organizations; and hire minority teachers.[93]

C. The Christian Friends for Racial Equality

The Christian Friends for Racial Equality had a somewhat different approach from that of the Council of Churches, and it was rooted in a different and more focused sense of purpose. Every issue of the *Racial Equality Bulletin*, their regular publication, contained the statement of purpose.

> As Christian Friends for Racial Equality, we seek to apply the Golden Rule. We stand for the equality of opportunity for all men of all races to exercise all rights and privileges guaranteed by our Constitution and the Bill of Rights. We protest by all peaceful means the denial of those rights and privileges, and strive to develop a public conscience against racial and religious discrimination. We endeavor to promote understanding by social acquaintance. Toward this end, we, Christian Friends, seek to welcome all people to our churches, and to strengthen those bonds which unite us all as one people in our democracy.[94]

As they became more active in the endeavor to protest by all peaceful means the social structures that promoted discrimination and intolerance, they adopted a further refinement of their purpose with this statement of method.

1. Direct nonviolent action seeking to develop understanding not resentment
2. Procedure of investigation, persuasion, and when advisable publicity
3. Welcoming cooperation[95]

The first issue that came to the attention of the CFRE was the fact that the Red Cross maintained two racially segregated blood banks. They began working on this problem in 1942 and approached it theologically. Since they believed that God made all humanity "of one blood," they could not agree with the racial theory used by the Red Cross that understood race as something that could be transmitted in the blood, or that the blood of people from one race was somehow different and incompatible with the blood of another race, or would somehow harm the person who received it. Characteristically, they began with the question, "Why does the Red Cross have this practice?" Then they began a long series of conversations and cooperative efforts to get the Red Cross to change its policy, which it finally did in 1951. They were not the only ones to note this discriminatory practice on the part of the Red Cross. The February 1942 issue of the Zion's Herald, a publication of the Boston Wesleyan Association with a nationwide circulation among Methodists, noted the inconsistency "of fighting for democracy abroad, but violating the rights of Negroes at home." Among the things the author suggested were serious problems, was the refusal of the Red Cross to accept Negro blood.[96]

The CFRE had a second problem with the Red Cross; the lack of racial minority nurses aids. They were successful in persuading them to accept a Chinese and three Negro applications for jobs as nurse's aides. This was part of a larger concern with the integration of health care providers in Seattle. Among those, they investigated were the Harborview Hospital Nursing School and the King County Medical Association. In addition, they paid visits doctors and dentists who refused to treat Negro clients.

The effort to integrate the sales forces at the department stores in 1947 brought forth a creative technique. They printed stickers, which people wore when shopping saying, "We would like to see minority sales people at this store."[97] Their sense of publicity as a tool for achieving integration was a strategy based on their confidence in the existence of a public conscience to which they addressed that publicity. Silently wearing stickers with such a request alerted everyone in the store that they were denying cherished community values. The tactic made everyone less comfortable, and support for the change could grow among the customers.

Another subtle CFRE publicity effort involved the collection of some sixty copies of restrictive real estate covenants in common use in Seattle and pointing out areas where church members owned property. These church members often attended churches that were on record as favoring the fair housing bill pending in Congress. A third example of their publicity strategy occurred during the effort to integrate the cemeteries. The CFRE first began to work for the integration of the cemeteries in 1945, using an educational effort aimed at the churches. Bringing the problem to public attention was more difficult. Their effort began to be more successful when the Seattle Times ran a series of articles on the cemetery situation in 1952 after the Presbyterians and Congregationalists gathered eleven hundred signatures on a petition to the cemetery owners. Again, this effort depended for success upon the existence of a public conscience. Nevertheless, the publicity effort itself helped to shape such a conscience in a public who may otherwise not have given thought to the morality of the situation. Finally, the cemeteries began to integrate after the public accommodations law changed making such discrimination illegal.[98]

Their primary goal of both ecumenical organizations remained the effort to integrate Seattle society at the level of individual relationships as well as in organizations. The monthly meetings of the CFRE bringing people from all races together to eat, talk, and share entertainment or informative presentations, were the primary memories of many former members.[99] As with the Seattle Council of Churches, the CFRE was also primarily interested in the integration of the churches. The CFRE was more energetic in this project than the Council of Churches. The Council, though integrated, focused only once a year on church integration during Race Relations Sunday. The CFRE paid it monthly attention. Both groups tended to understand the end result of this integration process as the gradual disappearance of any congregations identified with particular races. They did not foresee the unintended consequence of such integration policies in weakening the minority communities in society.[100] The exclusion of Filipino immigrant Christians from the churches of Seattle was one of the situations that drove the formation of the group; integration remained the central focus to the end. When the CFRE became too involved in efforts to bring about legal change, it always brought itself back to its central purpose of fostering an integrated society through personal relationships and the development of a public conscience through those relationships. In the next chapter, we will look more closely at what the Council of Churches and the CFRE meant by public conscience and how this concept was used to orient their efforts.

Chapter 2

The Development of a Public Conscience in Seattle

> "And our purpose was to seek to apply the Golden Rule, to stand for the Equality of opportunity for all men of all races. To Exercise all rights and privileges guaranteed by the Constitution and by the Bill of Rights. We protest by all peaceful means, the denial of these rights and privileges and strive to develop a public conscience against racial and religious discrimination."[1]

I. Public Conscience Seattle

Larger movements in the American scene influenced Seattle in its public conscience about race relations. The quality of Seattle's public conscience about racial justice waxed and waned through the course of its history. The influence of the churches in Seattle on the development of this conscience is difficult to assess. On the one hand, representing a minority of the population, the churches did not reach most of the population of Seattle on a regular basis because most residents of Seattle did not attend church. On the other hand, those who were church members were more committed than the norm for U. S. church members, and they took their religious outlook into their secular and political activities. Seattle had an early history of Progressive Christian voices for racial justice, Rev. Stanley Strong of the Queen Anne Congregational Church in 1919, Rev. Mark Matthews of the First Presbyterian Church throughout the first three decades of the twentieth century, Rev. Fred Shorter of the Church of the People, and Rev. Samuel McKinney of the Mt. Zion Baptist Church, and several others who took radically

Progressive stands with regard to the inclusion of all people in church and society and worked for the empowerment of racial minority communities, workers and the poor. Washington State was early in adopting anti-discrimination laws. In 1909, discrimination in public accommodation was illegal in the state. Seattle was one of the first cities to adopt an integrated schools policy responding to pressure from the black community, though such a policy was difficult to implement because housing discrimination remained prevalent. In 1967, an article in the *Seattle Post Intelligencer* noted that a person with an anti-integration opinion wanted to remain anonymous in when interviewed about apartment and home ownership integration.[2] By the mid Sixties, Seattle residents no longer considered segregation something publically accepted as right, though privately many still practiced discrimination. Quintard Taylor, in his history of the black community in Seattle, noted that Seattle was an urban frontier, where people were less inclined to duplicate all of the social structures of the older parts of the United States.[3] The population boom of the 1940s brought into Seattle habits of life picked up from more segregated areas of the country. As a result, segregated patterns, while not absent before, became the custom and public support enforced these patterns, and race relations deteriorated as a result.[4] The public conscience of Seattle had not developed to the point where this movement toward racial segregation could be prevented.

> The ideal of racial toleration and egalitarianism proudly espoused by the vast majority of the city's residents has been precariously juxtaposed against a background of racial fear, prejudice and discrimination.[5]

Taylor notes several differences between Seattle and the rest of the country. There was less pre- World War II migration of blacks from other parts of the country and thus fewer tensions with the other groups in the city. The prewar migration to Seattle tended to keep families intact and thus there was less social disintegration than in situations where men migrated alone in search of work, leaving women and children behind or where women migrated alone or with their children in search of a better situation. Poverty in Seattle was not so severe as to cause the breakdown of families and education remained integrated, though the pattern slowly changed as the Central District became more and more segregated. The tensions with the white working-class community were not strong in Seattle before the 1940s because black workers lacked the numbers to challenge the powerful white unions. African -American members of the community thought there was probably no better place for them to live in the United States. White society in Seattle was ambivalent toward them. On the one hand, whites could afford to be more open because their hegemony was not threatened; on the other hand, whites did not extend privileges to black residents. [6]

The black press in Seattle affirmed the ambivalence of the white community toward social and economic equality for African Americans. *The Seattle Republican* the oldest and one of the longest running black papers in the city regularly pointed out the difficulties people faced finding employment in Seattle if they were not white. For example, in June 1898, *The Republican* noted that the Aberdeen Packing Company "introduced the innovation of hiring only white labor. *The Republican* suggests they hire American labor whatever the color."[7] In 1907, *The Republican* suggested the Christian Endeavor [a popular national ecumenical youth organization] in its upcoming meeting in Seattle; hold a day of prayer to rid Seattle "of some of its unholy prejudices and unlawful discrimination."[8] The paper also regularly noted the ways in which the Republican Party ignored its African American supporters. While most African Americans of the early twentieth century registered to vote as Republicans, the *Seattle Republican* regularly discouraged them from voting a straight party ticket since Republican candidates seldom had their interests in mind.

A. Evidence for a Public Conscience: The 1924 Race Relations Survey of the Pacific Coast

In 1924, partly in response to the debate in Congress about the Asian Exclusion Bill, a group of sociologists at a number of Universities, headed by Professor Robert Park of the University of Chicago, undertook a survey of race relations on the Pacific Coast. The survey particularly paid attention to attitudes affecting Japanese, Chinese and Filipino immigrant communities who were most affected by the efforts to extend exclusionary legal sanctions against them. The records from Washington State suggest that the hostility toward Asian Americans was strongest in the rural areas, among farmers and communities depending on timber and mining. One white farmer interviewed noted that opinions of the Japanese, in particular, vary predictably according to economic status. Larger landowners who leased fields to the Japanese tended to have a positive view of them, where owners of small farms saw the Japanese as competitors and had a more negative view.

Among urban residents in Seattle, older Asian immigrant residents reported some experiences of prejudice and exclusion, but the interviews with Asian-American and Pacific Islander high school students suggested that the young people, for the most part, felt included among their white friends. Two specific incidents, which we noted in chapter 1, appeared in the survey records and offer a sense of the state of the public conscience. Both incidents appeared in the *Seattle Star*, a newspaper with a particularly anti-immigrant position, and people interviewed for the survey subsequently pointed these incidents out to those conducting the survey as particularly important. The incident of the Japanese boy, who played George Washington in a school play celebrating the first President's birthday, came to the attention of certain adults in the community, who called the *Star*, and the Sons of Veterans organization called for the resignation of the teacher who allowed a child who was not white to play the part of Washington. The school principal and the majority of the parents supported the teacher and the Japanese child.[9] In the interview with the Race Relations Survey, the principal indicated that the teacher remained on the job. The elementary school incident, with the particularly strong support offered to the child and the school officials by the white parents indicates the presence of considerable public conscience about race relations as early as 1924, at least in that neighborhood.

The other incident, also negatively reported in the *Star*, was the valedictory speech by Tadeo Kimura, the Japanese young man graduating from Franklin High School. In the Survey interview with him, Kimura noted the negative newspaper article, and said his teachers warned him that there might be such opposition, but that his classmates were uniformly supportive. He noted that because of the article, people recognized him as a result and he benefitted by the publicity.[10] The records of the Race Relations survey also contain a paper by Don Greiner, a high school student, who did his own survey of students in his high school and concluded that those who were informed about current events and knew about the Constitution of the United States had favorable views of immigrant students whereas those who were not informed tended to have more negative views. He noted the power of the press to sway people's opinions regardless of the facts. In the absence of education, or critical thought about the issues, the press tended to shape public conscience.[11]

B. The Seattle Council of Churches and the Seattle Public Conscience

Douglas Mark Dye, in his history of the Seattle Council of Churches, argues that not only did the Seattle Council of Churches represent an exception to the general decline of more established denominations before World War II, it also was influential in shaping public thought at a time when historians note the muting of the religious voice in American public affairs. Dye notes that the Council of Churches addressed several issues in an effort to shape the moral character of the city. They opposed the internment of the Japanese, they engaged the issues raised by the growing African American community, they worked with youth, particularly the young men in the armed forces, and Dye argues, this activity contributed to the revival of mainline Protestantism in the Post War years.[12]

The Japanese American Citizens' League noted the deterioration in their situation as the war developed and also deterioration in the efforts of the Seattle community to promote fairness.

> So far as we know, there was no sudden public reactions against Japanese aliens or their citizen children, although there were a number of cases where employers anticipating public disfavor discharged Japanese help. School authorities, church leaders and others, who knew the Japanese or were interested in preventing hysteria from rising against them, joined in these appeals [published in the newspapers and stressing the necessity of fairness to individuals and urging people to remember pre-war friendship.][13]

The Seattle Council of Churches made one such appeal to public conscience in urging the Christian treatment of the Japanese so that the world could not confuse American actions with those of the Nazis or other enemy powers. The head of the Seattle Council of Churches Emergency Committee on Aliens wrote to the President of the United States, Congressional Representatives and the Chiefs of the Armed Forces as well as the Attorney General of the United States, "We are mainly concerned that you, as government officials know of the reaction of the Christian Community."[14] The following year the Council of Churches issued a "Statement Regarding Minority Groups and the Bill of Rights." In this document, which they intended to be widely circulated in the Seattle churches, they argued that Christian principles urged the protection of civil liberties in the midst of war, and "that we should do all in our power as Christian citizens to understand minority groups and racial tensions, such as occasioned by the rise of Negro status during wartime, and recognize the common rights of all citizens, regardless of race, class, or creed, to equal opportunity for employment, housing, recreation, education, and political expression."[15]

C. The Seattle Council of Churches and the Formation of the Civic Unity Committee

The Seattle Council of Churches, recognizing the need for a more broadly based effort to address the problems of race relations as they developed during the 1940s, were among those calling for the establishment of a Civic Unity Committee. Sparked by concern about the 1943 race riots in Detroit, Seattle Mayor Devin appointed a Civic Unity Committee in 1944 comprised of representatives from business, labor, civic officials, Protestant, Catholic and Jewish religious leaders, and Negro, Chinese, and Filipino communities. After the Japanese returned from the Internment, representatives from the Japanese community were included as well. The committee had two purposes, fostering education about racial differences and hearing specific cases in order to find solutions to problems. Because of a grant by the Seattle Women's Service Club, the Civic Unity Committee was able to hire staff to assist their work. The Civic Unity Committee also sought to shape public conscience. Most important, they continually reminded people of the 1909 Washington State law, still in effect, prohibiting discrimination in public accommodation. They did so using off the record conferences with people in government and industry to improve policies and public recognition of those who followed non-discriminatory policies. They were able to achieve nondiscriminatory policies by the Housing Authority and published ways for people to end restrictive real estate covenants. They instituted training for police in human relations, and pressed for the integration of the National Guard. The committee was significantly involved in preparing the city for the return of the Japanese released from the internment camps after the war.[16] The Civic Unity Committee was able to address a number of problems, but was not able to fundamentally change the economic structures of the city which resulted in higher rates of poverty for people of color and the persistence of segregated housing, which if it was not the result any longer of specific racial restrictions, continued as a result of economic disparities between white residents and people of color.

In 1964 and again in 1966 grievances with the Seattle police resulted in The Seattle Human Rights Commission organizing Law Enforcement Conferences on Human Relations. In 1997, the Seattle Human Rights Commission received a report on Community and Police Relations that indicated race relations problems with the Seattle police continued to exist.[17] The Seattle civic efforts to shape a public conscience that would resist racial discrimination and prejudice have had mixed results. Not all groups have benefitted to the same degree from efforts to lessen prejudice. None of the efforts had been able to shift the prevailing economic inequalities that exacerbate racial prejudice. Quintard Taylor noted that the private practice of discrimination counterbalanced the public endorsement of equality celebrated by most of Seattle's population, creating uncertainty for all of the city's residents of color.[18] Other historians also noted this paradox of public support for equality and private discrimination. Jeffrey Zane and Judson Jeffries, in their study of the Seattle Black Panther Party, noted that Seattle had a reputation for its early laws against discrimination, its early adoption of bussing to integrate the schools, and the general lack of discriminatory laws, it was weak enforcement that created persistent problems, particularly for African Americans.[19] Nonetheless, our study of efforts to create a public conscience capable of shaping private practice, while not yet successful, are instructive for those who continue to harbor hope for racial equality.

II. The Secular Conscience

In the United States, liberal political traditions of the Enlightenment shape the secular conscience through principles enshrined in the Declaration of Independence and the Constitution. These ideals have been elaborated in law and transmitted generation by generation in a series of foundational stories such as those associated with George Washington enacted by the children of Seattle. Whether factual or not, these stories contain specific pictures of the kinds of behavior Americans consider to be ideal, particularly honesty, fairness, and bravery in support of liberty. National identity in the United States includes an awareness of these particular ideals and it creates a sense of disquiet when we violate them. Transmitted by education relying on persuasion, and by mass media, sometimes relying on a shared national identity and sometimes by desire, these ideals survive as long as people are prosperous, but over the course of United States history, the ideals have proved to be fragile in hard times. Economic uncertainty tends to erode the secular conscience, and sometimes individuals, groups, and the press, using fear, attempt to bypass the public conscience in order to preserve social or economic advantage. The American public conscience has roots deeper than the Enlightenment. The idea of a public conscience predates Christianity and is probably present in any organized human society, calling on the individual to attend to the whole community and its flourishing. As such, we could expect the shape of the public conscience to vary widely according to the context in which it arose and is active.

Within Western culture, even with the evident influence of Christianity there exists more than one public conscience side by side, sometimes based in values that originated in pre-Christian cultures. Isaiah Berlin points out the conflict of two such public consciences in the work of Machiavelli, famous for his depiction of the prince who seems to have no conscience at all. Berlin argues that Machiavelli makes a stark contrast between two different systems of public morality. The first kind of conscience originated in the pagan world and it values courage, vigor, and fortitude in adversity, public achievement, order, discipline, happiness, strength, justice and "above all assertion of one's proper claims and the power and knowledge needed to secure their satisfaction."[20] The second is that of Christianity which values charity, mercy, sacrifice, love of God, forgiveness of enemies, contempt for the goods of the world, faith in a life hereafter, and the incomparable value of the human soul and its salvation. Christianity also values justice, discipline, and courage in its own way. However, Machiavelli argued that Christianity does not have the capacity to produce a moral community because its ideals are unattainable, and it does not take account of original sin, ignorance, bad luck, and poverty and the ways that these powerfully motivate people to act without regard to others.[21] Berlin argues that a person must choose Christianity or political power; one cannot have both. The organized Christianity active in public life at his time, namely the Roman Catholic Church, Machiavelli thought, contributed to the destruction of civic spirit because the Church regularly misinterpreted Christianity and itself tended to be corrupt because it tried to achieve political power. He reminded his readers that Aristotle in his Politics pointed out that a good person may not necessarily be a good citizen. Christianity, originating in the oikos (the household), worked well as a private morality, but not as a public one. As a religion, Machiavelli thought that Christianity failed to take account of people's preference for vengeance and security rather than peace and liberty. Berlin points to Sophocles' play Antigone as expressing this classic conflict between polis (public realm) and the oikos when the king executed Antigone for attempting to bury her brother's body. The king could not allow her to perform this family duty because her brother committed treason. Machiavelli wanted us to understand that while we can never fully distinguish the two kinds of conscience, we cannot reconcile them either.

American liberals of the Progressive Era, whether Christian or not, tended to be idealistic about the capacities of humanity. The optimism of liberal Christian theology in the late nineteenth century is well known. Sigmund Freud, writing during this same era, punctured the hopeful balloon of Progressive idealism with regard to the nature of the conscience, reminding people that the public conscience is only as moral as the society that shapes it. Freud argued that the dread of society's opinion is the essence of conscience. From the liberal point of view, the much-lamented disappearance of conscience resulted from the lack of social commitment to the right and good rather than some corruption of the individual apart from his or her community. Thus, an individual can sway whole societies in the direction of destruction.[22] This vast shaping of public conscience is particularly evident in war and allows societies to overlook or deny the Holocaust or the Internment of the Japanese when otherwise their rulers could not achieve such things without public outrage.

Charles Long, the African American philosopher and historian reflects both Machiavelli's ambivalence about the effectiveness of Christianity in public life and Freud's more scientific approach to understanding group behavior. He notes that the scandal of slavery to Enlightenment and Christian ideals resulted from the silence of modernity (a modernity that celebrated its Christian roots). He located God in the Silence, "terrifying understanding knowledge." He argues for the development of a collective conscience based in a consciousness of exploitation, the working of greed, and understanding this, the courage to challenge authority and claim political freedom. Long argues that individual liberty is contingent and not absolute.[23]

The historian Roger Burlingame noted a persistent puritan conscience among the American people but that it tended too often to take as its reference point American interests. "It sleeps in prosperity, wakes in tribulation."[24] He noted that the American conscience is often divided, uneasy about slavery but reluctant to disrupt the union, seeing in the family farm the basis of social health but celebrating the wealth of the corporation as a blessing from God. Burlingame gives us the ultimate irony of "the victor's conscience," the conscience that does not have to look closely at what it took to win the victory. Where, Burlingame asks, does society get the capacity for reason and empathy? If the churches are corrupt or unable to supply a set of moral values sufficient for the cause of a just society, where does the public conscience find its ground? Austin Darcey, in *The Secular Conscience: Why Belief Belongs in Public Life* argues that the faculties of reason and empathy, a conscience which does not require a religious basis, is located not in a duty to God, but in our duty to each other.[25] This is what Josiah Royce might have meant by loyalty, though he understood our loyalty to each other to be the location of the presence of God in the Beloved Community.

An example of the working of the secular conscience is the repeal, in September 1971, of Title II, the law that authorized the Internment of the Japanese in World War II, "Through Title II repeal, Americans negotiated what it meant to be a "loyal American" and what a "free society" was supposed to look like, because they saw the specter of the barbed-wire fences and watchtowers, while violence rampaged in U. S. cities and Asian jungles."[26] The effort in recent times by many Americans, both liberal and conservative in their politics and religious commitments, to make color-blindness a characteristic of the American secular public conscience makes such racially specific historical memory invalid.[27] This is another illustration of the dilemma of the American Conscience outlined by Burlingame. That dilemma was present in Seattle and it complicated efforts to bring about racial justice without addressing underlying economic effects of years of discrimination.

III. Religion and Public Conscience

The religious influences on the public conscience are as complex as the secular influences. This is even truer of the public conscience on the Pacific coast because of the complicated meeting places of several major religious traditions. The original Native American traditions are still present. Despite centuries of effort on the part of the governments and cultures of the United States, Mexico and Canada to fold the Native Americans into the European population and dismantle their ways of life, philosophies, religions, and existence as distinctive peoples, the native communities survived. Native American survival continues to prod the public conscience though they still wait for the kind of acknowledgement of injustice the Japanese Americans received with the repeal of Title II. Few of the Native or First Nations religious practices or beliefs remained unchanged as they adapted to rapidly changing conditions. In urban areas such as Seattle, the Native voice remains muted in the shaping of public conscience, but is not absent altogether. It surfaces in several ways, the most prominent being the appeal for Native American rights to use natural resources and in white reference to Native spirituality and culture in the environmental movements of the twentieth century. White people seldom make such appeals because of deeply held acquaintance with actual Native thought and practice or commitment to Native communities, but they represent a conscious awareness on the part of some white people that their ancestors in the conquest destroyed something important and harm continues to result.

A. Layered Christian Efforts to Shape Public Conscience in the American West

Roman Catholic Christians have the longest presence of any European religions in the Pacific coast of North America. While tiny minorities of Christians existed on the East Asian Pacific coast a thousand years ago, the European expression of Roman Catholicism was the first form of Christianity well known in the Pacific region as a whole, almost always associated with Spanish or Portuguese trade and colonization efforts. Associated with colonial projects, no wonder that the Catholic approach to developing a public conscience tended to support the authority of the colonial government, and made its appeal based on fear of hell at worst, or appeal to reward for loyal obedience to the laws of God. Christianity contains unmistakably within it a sense of conscience placing the value of human beings over the value of riches and power and, from time to time, movements in the Spanish colonial communities toward justice for workers and compassion for the poor surfaced in appeals to Christian public conscience.[28] Native American observations of the Spanish colonial regime noted that the colonial project violated the stated values of Christianity in most regards. The Spanish colonial legacy of conflicted conscience was present in Seattle most strongly in the Filipino population, though by the end of the 1950s increasing numbers of Mexican and other Latin American immigrants also resided in the city.

In the seventeenth century, the Pacific coast of North America was the meeting ground between the Spanish, Roman Catholic empire and the Russian, Orthodox empire. Russian presence also touched Seattle. The Russian Orthodox church had a similarly ambiguous sense of public conscience, on the one hand loyal to the Russian colonial project, and on the other, critical, by virtue of Christian teachings, of the exploitation of the people and the resources of the land. By the 1940s, the Russians had become a major rival to the United States, linked to Communism as an ideology Americans tended to regard with distrust and fear. In Seattle, Greek, Russian or other Eastern European Orthodox traditions were largely silent in the organized efforts to achieve racial equality.

Other religious minority traditions were present in Seattle and in conversation with Christians in the effort to achieve racial justice. The Jewish community had several active members in the Christian Friends for Racial Equality, one reason the group considered changing its name to Christians and Friends for Racial Equality in the Sixties. The Christians and Jews in Seattle cooperated in many common efforts. Concerned with racially restrictive covenants that limited the neighborhoods where Jews were welcome, and generally concerned with race relations, the Jewish community cooperated in many ways with Christian efforts toward racial equality. Asian religious traditions such as Buddhism and Shinto, Chinese folk religions as well as more philosophical traditions of Confucianism had a lesser influence on public conscience in Seattle because the practitioners of these traditions were in such a minority. They more quietly supported the life of their own people than attempted to affect the larger public sphere around them. Since many immigrants from China and Japan were already Christian when they arrived, they participated in shaping Christian public opinion and conscience, and in groups such as the Japanese American Citizens' League, cooperated with Japanese Buddhists and practitioners of Shinto as well as with secularized Japanese citizens. The Chinese benevolent societies such as the Chong Wah played a similar role in the Chinese community connecting Buddhists, Taoists and Christians as well as secularized Chinese Americans.

B. The Protestants and the Public Conscience

Protestants undertook the majority of the effort on the part of religious people to shape the public conscience. While religiously affiliated people were a minority to begin with in Seattle, the largest affiliated religious group was the Protestants. Protestants varied considerably in their picture of the kind of conscience the public should have. As in the secular efforts to shape a public conscience based on national ideals, Protestant efforts followed several different methods. Some sought to shape the conscience of individuals and the community, as the Catholics did, by appeal to fear of God or fear of hell or fear of chaos. Underlining this appeal was the sense that misfortune would befall the community that did not so fear God as to live by particular precepts. This fear underlay many Christian justifications for restricting those whose difference seemed to them to be displeasing to God. Those who believed that God had decreed racial inequality appealed to fear of social disintegration should principles of racial equality begin to reshape society. Other Protestants appealed to obedience to God and to religious principles laid down in the Bible and the promise of reward for obedience. They read those principles or laws in different ways depending on the method of biblical interpretation generally applied in particular Protestant communities. Such an appeal to obedience, duty or loyalty to God could underlie an effort toward racial equality or toward maintenance of the status quo. Finally, many Protestants made an appeal based on love, Jesus summation of the Jewish law in the principles "love God with all your heart, and mind, and soul and strength and your neighbor as yourself." Such love could lead to actions well outside the specific teachings of the Bible though coherent with its spirit. The Christian Friends for Racial Equality sought to develop the appeal made on the principle of love of one's neighbor. To understand better the reasons that the Protestants were not able to give a completely united shape to the public conscience of Seattle, it will be necessary to look at the ways several of the larger Protestant groups represented in Seattle approached this issue.

1. The Baptists

The Baptists in the United States originated in the British context. They were part of the more radical reform movements of the sixteenth century, and came to the British colonies in the Americas as religious refugees. Puritan communities did not accept the Baptists though they shared many of the Puritan theological principles. The Baptists too divided by issues of race and slavery. Both the Baptists and Methodists together account for a majority of African American churchgoers today. In Seattle the Mt. Zion Baptist Church, affiliated with the National Baptist Convention and the Northern or American Baptist Convention, and the People's Institutional Baptist Church were the primary African American Baptist churches. Among the white Baptists, the split over slavery resulted in two denominations, the American Baptist Convention and the Southern Baptist Convention. Innumerable independent Baptist congregations and many small Baptist Associations and Conventions represent many differences of opinion about how best to be Baptist in the United States.

Most Baptists trace their understanding of the role of Christianity in public life to Roger Williams in the seventeenth century. Williams' theology was based in a largely Reformed approach derived from John Calvin's Reformation thinking with its roots in the thought of Thomas Aquinas from the Middle Ages. The human ability to grasp moral principles and the exercise of trying to apply these principles to life resulted in conscience. Calvin viewed a person with a conscience as both one who practiced moral discernment and good judgment. The Christian tradition has a long history of noting the inability of even well meaning people to act perfectly in accord with conscience. Williams viewed this conscience as what makes us human, and had an optimistic view of human efforts to overcome the sin that causes us to mistake evil for good and justify our evil deeds by appeal to good intentions. Collectively, the Christian community exercising its several consciences produces a public conscience.[29]

In 1964, the President of the California State Baptist Convention noted the silence of the churches on injustice, particularly on racial injustice.

> I feel that the church must continue to play a part in this march toward first-class citizenship. There are certain areas which we can help to bring about this bridge between the two races. We must continue to preach, believe and practice, the Fatherhood of God, and the Brotherhood of man. I am firmly convinced that it is the duty of the church to share with other secular movements, but be hesitant about letting all movements lead the church.[30]

The decade of the sixties produced in the Baptist Churches as well as in other evangelical denominations, what Timothy Tseng refers to as "the awakened generation," one that experienced the rising racial and ethnic consciousness of the 1950s and 1960s, and which argued, in the cases he studied, among the Chinese, Japanese, Filipino and Korean churches for a more effective political voice from the churches against racial discrimination.[31]

2. Establishment Protestants: Episcopalians, Presbyterians and Congregationalists

Unlike the Baptists whose identity was marked by a sense of dissenting from an established tradition, the Episcopalians, related to the Anglican Churches and the British state church, the Presbyterians, established in the Church of Scotland and in some of the American British colonies, and the Congregationalists, who were dissenters in Great Britain, but became established in many of the New England colonies, all thought of themselves as the denominations shaping the culture and ethos of the United States. All three of these denominations tended to assume that they represented the public conscience of the nation though all three appealed to the well-educated, business and intellectual elite and often represented those interests uncritically.

The Episcopal Church, as part of the Anglican Communion in its worldwide aspect, addressed issues of race from a broader context than simply the race relations developments in the United States. Great Britain had abolished slavery long before the United States, but maintained a global colonial empire into the twentieth century where racism flourished in conjunction with economic exploitation. The Anglican churches both supported and criticized this empire and its effect on human beings of many races. Within the United States, the Episcopal Church similarly was ambivalent about slavery and about the role of people of color in the church and society. In Seattle, the St. Phillips Chapel was an African American parish.

Of the three, the Presbyterians had developed the most extensive multi-racial church by the middle of the twentieth century. Valuing an educated ministry, the Presbyterian Church established schools in many areas where they started churches. Their primary concern was insuring sufficient educational opportunities for those who might feel called to be pastors. Grace Presbyterian Church in Seattle was an African American congregation.

The Presbyterian Churches split during the Civil War over the issue of slavery and later over the Fundamentalist/Modernist debates of the early part of the century. The denomination has had trouble finding a common voice on issues of social justice, even after the reunion of the severed parts of the church. Mark Matthews, the Social Gospel Presbyterian pastor of First Presbyterian Church of Seattle, was also a staunch Fundamentalist though he labored to keep the church from splitting over the issue. Within the Presbyterian Church, as in other mainline American Protestant denominations, theological divisions complicated the issues raised by race. While the

Presbyterian Church finds it difficult to come to an agreement on social justice issues because of its complicated process of coming to a consensus, once it does, that position tends to have widespread acceptance in the denomination.

The Congregational Churches on the other hand, though they were the established churches in New England through the early part of the nineteenth century, had a more difficult time forming denominational decisions about social justice policies. Over the course of the twentieth century, especially during the period we are considering here, the Congregational Churches were engaged in a complex negotiation to become part of a united church made up of several denominations. Joining in the 1930s with the General Convention of Christian Churches to form the Congregational Christian Churches, throughout the forties and fifties, the process of deciding how to unite with the Evangelical and Reformed Church consumed much of the denominational capacity and distracted it from attention to issues of racial justice. In the Seattle area, the Evangelical and Reformed Churches established only a handful of churches, and so the Seattle area Congregationalists may have felt less concerned about the effects of the union that eventually formed the United Church of Christ in 1957 on their local situation. Second to the Baptists, the Congregational churches were the most active congregations represented in the CFRE.

Because of the Congregational practice of leaving each congregation and each body of the church independent and able to decide its own affairs in its own location, some parts of the denomination may move much more quickly than other parts on issues of the day. Consensus was more difficult for the Congregationalists to achieve denominationally but they did not need consensus for any part of the church to act. In addition, Congregationalists often worked in voluntary, lay organized societies to further particular interests. These organizations did not need to receive approval from the denomination for their activities, but judged their support by the level of financial and voluntary contributions to their work.

From the anti-slavery movement forward, the Congregational AMA missionaries and many Congregational pastors emphasized that Christianity taught love for ones neighbor. Without such love, the Christian religion was simply a "sounding gong and tinkling cymbal.[32] The AMA noted after the Civil War, that it was easier for Congregational churches and pastors to take a stand against slavery than it was for them to support the rights of the Indians. "No religious denomination in the land makes an earnest protest; and few, if any, pulpits, which thundered so mightily against the wrongs of the blacks, raise a voice either in pleading for national faith with the Indians, or in denunciation of the crimes which the nation commits in its dealings with them."[33] The AMA also noted that the churches failed to protest the barbarous treatment of the Chinese on the Pacific Coast, which hampered missionary efforts with them.

Despite the AMA effort and the wide readership within the Congregational Churches of society's journal *The American Missionary*, prejudice still existed. A letter from George Shima, a Japanese immigrant to California printed in the journal summed up the contradiction between teaching and practice in the Congregational churches.

> As we listen to the passing storm of passion, of denunciation, of abuse and slander, we ask ourselves if we were mistaken in our belief in your honor, in our faith that you would not strip us of the protection of the common law of equity and deny us the equal protection of your laws.[34]

In the 1940s, evidence for a public conscience in Seattle appeared in the other popular Congregational paper in the early twentieth century was *The Advance*. This journal was more ambivalent about its political positions and more optimistic about the ability of American society to get over race prejudice by wider acquaintance across racial lines. It tended to emphasize the work of Congregational missionaries and not to cover the contradictory realities of American society. In November 1946, *The Advance* carried an article outlining the reasons why it was not a good idea for a white woman to marry a Negro. The article cited the loss of social status for herself and her children, the economic hardship, and the loss of white friends and family relationships as the important consequences of such a marriage. In April the following year, Harold Lindley, a Congregationalist from Seattle wrote to counter the fears of the previous author. He noted that he visits regularly in two happy interracial homes and added that other nations do not put up barriers "to the exercise of the God-given privilege of choosing one's companion and creating a home."[35] Seattle Congregationalists showed a sense of public conscience about race relations in 1947, but this was not the result only of efforts such as the CFRE and the Council of Churches in the 1940s and 1950s. As early as 1919, the Rev. Sydney Strong, pastor of the Queen Anne Congregational Church in Seattle, was preaching strongly in favor of racial equality.

> The early Christians believed in racial equality. . . . Strange that it should be left to Japan to mention racial equality [at the Peace Congress]. I know Japan is individually interested. But racial equality is a Christian note, Japan is not Christian. Why does not England or America boldly say, of course a league of nations is not to be considered, cannot be safely considered, without the assumption of racial equality. That was established 1900 years ago. . . .I wonder sometimes if America is to be punished afresh for her cruel treatment of the Negro, these past 150 years.[36]

Congregational publications consistently supported Federal

Council of Churches initiatives such as Race Relations Sunday and advocated support of Fair Employment Practices Legislation and Fair Housing legislation, but seldom went as far as Pastor Strong in locating racial discrimination and prejudice as sin for which God would hold the nation accountable. For the most part, Congregationalists advocated for education, cultivation of relationships across lines of race and culture, and tended to cite the American Constitution as often as the Bible in advocating for racial equality.

Because of their history dating to the British colonial era, and the influence of the Congregationalists, Presbyterians, Episcopalians, and Baptists in American society, they tend to assume they have a role to play in the larger public conscience. Because they were so large, they also tended to take a mainstream rather than a radical stance with regard to racial equality. In addition to these denominations with roots in the European Protestant Reformation, we need to consider the Methodists, a more homegrown denomination. It is particularly important because, like the Baptists, it has strong African American branches deeply involved in civil rights work. The Jones Street African Methodist Church was active in the Seattle area civil rights efforts.

3. The Methodists

Methodism, from its beginnings in Great Britain and the British American Colonies in the eighteenth century, has strongly attracted the working class. By the beginning of the twentieth century, wealthier people filled many of the prominent Methodist churches nationwide, but the denomination as a whole did not forget its working class roots. The white Methodist Episcopal Church splintered into northern and southern branches before the Civil War, parting ways over differences in policy about slavery. Earlier splits occurred when African American Methodists, tired of having second-class status in the northern

Methodist Episcopal churches, formed their own denominations. Richard Allen from Philadelphia formed the African Methodist Episcopal Church. The African Methodist Episcopal Church, Zion soon followed. In the South, after the Civil War, the Colored (later Christian) Methodist Episcopal Church formed among free African American Methodists. By 1939, the two large white Methodist churches had reunited to form The Methodist Church, but their union has not yet encompassed the AME, AMEZ or CME Churches. In Seattle, the Methodists were mostly representative of the northern white Methodist Episcopal Church, but the First African Methodist Episcopal Church (Jones Street), Walker Chapel AME, and the Ebenezer Methodist Episcopal Church Zion formed the heart of Seattle's black Methodist life. Seattle also had Japanese, Chinese and Filipino Methodist congregations as well.

The working-class roots of the Methodist movements caused the church to be a public voice for labor rights and supporters of labor unions from the beginning. While the Methodist churches along with most of the mainline Protestants of the nineteenth century tended to equate Protestant Christian values and culture with American patriotism, the Methodists in their effort to create a Christian Republic, emphasized the working people of the country.

> The Methodist Episcopal Church has always been a church of the people and identified with their interests; it is now in completely sympathy with every rational effort for their betterment. Not only has the church espoused the cause of laboring people, but it is from them that its membership and its benevolent contributions have been most largely drawn, and we seek the closest affiliation with them in all matters pertaining to the extension of the kingdom of Christ.[37]

The Methodist Episcopal Church extended its concern for labor to the anti-slavery cause as well as to the cause of labor organization in the cities. It recognized the plight of Chinese, Japanese, Korean, and Filipino labor in the American West. Herbert Johnson, the Superintendent of the Pacific Japanese Mission of the Methodist Episcopal Church, considered the conduct on the part of those seeking Asian exclusion from the United States to be unchristian and un-American. He believed this negative attitude had the effect of making Christian missions among the immigrants from East Asia and the Pacific Islands difficult. Such anti-immigration activity went directly contrary to Christian principles. Most of the Methodist publications, some official reports of conferences and mission activities, and some of them like the Zion's Herald being read by millions of Methodists each week, regularly connected Christian principles to public life and argued on behalf of the laborer of whatever race.[38] Guy Emery Shipler, Jr. writing for the *Zion's Herald* in 1942, noted that the discrimination against Negro labor at home, denying them work in war industries, segregating the military, and the Red Cross refusing their blood donations, causes American national prestige to suffer everywhere, especially among close allies in Latin America. The article supported A. Philip Randolph's planned March on Washington and the passage of a Fair Employment Act.[39] An article, in the Spring issue the *Zion's Herald* in 1942, lamented the inability of the Methodists, with their millions of members, to speak against racial discrimination. "We have bowed to segregation. No wonder the life has gone out of us."[40] In July, a related article noted that in integrated settings, people learn to get along with people different from themselves. "Unless the church soon squares itself with the social teachings of Jesus, its noisy utterances upon other questions of lesser import will eventually die away in the bleak stillness of its own moral and spiritual ineptitude."[41]

In the 1950s, the Methodist Church Board of Social and Economic Relations began a series of Interracial Conferences across the country. Two held in the western states were in Phoenix, Arizona and Glendale, California. The purpose of these conferences was "to discover the role and improve the skill of the local church in changing personal attitudes regarding race, changing community patterns of interracial relationships,"[42] and to create Methodist congregations with a conscience that knew how to be welcoming and affirming of people of other races, how to include others in worship and how to have direct fellowship across racial lines. They argued that interracial living was natural.

4. Other Churches involved in Civil Rights Efforts in Seattle: The Lutherans and Quakers

Though Seattle has large Lutheran population, representing several immigrant communities, the Lutherans were surprisingly absent from the Christian Friends for Racial Equality. The Lutheran churches had few members from outside of the European American community, though one Lutheran cemetery made an exception to its policy of burying Caucasians only for Chinese members of Lutheran churches. On the other hand, the Lutheran churches were among those most active in the effort to integrate the cemeteries in Seattle. Lutherans have not had many African American members or congregations, though through a worldwide presence, Lutherans have members of every race. In the United States, various Lutheran denominations have supported the civil rights movements of the twentieth century. Lutherans make up a large proportion of the Protestant Christian adherents in Seattle, but there were no black Lutheran congregations. The Lutheran theological tradition calls for a strong sense of civic conscience and for the church to serve as a public conscience.

The Quakers had possibly the strongest public conscience toward racial justice of any of the predominantly white American churches. They located their racial justice work in the

American Friends Service Committee, though the denomination as a whole had been among the earliest supporters of the anti-slavery movement as well as the inclusion of African Americans in their churches. The publication, The *American Friend* contained articles about racial justice and justice for workers regularly. They covered activities of other churches as well as their own. They were not a large group in Seattle, but they had considerable influence especially through the work of the American Friends Service Committee.

IV. Josiah Royce and the Beloved Community

The shape of the Public Conscience in Seattle, influenced by both secular and religious efforts, represented the result of a complicated and difficult negotiation of competing interests in a rapidly changing social environment. To make clear both the difficulties and the outcome of this negotiation, I turn to the philosophical framework developed by Josiah Royce, an American philosopher writing in the Progressive Era who had an acute awareness of the difficulty of establishing community in the American West. He was born in Grass Valley, California, in 1855 and grew up in Gold Rush California. His family was the last party over the passes in the Sierras before the snow fell in 1849, and his father made his living selling supplies to the miners. In the Gold Rush environment, first in the mining towns and later in San Francisco, he witnessed both the fragmentation of humanity in the mad rush to get rich and the successful efforts of a few to create community here and there. He graduated from the University of California in one of its first classes, studied philosophy for a year in Germany, and returned to the United States to finish his Ph.D. at Johns Hopkins University. He returned to the University of California for a few years teaching English and was invited by William James to teach philosophy at Harvard in 1882 where he remained for the rest of his career.

At Harvard, Royce gained a reputation as an idealist

philosopher, but was probably just as interested in the ideas of the American Pragmatists. Among his writings are a history of California, *The World and the Individual, The Philosophy of Loyalty, The Problem of Christianity*, and essays on race questions. In these works, he stresses the importance of understanding the individual as a dynamic creation in relationship with the community. The problem of understanding Christianity as a religion simply of the salvation of the individual, he argued, discounts the importance of humanity, community, in the redemption Jesus, as presented in the biblical texts, taught and lived out. For Royce, Christianity was best understood as teaching loyalty; expressed ethically in loyalty to humanity, and loyalty to what Christianity means by God expressed in loyalty to loyalty. This loyalty requires us to decide to work for causes that foster the flourishing of humanity and the whole environment that sustains humanity. Since human life is complex, there will be conflicts among causes that could equally foster human flourishing. In his work *The Philosophy of Loyalty* he gave the example of a young woman who is educated and whose profession serves the greater community. She faces a family crisis and the choice of continuing her profession or resigning to serve her family in its need. Royce did not suggest the solution to the problem, but noted that both causes, her profession and her family, are causes that legitimately call forth her loyalty to humanity. The woman has to decide which she will work for, but she cannot do so being sure she has made the right choice.[43]

Royce entered the debates about race in his day from this perspective. He was educated in the first generation of thinkers who came to terms with Darwin. Darwin published *The Origin of the Species* in 1859 when Royce was ten years old. By the time he was teaching at Harvard, Spencer's Social Darwinism was shaping much of the effort to understand race and cultural differences. Royce recognized the existence of such differences, and struggled to make sense of them in his philosophical thinking. In his essay "Race Questions and Prejudices," a skeptical survey of theories about race, he allowed that science may one day find real differences among the races that bear upon intelligence or ability to develop culturally, but so far, in his experience, scientists who try to do so seemed to find evidence that supports their own prejudices.[44] Similarly, he allowed that the white race may be the superior one, but if so, it gives little evidence of being superior. Its behavior to races it regards as weaker is for the most part barbaric. He applied his principle of loyalty to the race relations question. All people of whatever race, he suggested, are human beings and included in the Beloved Community to which we are called to be loyal.

In addition to his notice that scientific evidence of difference tends to reinforce the prejudices of the scientist, he also noted that most race theories make the philosophical error of confusing the accidental and the essential. He asked what race actually consists of, and what the concept of race is good for; is it inherited and constitutional or changeable and learned? He clearly connected our ideas about race to power. "For man, whatever his race, is an animal that you unquestionably can debase to whatever level you please, if only you have power, and if you begin early enough, and devote yourself persistently enough to the noble and civilized task of proving him to be debased."[45] The race problem is, he argued, caused not so much by any essential difference, but by fear and antipathy, and we are capricious and suggestible.

> For my part, then, I am a member of the human race, and that is a race which is, as a whole, considerably lower than the angels, so that the whole of it very badly needs race-elevation. In this need of my race I personally and deeply share. And it is in this spirit only that I am able to approach the problem.[46]

Royce is fruitful for considering the work of the CFRE and Seattle

Council of Churches in the 1940s and 1950s because he was doing his work during the Progressive Era, and the period of greatest development of what became known as liberal theology in the American Protestant churches. His thought captures some important elements of that cultural stream. He was familiar with and engaged the thinking of both Darwin and Freud, though his psychology is closer to that of William James, and he was more favorable toward religion, particularly Christianity than Freud was. His use of the concept of Beloved Community also provides an entry into considering what the CFRE understood to be their ultimate goal.

For Royce, Christianity was not merely a religion of personal experience and sentiment, though it was in part that. He stressed the unity and coherence of the common experience of the community rather than that of the individual.[47] He was interested in the role of the will in religious life. "The true lover of religion needs a conscience as well as a joy in living."[48] The mutual ties between the community and the individual rest for Royce in memory, the community of memory shaped by individuals sharing common and related experiences and the community of hope shaped by shared expectations for the future. The community's ability to interpret shared memories and hopes in turn shapes the identity of the individual. The community exists because its members can engage in communication.[49] Language is the product of a whole people and shapes the individual self. Community for Royce is not simply shared experience, not simply cooperation, and not simply shared expectations and hope, but all of these are necessary for it to come into being. For Royce, loyalty is what makes community possible; we are loyal to each other by looking out for each other's needs, and paying attention to each other's experience and hopes rather than our own alone. He defined Christianity as a religion of loyalty. "The name of Christ has always been for the Christian believers, the symbol for the Spirit in whom the faithful - that is to say the loyal - always are and have been one. . . . Let your Christology be the practical acknowledgment of the Spirit of the Universal and Beloved Community."[50] The task of the Christian life then he argues is to realize the presence of the Spirit in the Community. The sign of this presence will be the creation of Beloved Community.

V. The CFRE and the Council of Churches: The Project to Establish the Beloved Community

The Christian Friends for Racial Equality recognized two aspects to the creation of a public conscience: relationships and education. The means of relationship counted on conscience shaped by people coming to understand one another as friends or perhaps as brothers and sisters in the sense of the Beloved Community. While the member of the CFRE did not use the term Beloved Community, Martin Luther King certainly did. The concept dating back at least to Josiah Royce, expressed a longing and goal toward which people in the new cities of the American West worked. In a setting where practically everyone was a relative newcomer, however, people of color still found themselves in a society shaped by color prejudice and discrimination. The CFRE believed that deliberate engagement of people face-to-face makes is difficult to define those people as "other." Society's creation of racial identity is the abstraction of people into stereotypes, the working of prejudice married to political and economic power, that allows a society to isolate certain people by arbitrary categories (in this case skin color) and define them as enemies.[51] When the prejudice becomes enshrined in law, such as the Jim Crow laws in the American South, or the real estate contracts governed by racially restrictive covenants, membership in the stereotyped groups confers specific disadvantages in society and works deliberately to limit contact between people of different races. Since separation was the main goal of the legal system bent on preserving white power in the United

States, integration became a natural goal for those who worked for racial justice.

Working as they did, in the period when people defined race relations objectives in the United States in terms of integration, fostering face-to-face relationship across racial lines made sense to the members of the CFRE. It was also revolutionary because in the growing tendency toward segregation in Seattle, the real fear of loss of business and property value, and the terrorist activity of Southern based white supremacist groups such as the Ku Klux Klan as close by as Oregon and organizing in Washington, particularly in rural areas, integration could be a dangerous business. In this period Washington was one of the few states that did not enact a misogeny law forbidding marriage between people of different races. Nonetheless, parents did not encourage such relationships and society frowned on them. Interracial friendship was a highly suspect activity because of what (they feared) it might lead to.[52] Face to face friendship building was probably one of the slowest ways to create a public conscience in a group, but also probably one of the surest. The more friendly we feel to others the less likely we are to accept their mistreatment.

The second method of the CFRE in creating a public conscience rested on a long-standing principle of liberalism, the value of education. In sponsoring regular, well-publicized educational events, the CFRE counted on the power of knowledge to shape morality. The American liberal support for public education was rooted in the Enlightenment confidence in human rationality, properly trained, to create a better society. The theological liberals of the nineteenth century and early twentieth century envisioned education as a primary means of creating a Christian society. Horace Bushnell challenged the Puritan Calvinist insistence that conversion came by divine intervention and instead argued that a person could be educated into the faith, in fact would be more deeply rooted in it if they understood it to be part of one's upbringing. The 1940s and 1950s world events severely challenged these forms of Christian liberalism and revealed the liberal failure to achieve their more optimistic dreams of creating a better society and converting the world to Christianity. Nevertheless, the faith in education, that if people only knew the truth, they would do the right thing, still held.

Chapter 3

The Network of Civil Rights Work in Seattle

> By welcoming the cooperation of other individuals and organizations in the mutual working out of community problems, remembering that the matter of who accomplishes the good result is of little concern, just so the good result is actually accomplished.[1]

The core members of the Christians and Friends for Racial Equality were well-connected people who were often active in more than one community organization. In the statement of method in their founding documents, they made cooperation with other organizations a key component of their way of working. They were not people who simplistically saw personal relationships as the only road to racial equality. They did believe these relationships were important to the success of their effort to achieve racial equality. All of them were involved in the work for racial justice on several fronts at the same time.

The members of the CFRE had an intuitive understanding of the way in which social isolation contributes to prejudice and persecution. The isolation of the Japanese community before the internment is one example.[2] In their case, public pressure resulted in segregation, exclusion from privileges of citizenship, and finally the internment of the Japanese during the war. Propagation of stereotypes and racial segregation aimed at producing just this pattern of isolation strongly influenced government policy, creating public pressure to enforce this isolation. This, in turn, lent authority to the stereotype, as it was publicized and shaped public opinion toward agreement with exclusionary policies.[3] The CFRE believed that the existence of cross-cultural or cross-racial friendships could act against this pressure of public opinion by creating another body of public opinion based, not on isolation, but on a sense of shared experience. Both the Christian Friends for Racial Equality and the Seattle Council of Churches, as religious organizations, based their project of creating a public conscience on the possibility of cross-cultural friendship.

I. The Network of Seattle Civil Rights Organizations in the 1940s and 1950s

People working for racial equality in Seattle in the mid-twentieth century tended to be involved in more than one organization. The key people in most organizations were well acquainted with each other. Each group, the Urban League, the NAACP, The Chinese Chong Wah charitable organization, the Japanese American Citizens' League, the Filipino Christian Fellowship, CORE, the Civic Unity Committee, the Jackson Street community organization, the Central Area Civil Rights Committee, the Council of Churches and CFRE, was the center of a network of organizations. Describing the relationship of these networks to the development of a public conscience in Seattle leads us to a relatively small group of interrelated people, who were yet able to influence a city toward racial justice.[4] While they imagined that they imparted this conscience to the larger community in the form of an influence on public opinion; in fact their most effective strategy was to develop the conscience located among decision makers. In a secular society such as Seattle, religious or theological understandings of justice and equality played a smaller role in the developments of public conscience. Nonetheless, religious commitments of many key people in the city's civil rights organizations influenced a religiously based general concept of justice among their constituents and the public without conveying a specific religious belief.

In 1959, the *American Sociological Review* published an article about the structures of influence in the Seattle Central District. The authors, University of Washington professors of sociology, Ernest A. T. Barth and Baha Abū Laban, interviewed thirty-six leaders in the black community in the Central District asking them which organizations were channels of influence in the city. These leaders identified the CFRE as one of the four most influential out of the thirteen identified organizations; after the NAACP and the Urban League, the CFRE ranked third equally with the Jackson Street Community Association. Most of the leaders the authors interviewed were professional people and all but four were recent immigrants to Seattle, mostly from the American South. The authors noted the general absence of churches from the list of influential organizations though two of these identified leaders were ministers. The CFRE and the People's Institutional Baptist Church were the only religious organizations of the thirteen. The leaders also rated each other regarding their perceived power and influence in the community. They noted that the most influential leaders in the community were well known to each other, active in multiple organizations.[5]

The network of civil rights organizations and religious groups interested in racial equality or racial justice within which the CFRE and the Council of Churches worked was mostly a middle class set of organizations. Seattle also had a thriving black ecumenical cooperation among the churches in the Central Area. The development of the Central Area Civil Rights Committee in the 1960s was an outgrowth of this black ecumenism.[6] With the exception of CORE, which the CFRE supported but did not directly participate in, and certain radical clergy such as Fred Shorter, the religious organizations, whose goals tended toward integration of social venues, schools, housing and employment, explicitly avoided strategies of direct confrontation, coercion and especially violence. Some of the groups in the network, particularly the Urban League, CORE and the NAACP, The Japanese American Citizens' League, and many churches carried out systematic programs aimed at improving conditions and race relations using legal procedures, political pressure on elected officials, or directed economic activity including boycotts. For the most part all of them dealt with local cases as they presented themselves but not all analyzed the deeper structural connections among them.

A. Who was Involved in the Network Inhabited by the CFRE and Council of Churches?

The Christians and Friends for Racial Equality had as many as a thousand people involved in some facet of its work during its existence. It would be impossible to map the complete network of these relationships in comparison with other organizations doing civil rights work in the city. A core group of people was present for most of the organization's twenty years of active life. This core of people included names that regularly appeared in the membership and activities of other civil rights organizations in the city.

The CFRE was certainly not the hub of this activity. Probably one could map any organization as if its members were a core of people who linked together other organizations by their network of connections. The CFRE had a unique sense of mission to foster just such relationships and connections among activists, and people joined their project in addition to other organizations because they valued the contribution made by the CFRE. Johanna Phillips suggests that, though it was not one of their stated intentions, in fact, the existence of CFRE fostered cooperation among the many civil rights organizations in the city.[7]

> By its fourteenth year (1956), CFRE had become the largest interracial civil rights organization in Seattle's history. . . . Firstly, . . . cross- membership expanded cooperation between

> organizations. Secondly, cross-membership indicates that CFRE performed a function that was not served by the other organizations. Thus, CFRE occupied a niche in the Seattle community. The social focus of the Christian Friends was its rare and appealing function. The Christian Friends aimed to create an enjoyable social environment in which interracial and interfaith exchanges could take place.[8]

That the majority of the members and leadership of the CFRE were female may have contributed to this important function of the group. We will consider this and other gender-related issues more fully in Chapter 4. While the founders of the CFRE wanted primarily to foster social relationships across racial lines, at its business meetings it quickly became clear that these relationships led to greater awareness of the discrimination faced by the racial minority members of the group. Thus from the beginning the CFRE also began to design strategies to address discrimination. The network within which the CFRE worked was the site of much of their effort to develop a public conscience.

The Seattle Council of Churches similarly contained people who participated actively in other organizations. Since the Council of Churches was not in itself a civil rights organization, but had a component of its work focused on civil rights and race relations, I will pay most attention to the individuals involved in the Race Relations Committee of the Council of Churches. Several important groups of people made up this network. The committee included older members, for whom civil rights activities were their main work after retirement, and younger people active both in voluntary capacities and often in their employment. The committee included several active clergy. The CFRE had several younger members who lived to see the demise of the organization and the development of new kinds of civil rights work. In addition to their participation in the CFRE, its members also belonged to many churches, religious organizations and secular civic organizations that were active in the city.

1. The Founders of the CFRE and their Connections[9]

Edith Steinmetz played the most prominent role in the life of the CFRE over its history. Those who have recorded the history of the group often assumed she was the founder of the group, and honored her for having done most of the initial work. Steinmetz herself gave credit to Victor Carreon for actually having the initial idea. Steinmetz served as the first president and also as honorary president long after she had left the city. She was active in a wide range of Baptist circles, which may account for the large number of Baptist participants in the CFRE. She appears as a missionary associated with the First Baptist Church, was later a member of the Chinese Baptist Church and they held her funeral at the Mt. Zion Baptist Church.[10] In addition to her church affiliation, she was active in the Seattle Council of Churches.

Edith Steinmetz and her husband were missionaries in the Philippines for several years. The two of them served as missionaries of the Northern Baptist Convention (later renamed the American Baptist Convention) from 1907 until 1918. On Negros Island, they also had a boys' dormitory in Bacolod for young men attending school there. Harold and Edith Steinmetz lived in the dormitory with the students.[11] She was a teacher and Harold started hospitals in the Negros Island in Bacolod, Iloilo and Capiz, which they gradually turned over to Filipino leadership until they were fully self supporting.[12] After they left the Baptist mission, they remained in the Philippines for a few years and at that time Edith Steinmetz was associated with the YMCA as a teacher. The YMCA school was among the oldest Protestant educational institution in the Philippines, established in the 1890s to teach English.[13]

Steinmetz pursued the same racial justice concerns in the CFRE and in the Council of Churches. One example of her joint work was the issue of integrating the nursing staff at the

Harborview Hospital and the Red Cross. Both the CFRE and the Council of Churches investigated the Harborview Hospital because of someone's perception that they did not hire African American or Filipino nurses or accept them into its nursing school. Steinmetz reported on the results of the inquiry to both the CFRE and the Council. The hospital claimed that it did not discriminate, at least in its nursing school. The source of the perception is not clear in the records. Often institutions with non-discriminatory policies in place still do not have racial minority students, clients, or employees. Steinmetz's strategy began with such simple inquiries. Members of the CFRE would personally check out such stories if the perception of discrimination persisted. One CFRE member, Rev. Fountain Penick, pastor of the People's Institutional Baptist Church, particularly worked to recruit an African-American young woman willing to apply to the nursing school at Harborview to test the seriousness of their claim to non-discrimination.[14]

Fountain Penick was another of the charter members of the CFRE along with his wife Vivienne. Penick was the founding pastor of the People's Institutional Baptist church. Penick was a prominent member of the CFRE advisory board for many years. Vivienne, his wife, came to Seattle in 1940 as a graduate of Atlanta University and organized a day nursery during the war. She was a founding organizer of the CFRE as well as the Cosmopolitan Century Club, a black women's club, in 1947. She was active in the YWCA, the Seattle Urban League (where she served as secretary to the Director), the Civic Unity Committee, and the New Year's Callers in addition to the CFRE.[15]

Active in founding more than one civic organization, most people knew Bertha Pitts Campbell (1889-1990) for being the one of the founders of the Delta Sigma Theta, a national black women's public service sorority. She was active in the organization of this sorority while she was a student at Howard University. She began her civil rights work in the women's suffrage movement in the early twentieth century, leading the Delta Sigma Theta members as they participated in the women's march on Washington in 1913 for woman suffrage. Campbell moved to Seattle in 1923 and was active in the Urban League and in the YWCA for over thirty years in addition to the CFRE. She was a Grey Lady for the Red Cross visiting soldiers in the hospital.[16] Bertha Campbell was a religious person and was an active member of the First African Methodist Episcopal Church in Seattle. When she arrived in Seattle in the 1920s, she remembered that Seattle did not have very many African Americans, ". . . there weren't enough to make that much of an impression. That is, their political strength, their voting strength, would not have been very much."[17] Campbell's network of involvement illustrates the ways that the sorority fostered civic responsibility in its members during their college years. Campbell used her organizing skills all of her life in working for women's rights and racial justice.[18] She was the first black member of the Board of Directors of the Seattle-King County YWCA. She died at the age of 100 in 1990.[19]

Campbell was active in the CFRE from its founding and served on its permanent committee dealing with racial discrimination issues.[20] The formation of this committee allowed CFRE work against discrimination to proceed in a more organized manner. Campbell, in an oral history interview with Esther Mumford, placed her work with the CFRE at the heart of her race relations work.

> As a result of some if it [CFRE work to abolish discrimination], for instance, the Red Cross trained three Negroes and one Chinese, as Nurse's Aides. They were trained by the Red Cross. [Before] Red Cross refused to have Negroes in their thing. And the Red Cross also refused to allow Negro women to act as Gray Ladies. Because they said their quota was filled, gray Ladies, to visit the boys. So we kept hammering after that

> all during the war time until they finally broke down and we were allowed to visit the boys. I don't know that we ever took the Gray Lady training, nobody that I knew of did. But we were allowed to visit the boys. 'Course I don't know how you'd have to be trained to go up and visit a boy and write a letter for him.[21]

Campbell noted the difficulty of finding an office for the CFRE in the increasingly segregated city.

> This was an interracial group. And do you know that for a long time we tried our best to find a place for an office. And we couldn't get a place rented to us for an office because it was an interracial group. But we finally did, we finally made it and got one good place up in the center of town for our office, after much striving. This was in '42 [that] we began, so that was almost at the beginning of the war, you see. And from then on, we worked on discrimination in restaurants, hotels, Red Cross, theaters, housing projects, and urging that discrimination be abolished.[22]

One article about Campbell stated that the a group of women from the Council of Churches started the CFRE.[23] While the perception is not strictly accurate, it does indicate the complex web of relationships that sustained work for racial equality in Seattle. Many of the founders of the CFRE were members of the Council of Churches. Campbell was one of the middle class women actively involved many clubs and organizations centered on the achievement of a better society and service to others. The sorority she helped to found was one of several African American Greek-letter organizations founded "on principles of black pride, service and justice . . . to advance black democratic rights." Stephanie Evans in her study of these organizations also pointed out the extensive network to which members of these sororities and fraternities also belonged. Often these Delta Sigma Theta sorority members were leaders in other organizations.[24]

Arline (1912-1999) and Letcher Yarbrough (1908-1992) provide another example of the complex network of organizations members of the CFRE brought with them to their inter-racial concerts and potluck suppers. Both Yarbroughs had extensive active careers in civil rights. Letcher Yarbrough (1909-1992) was one of the early sponsors of the CFRE and served as head of the Seattle NAACP.

Letcher Yarbrough came from an old family in Seattle, who arrived in the city in the 1890s, though he was apparently born in Pittsburgh, PA.[25] He graduated from Garfield High School in 1927 (about the time of the Pacific Coast Race Relations Survey). He attended the University of Washington for one year but financial difficulties forced him to discontinue his education. After World War II, the influx of people brought "patterns and attitudes that were not acceptable in a multi-racial community." As a result of the deterioration of race relations, Yarbrough became involved in a number of organizations. He was president of the Seattle NAACP in the 1940s and was involved through that organization in the effort to secure fair employment practices legislation (successfully in 1949 when the State legislature passed the Fair Employment Practices Bill). He was also active in the effort to desegregate the court system in the 1950s. In addition to the NAACP, Yarbrough was active in two faith-based organizations, the CFRE and the National Conference of Christians and Jews. The mayor of Seattle appointed him to the Civic Unity Committee and he was active in the Urban League. During his retirement in the 1970s he served as assistant director of the Urban League.[26]

Arline Yarbrough (1912 - 1999) married Letcher in the 1930s. She was born in Colorado and attended Garfield High School when her family moved to Seattle. She also attended the University of Washington but had to leave school to earn a living.

She worked as a secretary and businesswoman, and was active in several organizations, among them the Urban League, and was on the staff of the University of Washington in the School of Social Work.[27] Arline Yarbrough was the mind behind the CFRE effort to integrate the cemeteries enlisting the Seattle Times in the effort. She later sold cemetery plots for one of the first cemeteries to integrate, Sunset Hills. Seattle remembered her for her activities in historical organizations, the Black Heritage Society of Washington, the King County Landmarks Commission, and the National Council of Negro Women.[28] Arline and Letcher were not apparently religiously affiliated. Their obituaries noted no specific church membership. Their participation in the CFRE and the Conference of Christians and Jews gives evidence of a religious sensibility that transcended denominational lines.

The network represented by the members of the CFRE stretched beyond the white and African American communities from which many of its most well known members came. Rev. Paul Fong, pastor of the Chinese Baptist Church, was one of several Chinese members of the CFRE. He was also active in the Seattle Council of Churches where he advertized the CFRE social activities. Several other members of the Chinese Baptist Church were part of the CFRE, though the record does not indicate what their particular efforts were. While Rev. Fong appears by name in many CFRE and Council of Churches records and appears to have been the primary link of these groups with the Chinese Christian community in Seattle, he was relatively quiet. Work done by a number of Chinese-American historians and theologians later in the twentieth century suggest several reasons why Rev. Fong was not as prominent though persistently present in the records. First, language barriers continued to affect Chinese immigrant participation in social situations.[29] More than language, cultural differences in the ways Chinese and Americans approached problems associated with racial discrimination and prejudice affected Chinese participation in the kind of projects undertaken by the CFRE and the Council of Churches. David Ng, a historian of Asian American religion, noted that

> Asian-Americans, including the Chinese, have suffered many years under stifling stereotypes held by the majority of Americans. . . . Difficulties with languages, differences in culture, the prevalence of poverty, the isolation of ghetto living, and age differences put pressure not only on the Chinese in relation to the majority culture, but also among themselves.[30]

Paul Fong had to negotiate this distance between his Chinese constituents and his participation in ecumenical, interracial efforts to shape Seattle society. In the Council of Churches, he worked in a majority white group with a project shaped by European and American ecumenical ideals. In the CFRE, he was in an interracial situation, but where the majority was African American and white, with the Asian and Asian American parts of the Seattle church-going population still in a distinct minority. Fong's church, the Chinese Baptist Church of Seattle, was located in the Jackson Street Neighborhood in the Central Area, one of the most diverse neighborhoods in Seattle. The CFRE regularly met in their building. Many members of the congregation served on the Jackson Street Community Council. The church was active in many neighborhood causes and housed a well-baby clinic in its building during the 1940s.

In the 1970s Frank Mar, a Chinese-American church leader reflected on what happened to the Chinese American churches in their earlier history. "We have been functioning as little religious enclaves in the midst of a vast sea of predominantly white churches. That kind of mentality has permeated almost all our religious life and witness."[31] The trans-Pacific complexities of Protestant Christianity in China complicate the understanding the Chinese American Protestants in the situation of Seattle. The associations of Protestantism with American cultural ideals on the one hand and with Chinese nationalism on the other hand created complex sets of loyalties, and served to create internal conflict among different generations of Chinese-American immigrant Christians. In addition, the activism of the Chinese Protestants of the same generation as the American Progressive or Social Gospel Protestants was in contrast to the quieter demeanor of the American Chinese Protestants who had to live with the discrimination and exclusionary rhetoric of the American context.[32] The Chinese Christians not only crossed cultural lines within their own nation and its people, but also always negotiated a complicated and often contradictory set of expectations of them as Protestants, as Americans and as Chinese. Perhaps this is why Fong was particularly interested in the cultural exchange that took place in the CFRE. His church was emerging from any isolation it had experienced and was becoming active in its multi-racial community. In addition to Rev. Paul Fong, another Chinese pastor, Rev. Ai Chih Tsai and a laywoman, Mrs. Loun Lew participated actively in the CFRE.

The Filipino Christian community in Seattle faced similar problems and shared with the Chinese a sense of the deep connections between Protestant Christianity and American culture, but also the contradictions of racialized identity as people of color in a majority white society. One of these Filipino Christians was Victor Carreon, the person whose vision of a just society in the United States was the catalyst for the formation of the CFRE.[33] He was not the only Filipino member of the CFRE. Like Victor Carreon, Grandino Baaoa came to the United States from the Philippines. He was aware of the idealized presentation of America presented by the Protestant missionaries. Grandino Baaoa and Victor Carreon were part of a network of Filipino Protestants centered in the Methodist church and related also to the YMCA. Through the YMCA in the Philippines, and later through the Filipino Christian Fellowship, Carreon was acquainted with Edith Steinmetz, a Baptist missionary. These two men came to the United States seeking greater educational opportunities, but found it difficult to pursue that path. The economic struggles of labor in the developing transpacific economy, which forced labor into ever-lower pay brackets, caught them in low paying jobs that would not cover the cost of the education they sought.

The Filipino community in Seattle organized itself primarily by kinship groups, networks of extended families crossing the Pacific. The mobility of the individuals coming to the United States for employment separated people for long periods from their primary familial networks and in many cases, the churches served as alternative families. The Seattle Maryknoll Church, Our Lady Queen of the Martyrs and the Filipino Christian Fellowship Association of the First Methodist Church serve as examples.[34] Despite the tie of Edith Steinmetz, one of the founders and leaders of the CFRE, to the Philippines, after the first two or three years membership of the organization did not include many Filipinos, though Chinese and Japanese Baptist churches remained active. The Filipino community faced many of the same language and cultural difficulties as the Chinese along with the experience of exclusion and legal restrictions. The community continued to face the ambiguous identity of their former status as belonging to the United States but with the independence of the Philippines, suddenly becoming aliens. The limitations of poverty curtailed their participation in such organizations as the CFRE, though Baaoa continued to participate and Victor Carreon remained a member of the Advisory Board for many years.

Other ethnic groups participated in the CFRE and Seattle in the larger networks. Rabbi Raphael Harry Levine (1901-1985) and several members of the Reformed synagogue, Temple de Hirsch, were active in Seattle efforts to achieve racial equality. The Council of Churches and the Jewish organizations in Seattle cooperated on several projects as religious leaders found common ground in the civil rights movements. Levine himself was active in a number of organizations. He came to Seattle in 1942 and became the successor of Rabbi Samuel Koch at the Reform Jewish congregation Temple de Hirsch. Levine was particularly present in many efforts to create dialogue between Christians and Jews; he organized summer camps for young people of diverse religions. He was active in the fair housing movement and participated in the civil rights protests of the Seattle Public Schools in 1966, opening a freedom school in the temple.[35]

The Jewish Reformed synagogue, Temple de Hirsch was not the only synagogue involved in the CFRE; another synagogue, Congregation Ezra Bessaroth, was one of their regular meeting places. Occasionally Buddhist members of Chinese and Japanese civic groups joined in CFRE events or projects. The CFRE willingness to include other religious traditions in their work led the CFRE to consider changing their name later in 1967 to Christians and Friends for Racial Equality.[36]

The Japanese community, as we will note below, was notably missing from the early activities of the CFRE, though a Japanese woman had been involved in the initial conversations that took place before the group formally organized. Later in the 1960s, several Japanese members of the CFRE were associated also with the Japanese Congregational Church in Seattle. Mrs. J. Hayakawa served on the program committee of the CFRE in the late fifties. Mrs. Ted Hayashi served on the Church Committee along with a Chinese member Chin Tsai Hung, keeping the Asian-American churches connected to the work of the CFRE and the wider community.[37]

Though one cannot always judge simply by names what the ethnicity or race of a person might be, there seems to have been only one Native American in the group. He went by the name Yellowhorse and was present at the initial meetings of the group.

An article in the *Racial Equality Bulletin* (January 1954) by Edith Steinmetz indicated that he lived near the CFRE offices in the downtown area and that he was often in the office or nearby. Steinmetz indicated that he thought it best to keep an eye on the office when she was working there alone at night. Though Native American issues did not occupy much space in the deliberations recorded in their minutes, hardly any issue of the *Racial Equality Bulletin* failed to include a report on some issue of concern to the Native American communities, particularly those of the Washington State area.

Among the long term members of the CFRE and the Council of Churches were several pastors. Fred Shorter of the Church of the People was among the most active white pastors in both groups. Shorter was a pastor from the Congregational tradition whose labor activism and participation in the International Workers of the World earned him the displeasure of Pilgrim Congregational Church in Seattle. After resigning that position, he founded an independent non-denominational church near the University named The Church of the People. This non-denominational interracial social justice oriented church was short-lived, organized in 1937 and disappeared in the Fifties.

The congregation thought of itself as a "frontier of the Spirit." It appealed to apartment dwellers near the University, had a large young people's group that discussed the issues of the day, and addressed the public on these issues through a newsletter, *New Religious Frontier* ("Organized Religion must go beyond the old frontier of theological liberalism to a new frontier of economic radicalism.").[38] Through more innovative means such as painting murals on issues of lynching, armament industry, and starving farmers plowing under the crops they cannot afford to send to market they sought to form a public conscience about economic injustices.[39] The church organized a memorial society to offer affordable funerals, a birth control clinic as early as 1939, a cooperative credit union and grocery store, and worked for labor rights and low cost housing. The pastor Fred Shorter was the only white local branch president of the NAACP in the 1930s.[40]

The pastor was not the only one active in the community. By 1938, the congregation had five members of the church running for public office in Seattle. The Church of the People focused its energy during the Forties and Fifties in efforts to address issues of labor, including the integration of the workplace and the Fair Employment Practices Act, and on issues of peace during a time of war. Throughout the issues of the *New Religious Frontier*, in considering the problems of both labor and peace, race was a component of their concern.

The congregation focused particularly on class issues and worker's rights, but was interested in race relations because they realized the influence of racism on employment discrimination. They were active during the trial of white Seattle police officers for the abuse of a black Seattle citizen in 1938. Shorter was involved in the CFRE in its early years and wrote for the *Racial Equality Bulletin*. More than other CFRE members, Shorter was connected with the labor unions of Seattle as well as being aware of racial prejudice and discrimination, bringing the issues of workers to largely middle class civil rights organizations.

Another such white pastor was Harold Jensen, the pastor of the First Baptist Church during the war years, who was active in the CFRE. First Baptist Church was a mostly white American Baptist congregation, but was an active part of a larger network of American Baptist Churches of many ethnicities. The First Baptist Church had a long history of involvement in social justice ministries in Seattle, beginning with concern for temperance, cleaning up skid row, and corruption in city hall during the Progressive Era, protest of the internment of the Japanese during World War II, and fostering racial justice. In keeping with its Baptist heritage, it welcomed diverse theological perspectives and its pastor was free to preach from his (or her) conscience. Also in keeping with its Baptist heritage, it placed a high value on religious freedom in society.

Jensen was a vocal advocate for racial equality from his pulpit and in other public speaking in Seattle. He publically challenged the internment of the Japanese. "It [his appeal to the courts] didn't work, but it left a lasting impression on the church and the community as to what Christianity was really all about."[41] In the early 1950s, the CFRE began a campaign to have the ministers in Seattle write articles giving the theological reasons to support racial equality. These were published in the *Racial Equality Bulletin*. Jensen wrote one of the earliest of these articles for the December 1951 issue. He based his brief article on a verse from 1 John: 1-7, "If we walk in the light as He is in the light, we will have fellowship one with another." In the article, he reported an experience from the National Evangelical Preaching Mission, a preaching conference the previous year, sponsored by the Council of Churches in which Rosa Paige Welch, a nationally known southern black Gospel singer, sang a Negro Spiritual lullaby to a black baby, as the Christ Child. Jensen noted, "It startled me and humbled me. I knew it was right and I really should not have been startled at all. We know of course that Jesus was born a Jew; though one would never guess it from many of the paintings which make him look more like an Anglo-Saxon."[42] Jensen's theological perspective grounded racial equality in the Christian belief that Christ emphasized the supreme worth of all people because God made them in God's own image. Jensen's successor, John Skoglund was also involved in racial justice efforts in Seattle; a member of his church once challenged him because of his preaching about issues of racial equality, but the church Christian Citizenship Committee supported his freedom to preach according to his conscience.[43]

Other early or long-time members of the CFRE included Emma Chainey, also an active member of the First African Methodist Episcopal Church, who died in 1945, shortly after the CFRE was organized, and Frederica and Walter Hiltner who were newcomers to Seattle at about the time the CFRE began. The Hiltners were missionaries earlier in their careers. Water had served as a medical doctor in Shanghai and Frederica was on the faculty of the Ginling College in Nanking. The Hiltners moved to Seattle in 1925 and became members of Plymouth Congregational Church. They were active in the University YMCA, serving on its board; they participated in the CFRE and Frederica served as president in the early 1960s.

Later arrivals included Alice Nugent, the wife of the Evangelical and Reformed Church pastor, Carl Nugent. Both of the Nugents were active in ministry and advocacy for the Japanese in the Internment camps. Alice Nugent was the editor of the *Racial Equality Bulletin* for many years and was still a member of the group in the late sixties as they debated their future.

Mrs. Albert Chaney also was active in the group from the beginning and into the sixties. She served as first vice president of the CFRE for many years and in 1962 the CFRE elected her to be the organization's first black president. LeEtta King came to Seattle with her parents from Illinois. Her father began work as a strikebreaker in the coalmines of Roslyn Washington. Her parents died early, and friends in Yakima raised her; she moved to Seattle with them at the age of seventeen. She worked for a black lawyer and for the Federal Government during World War I. Later she supported herself as a music teacher. She was active in the Seattle Urban League, the NAACP, the YWCA, the Delta Sigma Theta Sorority (founded by Bertha Pitts Campbell), and the CFRE.[44]

A few younger or newer members of the CFRE joined the group after the Second World War. Dorothy Hollingsworth grew up in North Carolina and moved to Seattle in 1946. She was involved in the YWCA, the Delta Sigma Theta, and was involved in the open housing efforts of the CFRE. She was a social worker in the 1950s and 1960s focusing on educational issues in Seattle's

Central District and was the first director of Seattle's Head Start Program. She was active in the Central Area Civil Rights Committee and was the first black woman elected to Seattle's School Board, at the time when the Board voluntarily developed a bussing program to help integrate the city public schools.[45] Hollingsworth was a member of the First African Methodist Episcopal Church and the NAACP.[46]

Samuel McKinney was the pastor of the Mount Zion Baptist Church from 1958 until well into the 1990s. Early in his ministry, he invited his friend Martin Luther King Jr, to speak in Seattle. Since the Mt. Zion church building was too small, he sought a different venue. The First Presbyterian Church agreed to hold the meeting until the publicity went out and then withdrew its offer. Eventually King spoke at Temple de Hirsch with an additional appearance at the University of Washington and at Garfield High School. The CFRE criticized the Presbyterian cancellation, as did several other religious leaders in the city. McKinney reported that King was "impressed with the progressive attitude he saw in the city, especially in the African American Community."[47]

Two of the most active younger people were Mary Lund, a white woman who joined the CFRE just after her graduation from the university and Lola Day, a black woman. For several years beginning in 1948, Lund worked as the paid Executive Secretary for the group. She was the only paid staff member the CFRE had during its history. She kept the group in the news; most of the newspapers of the day quoted her when they published articles about the CFRE and its activities. Lola Day was active in the CFRE and the New Year's Callers later in that group's history. She was also active in the national social justice work of the Congregational Churches, and later the United Church of Christ. Seattle remembered Day for her work in helping to organize inter-racial home visits during the early years of the 1960s. She described the project in this way in the advertizing flyer she created for the events.

> Lola Day just can't help talking about the fun, the enjoyment, the enriching experiences to be had from participating in the home visitation day coming up Apr 25.
>
> Beneficiaries of past interracial home visitations are telling their friends of the fun, excitement, enjoyment, enriching experiences to be had from participating in the Interracial Home visit Day Apr 25. This is an opportunity to share in great sociological experiment in contrived association with an unknown person. You may meet a family that are your peers. They may have about the same job level or be above or below you. Your guest may be a Ph. D. or he may have only finished the 6th grade. It's guaranteed that you will meeting interesting people of varied interests and background.
>
> Your discussion with your guest may range over many mutual problems of schools, church, jobs, housing, little league or summer camp for children.
>
> Most parties have gained a friend through the exchange. If not they are better informed than they were before the visitation.[48]

The kinds of things she went on to suggest they discuss at such exchanges included such questions as how black parents prepare their children for prejudice and segregation as well as what they think of the activities of various civil rights groups. The CFRE held three successful inter-racial visiting events. Like Alice Nugent, Lola Day was part of the discussions in 1966 and 1967 about the future of the group, when they realized that many other civil rights organizations were doing a more effective job, and that the methods of civil rights work had changed over time as conditions had changed. The CFRE returned to its focus on building inter-racial friendship but not long after these discussions faded from the scene.

B. The Limits of the Network

The network of organizations did not include everyone, though it sustained connections to practically every social and religious organization in the city. Those who were missing from the network, or who were not as visible within it offer clues to the means by which they could do civil rights work in Seattle and their limits.

The case of the Filipino community illuminates the issues involved. While the Filipino community was present at the origin of the Christian Friends for Racial Equality, it quickly disappeared from active named membership. The letter from Victor Carreon giving the reasons for his need to resign from his position as secretary and member of the board indicated that class was an issue; Carreon had to work at the time that the group met, and he had to work too many hours to allow him the time to be an active member of the group. The majority of the core CFRE members were retired or they were younger middle class women who had time to participate actively in a volunteer organization. Though they held their meetings in the evenings when working people could attend, those who worked in the blue-color world often worked evening and night shifts. Even these meetings were difficult to attend if someone worked long hours and also had family responsibilities. The Filipino example shows that the CFRE was largely a middle class organization. While it attempted to include the Filipino community out of its commitment to racial equality, it was not able to find ways to keep working class people involved in the core group. The working class people were largely missing from its sphere of activity.

While the CFRE and the Council of Churches were in close contact with the Japanese Citizens Association, and the Japanese churches were part of the Council, the Japanese community too was conspicuously absent from the story, especially during the 1940s. The Japanese are a particular example of an exceptionally isolated group. One Japanese person was involved in the initial meeting of the CFRE, but abruptly stopped participating with the internment of the Japanese community several weeks later. The newly formed CFRE did not have time to develop any real relationships with the Japanese community before the internment, but the Council of Churches had a long history of active support through their relationships with the Japanese churches. After December 7, 1941 the Council of Churches mobilized their network of assistance organizations, cooperating with the Red Cross, Traveler's Aid, and others to enhance the safety and survival of the Japanese in the city. Through the 1940s, the Japanese remained in the background conversation of both religious organizations. The CFRE as well as the Council of Churches kept themselves informed about the conditions in the internment camps and advocated for the release of those for whom there was no evidence of enemy activity. One sponsor of the CFRE, the attorney Arthur G. Barnett, who was also President of the Civic Unity Committee, took the case of Gordon Hirabayashi, challenging the legality of the internment, to the Supreme Court where he lost.[49]

The younger generation was also missing from the network connected to the CFRE, with the exception of a handful of members such as Mary Lund. In her article about the CFRE, Johanna Phillips notes the perception that the members of the group were of an older generation.[50] Many of the core members were born late in the nineteenth century and were retired by the 1940s. We will consider the influence of this generation more fully in Chapter 4. The CFRE did not ignore the concerns of young people. Some of their projects related to youth, the efforts to integrate a skating rink, concern about discrimination in the Blue Birds (a youth organization for girls much like the Girls Scouts) and their concerns for the soldiers at Fort Lewis. They noted and protested the U. S. Army's separate beach designated "Negro Beach.[51] The CFRE also prepared a list of churches that would welcome racial minority soldiers. As a result, they counted several soldiers among their members, a transitory but younger constituency. This did not mean that younger people were present in the working life of the group. Few adult organizations invited the participation of school-age youth or post-high school college students or those just establishing themselves in work and family life. These young people were not usually fully involved in civic or church organizations. Many civil rights organizations, religious or secular, provided programs for younger people, but the CFRE and the Council of Churches left youth work to the churches or the YMCA and YWCA and other established organizations. The CFRE had a few programs designed to interest youth, and neither ecumenical organization had young people among its leaders.[52]

The CFRE was the product of people of a particular generation, one that came of age and did its active work during the Progressive Era. Those who were Protestant Christians were active in churches heavily influenced by nineteenth-century liberal theological developments and the conflicts generated between those of a liberal outlook and those holding an increasingly fundamentalist position on the practice of Christianity. Chapter 4 will address the generational aspect of the CFRE, but it did shape the visible network of people involved in the group.

Finally, among groups of people missing from these ecumenical efforts toward racial justice were the more theologically conservative churches, or those who did not typically involve themselves in ecumenical relationships. The CFRE and the Council of Churches drew from roughly the same constituency. The CFRE cultivated relationships with a wider group of churches including, the Full Gospel Pentecostal Temple, Our Lady Queen of the Martyrs, a Catholic parish in the Central District serving both Filipino and Japanese Catholics, the Reorganized Church of the Latter Day Saints, the Tabernacle Missionary Baptist, and on the more liberal side, the University Unitarian Church, but none of the Russian or Greek Orthodox churches and few of the smaller fundamentalist churches were involved. Other religious groups who were willing to engage in inter-religious activities cooperated with the Council of Churches and the CFRE from time to time but were missing from its ranks of members.[53]

II. The Shape of the Network of Civil Rights Organizations in Seattle in the 1940s and 1950s

The majority of the organizations in this network were middle class people, whether they were part of the Japanese Citizens League, the NAACP or their local churches. Some communities such as the black community of Seattle had a very small middle class due to a complex set of social restrictions and resulting economic circumstances, in addition to the persistent legacy from centuries of oppression. Quintard Taylor concludes that Seattle's failure to achieve the racial equality it desired lay in overlooking the connection between race and economic disparities in society and thus failing to address them.[54] The white majority in Seattle was largely middle class people who took for granted the right to succeed or fail based on their own efforts.[55] The Japanese had a historic middle class presence, but that status had been lost to many of those returning from the Internment. The Chinese and Filipino communities faced many of the same social and economic restrictions as the African Americans and, while some in their communities had created successful businesses and become professionals, many remained among the economically marginalized.

The majority of the churches represented in the CFRE were mainline Protestant or from other large national or international denominations. Because their communities were more prominently Christian, the white and black members of the CFRE outnumbered the other racial groups in the organization. The white Protestant churches participating in the CFRE were among the more progressive on issues of racial integration and justice.

The CFRE members were not exclusively from more theologically liberal churches, but the few were fundamentalists. Most of the churches, though not all of the individuals, in the CFRE were also active in the Council of churches. Not all of the churches in the Council were in agreement about the importance of the integration effort put forth by the CFRE in the 1940s and 1950s. Small non-denominational or Pentecostal churches attractive to the working class or low-income population of Seattle did not participate in many of the organizations in the network though the CFRE met in one of the Pentecostal churches in Seattle from time to time. Working-class volunteers had to organize their time differently from the heavy daytime commitments of time made by members of most of the organizations we consider here. Victor Carreon, one of the founders of the CFRE had to drop his active role because of the heavy burden of work.

A. Integration as the Encouragement of Loyalty to the Beloved Community

In Chapter 2, we looked at the possibility and process of creating a "public conscience." The Christian Friends for Racial Equality avoided overt secular political activity and did not understand their project as entailing the establishment of a particular political ideology. Their sense of conscience was not simply individualistic though. What the CFRE meant by public conscience is akin to the idea of beloved community put forward early in the twentieth century by the philosopher Josiah Royce.[56] The conscience they aimed for was a sense of loyalty to the beloved community, what Jensen understood to be the connection among human beings by virtue of their value to God. The CFRE argued that it was best to influence political activity with the long-term future in mind, by changing the attitudes of individuals. They argued that this required a face-to-face effort. Most active members of the CFRE, as we have seen, were also active in one or more other civil rights organizations. Through the *Racial Equality Bulletin*, the CFRE reached out beyond the organizations to which they belonged as individuals and made their members and others aware of political efforts for racial justice and individuals in the group supported or even led political efforts. The organization as a whole did not take overt political stands though by their activities they inevitably supported some political views over others.

The Seattle Council of Churches, as a body made up of churches, on the other hand often acted as a political voice of the Seattle churches. The Council too understood itself to be shaping the public conscience, but were more likely to locate that conscience in organized power structures, legislatures, city councils, churches, civic organizations and institutions such as schools and businesses. Where there was widespread agreement among the clergy and other religious leaders, the voice of the council as a representative body could have considerable influence in public affairs. Where such widespread agreement was absent, the Council would remain guarded or even silent. As a group, the Council could have a more active voice in unpopular causes than a single individual or congregation, but the Council was never a radical body. Conservatives accused it of being liberal or even communist in its views and its more liberal critics decried it for being too timid or conservative. The Council did not see itself primarily as a political advocate for racial justice, but rather as an advocate for the goals of the member churches. Thus, the Council undertook political advocacy only when it was clear that its member churches largely agreed on something.

Both the CFRE and the Council of Churches were networking organizations. The CFRE formed a web of relationships among the churches and civil rights organizations of Seattle through the participation of its core members in multiple groups. The CFRE fostered informal relationships that eased the more official work of other organizations. The Council of Churches also formed a web of relationships through individuals who often represented more than one group. The Council of Churches was fundamentally a collection of churches rather than individuals. The individuals involved were representing larger bodies, and thus not completely free to simply follow their personal views of things. Because it was representative of larger church organizations, it had more political influence than the CFRE, but at its height in the late 1940s and early 1950s, the CFRE brought together a wider range of individuals and was able to act earlier on issues like the integration of housing because they did not have the constraint of having to follow their church or denomination's official policy or to have to work from the larger silence of the group they might represent.

Late in the 1950s, the CFRE confronted the problem of declining participation and faced a question of identity and purpose. The people in the CFRE were extraordinarily loyal to an ideal of racial equality that was not yet evident in their society. Were they as loyal to the CFRE itself? In the 1960s, the group had dwindled from some thousand members in the 1950s to less than twenty. They had a meeting at the Mt. Olive Baptist Church in 1966 to decide whether to continue and voted to do so. At the same time, they realized that their kind of race relations work was not on the cutting edge any longer. While they had been able to bring important issues to the attention of the community and to raise the public conscience, that alone was not enough to solve the problems. No one recorded the actual end of the group, but it ceased to try to compete for time from individuals who were deeply active in other, more effective groups. Their loyalty was not to the CFRE as such, but rather to the project of racial equality.

Josiah Royce who was doing his major work during the period in which the majority of the CFRE members were young or getting started in their working lives, and who was a child of the American West, specifically Gold Rush California, was interested deeply in the nature of human community and the relation of Christianity to it. In his work *The Problem of Christianity* he puts forward a thesis about the nature of Christianity that works well to describe what the CFRE was aiming toward even if they did not themselves take time to think philosophically about what they were doing. Royce conceptualized Christianity as fundamentally a loyalty to the Beloved Community. The Beloved Community, in his definition, was that universal community of beings loved by God, but was dependent upon the union of members who first love it.[57] The task or ministry of the Christian and the Church was to express that love toward all beings loved by God. Racial equality, racial justice was such an expression of that love. In this world, Royce pointed out, we live in a highly developed complex society whose very structure turns us into individualists, concerned primarily for our own interests, and thus disloyal to the Beloved Community. He went on to give a philosophical discussion of grace and the nature of atonement, but for our purposes, he outlined a philosophical picture of the difficulty of race relations in spite of the clear Christian mandate to "love your neighbor as yourself," or to "Do unto others as you would have them do unto you."[58]

The CFRE wanted to put into practice the ideal of Christianity and yet they faced the reality of the society Royce described in its structural forms that worked to prevent that very practice. A network of organizations, of which the CFRE was one important node, created by a kind of religious practice, extended the visible manifestation of the Beloved Community as far as they could as an expression of their loyalty to it. Each member of the CFRE had multiple loyalties in one sense, to family, to race, to church, to country, to class, to gender. Even so, members also gave priority to their loyalty to this Beloved Community, this vision of a society where racial equality was a reality.

B. Cross Race Friendships and Engaged Spirituality

Johanna Phillips, the first historian to consider the Christian Friends for Racial Equality as an important organization in Seattle civil rights history, suggested that one of the difficulties faced by the group as it tried to develop cross-race friendships, through its annual picnic, dinners, concerts, and on a smaller scale, its Home Visit program in the early 1960s, was that those who participated were already convinced that such relationships were important. Those who retained prejudiced ideas about people of other races were not likely to be attracted to mixed-race social events.[59]

The effort to form friendships across racial lines took effort that many otherwise well-meaning people were not willing to expend. The CFRE regarded it as a kind of spiritual practice. Developing loyalty to friends of other races required regular time to be with them without the distractions of business, voluntary or not. They also cultivated an activist style of friendship. In the September 1958 issue of the *Racial Equality Bulletin,* Edith Steinmetz proposed several things the Christian Friends could do to "speed up brotherhood:" 1. Be friendly to those of other races; 2. Vote and encourage others to vote in an informed way; 3. Move out of segregated areas into neighborhoods where people of other races live as neighbors; 4. Finding that this will be difficult for people of minority races, encourage open housing, talk about it widely; encourage the integration of our churches, schools and other places where people meet; and 5. Do these things as a mental and spiritual discipline. "Find the mental and spiritual aeroplane that will take us there."[60] For Steinmetz, the creation of the Beloved Community was an engaged spirituality; she did not practice Christianity as a private solace, but as an active and creative force in society.

Readers of the *Racial Equality Bulletin* received advice from time to time on what to say in conversations about civil rights. In November 1963, published just before the assassination of

President John F. Kennedy, the *Racial Equality Bulletin* printed nine common questions that come up in conversations about why civil rights organizations take confrontational approaches. The NAACP compiled the list. Examples of the queries and answers include, "Don't protest marches and demonstrations create unrest and race hatred? Aren't they delaying integration by stiffening the opposition?" The answer was provided; "Some unrest is stirred up, but this rarely slows integration. It brings to the surface attitudes that need exposure." One question actually called into question the CFRE's central premise. "Can successful integration be forced by law? Doesn't there have to be a change of hearts and minds of men first?" The answer for this question; "Law has always regulated conduct quite apart from attitudes. The problem must be solved to save the whole."[61] The CFRE were also not willing to let racist remarks go by in private conversations without comment. In the 1950s, the CFRE held workshops for its members to practice responses to such racist remarks or jokes.

In a secular society such as Seattle, the role religious or theological understandings of justice or equality played in the developments of relationships lay in the background. The network formed by these individuals and organizations did not describe the relationships in overtly religious terms. The ethical principles from which the CFRE and the Council of Churches pursued their project of developing a public conscience were widely shared norms in most religious traditions. Among themselves, with the assistance of the public voice of the clergy, both groups cultivated a set of theological arguments to support their work for racial equality for the purpose of strengthening their appeal to the churches. Their overtly religious appeal allowed them to bring into the citywide conversation some people who otherwise would have remained on the periphery, people in more conservative churches, and mainline white Protestants who did not otherwise think race relations was an important issue for themselves. The loyalties within the CFRE to each other and the cause of racial equality helped them to cross color, culture, and class lines to advocate changes in public policy. The conscience they strove to develop in the larger community and particularly among the decision makers spread more widely because of the networks of relationships represented by the individuals engaged deliberately in the effort to shape such a conscience.

C. Integrating the Cemeteries

The issue of the cemeteries first came to the attention of the CFRE in 1945.[62] The case they learned about involved the case of a cemetery that did not allow an African American woman to purchase a plot in the same cemetery as her white mother, and the case of a cemetery that did not allow a Japanese American to purchase a plot for his father because of his race. The CFRE began a survey of the Seattle cemeteries to find out which had restrictions based on race.

Mary Lund, the executive secretary of the CFRE, in a letter to Chester Kingsbury, president of the Methodist Federation for Social Action, dated December 30, 1948, wrote that the CFRE effort had been in progress for some time already and the proposal of one of the mortuary companies in Seattle to open a new, unrestricted cemetery had been the catalyst for a renewed effort to end all restrictions in cemeteries. The CFRE was seeking allies, which it found early among the Methodists Federation for Social Action and the Congregational Minister's Association. In a note added to the bottom of the letter, Lund stated the problem briefly.

> We have not been able to find any Seattle (public) cemetery, which does not discriminate in any way because of race or color. Many of them will not accept non-Caucasians for the burial at all, others will permit them to be buried only in

> segregated areas. The basis for most of this discrimination seems to be restrictive covenants which were written into the property deeds many years ago, and which state that lots shall be sold to "Caucasians only." However, we maintain that the spirit of the Supreme Court decision, which declared legally unenforceable such covenants in real estate property, should also be applied to cemetery lots.[63]

The mobilization of the network that linked the CFRE and the Council of Churches shows in their approach to this problem of segregated cemeteries in Seattle. After gathering their facts, they approached the churches for support for a change of policy. The enlisted the support of a wide variety of church-related organizations. Local churches such as the University Unitarian Church, the Church of the People, the Green Lake Congregational Church, the First Baptist Church, the Seattle Presbyterian Church, and the social action committee of the University Congregational Church were prominent in the effort. In addition, several minister's associations became involved: the Puget Sound Association of Congregational Ministers, Baptist Ministers and Missionaries, the Methodist Ministerial Association and the Methodist State Federation for Social Action. The ecumenical Puget Sound Minister's Association declared such segregation and restriction as "unchristian, uncivilized and unintelligent."[64]

In 1948, the Supreme Court decision in the Shelley vs. Kramer case declared that racially restrictive real estate covenants were unenforceable and the CFRE used that decision to argue that restrictions in the cemeteries were equally unenforceable. The cemeteries made no change for several years. The cemetery owners argued that unless they all integrated, those that did would lose business and have to close. In 1951, the *Racial Equality Bulletin* included a special section on the matter.

> Our beautiful city of Seattle has an enviable reputation for freedom from race prejudice. Our citizens are proud of their high ranking in this regard. The facts in this bulletin are presented because we believe Seattle citizens are quite unaware that prejudice is being carried beyond the grave. . . . Is not prejudice present unless all cemeteries are unrestricted? All correspondence in evidence of the above statements may be seen at the office, 5145 Arcade Building.[65]

Four cemeteries of thirteen listed were not restricted by race, Catholic, Jewish, Veterans' and Resthaven. Three cemeteries, Lakeview, Mt. Pleasant both of which were nearly full, and Crown Hill contained both restricted and unrestricted sections, but Crown Hill, the only one with room, discouraged though it did not prohibit burial of non-Caucasians. The remaining six cemeteries were restricted to Caucasians only, thought the Pacific Lutheran Cemeteries would accept certain Asians, presumably members of the Lutheran Church.

After the printing of this pamphlet, the Seattle Civic Unity Committee joined in the effort and met with the cemetery owners. In 1951, the *Racial Equality Bulletin* published the policies of fourteen of the city's cemeteries. The Catholic, Jewish and Veteran's cemeteries did not restrict burial by race. Eight restricted burial to Caucasians only, with the exception that the Lutheran cemetery accepted Asian Lutherans and one would accept non-Caucasians in a segregated area, but did not encourage the practice. Two that were unrestricted had little room left and one new cemetery, Resthaven, incorporated as unrestricted.[66] A history of Seattle cemeteries indicates a long standing practice of different ethnic and religious groups purchasing land and arranging for the burial of their own dead. A history of the Queen Anne area Mt. Pleasant Cemetery (listed in the CFRE list as unrestricted but almost full) contains areas originally established by the Odd Fellows, the Free Methodist

Church, the Congregation Chaveth Sholem, and the Chinese Chong Wah Benevolent Society. The Mt. Pleasant Cemetery practice of setting aside sections for particular people continues today with a new area for Muslims arranging the graves pointing toward Mecca.[67]

Calling upon their friendship networks, in April 1952, the CFRE gathered letters from the Caucasians who owned lots in segregated cemeteries saying that they would not object to having non-Caucasians occupy graves nearby.[68] In February 1958, the *Seattle Times* reported that several religious groups asked for a ban on the Easter service customarily held at the Washelli Cemetery because the cemetery practiced segregation. The Seattle-King County Council of Churches made the request, but also the Association of Congregational Christian Churches took separate action. The precipitating event was the denial of a burial place in "Babyland" in the Evergreen Cemetery (owned by the same company) for the infant of Mr. and Mrs. Milton V. Price because they were Negro. They had filed suit against the cemetery. The *Times* article reported that the cemetery officials explained that their burial policies resulted from contracts with individuals and could not be broken except by court order. The Council of Churches noted that non-restricted sections existed in the cemetery, but Babyland was not one of them.[69] Some of the cemeteries in Seattle were restricted by such racially based contracts, but some cemeteries such as Mount Pleasant Cemetery in the Queen Anne district were not so much segregated as historically allowed different ethnic groups such as the Chinese benevolent societies and the Jewish synagogue to purchase sections of the cemetery for the use of their own group resulting in ethnically or racially defined sections of the cemetery without a policy of segregation on the part of the management.[70]

The CFRE and its allies accomplished the integration of the cemeteries after nine years of effort. Washington State passed a law making discrimination in cemeteries illegal in 1953, though the incident in 1958 indicated integration was still not common. The CFRE was the catalyst for the effort, though it took the entire network of religious organizations to influence the public policy decisions at the state level. Their effort also illustrates the basic method by which the CFRE addressed policy issues that came to their attention, usually in the context of their social activities. First, they gathered the facts. Then they made an attempt to correct the problem by approaching the individuals involved directly, in this case they visited the cemetery owners. Finding this did not produce the change they desired, they began to make the issue public and enlisted their allies. The final tactic was, as they reported it, to persuade the *Seattle Times* to do a series of stories on the issue, taking it out of the religious network all together.[71] The public pressure they were able to generate finally made a policy change possible.

The CFRE was part of a complex network of organizations and individuals, including religious bodies, churches, and secular organizations all working toward similar goals. At first glance, it might seem that having so many organizations working in somewhat different ways would dilute the energy for civil rights work. When we note the ways in which the CFRE and the Council of Churches deliberately allied themselves with other groups, it becomes clear that the network functioned more as a flexible pool of organizational resources deployed in different ways according to the issue at hand.

Chapter 4

Ambiguous and Limited Success

Issues of Gender and Generation in the Life of the CFRE and the Seattle Council of Churches

I. Women's Leadership in a Man's World

In 1959, the Seattle Civic Unity Committee gave its annual award to Edith Steinmetz for her work in establishing the Christian Friends for Racial equality. The Seattle paper, Filipino Forum described her as a frail, white-haired little woman who had been a missionary in the Philippines for thirty years.[1] Her photo accompanying the article confirms the impression. She must have been around eighty years old at the time. She and her husband began their missionary work in the Philippines in 1906. In accepting the award, Steinmetz gave credit for the founding of the organization to the Filipino Victor Carreon, a somewhat younger man, though old enough to have been a teacher in the Philippines when he first met Steinmetz. P. Allen Rickles, an attorney who had served as president of the CFRE as well as a member on the Civic Unity Committee, presented the award. Rickles was sixty-three at the time; he had been a member of the CFRE from the beginning and still participated in a number of civic organizations.[2] The story illustrates two important aspects of the CFRE, the gender and the age of its prominent members. Over the years, most of the leaders in the organization were female. The group largely represented a particular generation, the one whose careers began during the Progressive Era (from approximately 1890- through World War I).

A. Women's leadership in the Churches

Edith Steinmetz represented two aspects of the work of the CFRE that are important for understanding both its approach and its ultimate influence. The growing leadership of women in the Christian churches of the world is one important aspect of Modern Christianity. Women, as lay people, had been in leadership in the Christian religion from the founding of Christianity in the first century of the Common Era. Women were always among the influential spiritual leaders of the Church, especially in ascetic and monastic movements. Women's influence, while present to a degree in Christianity, often aroused suspicions of unorthodoxy rooted in generally negative social views of women's roles outside the household. In the earliest years, Christianity developed in households where women, particularly women of wealth, had more freedom, but as it became a public religion women faded from prominence. If they assumed roles of authority within a circle beyond their own household, most people of their day regarded this as unusual or inappropriate at best or worse harmful or even evil.

In the Middle Ages, a resurgence of women's creativity and leadership manifested itself especially in the European monastic world. Several prominent female mystics gained recognition as theologians and spiritual advisors. A few were influential in political affairs. In the period leading up to the Protestant Reformation, that influence had been significantly curtailed by the Roman Catholic Church. The Protestant reformers did not all agree about women's role in the churches. Some occasionally allowed women to preach and teach, especially the more radical traditions, the Anabaptists, Quakers, Unitarians, and Methodists who came in large numbers to the British colonies in the Americas. These more open traditions became enormously influential in the United States and kept open the possibility of women's religious leadership.

During the nineteenth century evangelical revivals in Europe and North America, the ministry of ordinary converted believers became a significant sign of the reality of one's conversion. Revivalists such as Charles Finney urged women to live useful lives alongside men in the effort to spread Christianity into the world and in the effort to shape their societies according to Christian teachings. Christian leaders often welcomed the revivals, in part because they were concerned about a perceived decline in church going. Anne Braude analyzed this concern and discovered that it was a decline in male piety that prompted this anxiety. She found in addition, that women's participation had actually increased.[3]

The encouragement to increase her usefulness to the world resulted in an expansion of the idea of the household, women's proper sphere of influence, to include the larger society as it impinged upon the household.[4] Women began to alter the social definition of the female and expand its scope as they included the larger world outside the household into their sphere. This move also resulted in a heightened sense of women's self-sacrifice as part of her essential nature.[5] Women began to expand their charitable activities to a wider circle, to become concerned for the education of all children, not just their own, to participate in the anti-slavery movements and other social reform efforts. In particular, women became increasingly involved in the missionary efforts of the American Protestant Churches because they were necessary to the conversion of non-Christian women to Christianity. Women in several denominations formed their own missionary societies to foster the conversion, education, and ministry of other women. Numerous voluntary societies organized by lay church members rather than clergy, offered expanded scope to women and addressed economic and political issues, among them the right of women to vote.

Several Protestant denominations began to open the ranks of authorized ministry to women in the nineteenth century. The Methodists had already occasionally licensed women to preach.

Some smaller groups such as the Christian Connection also licensed women preachers early in the nineteenth century.[6] As the nineteenth century progressed, in part encouraged by the theology of the revivals, and resting in older arguments from the Enlightenment, some schools began to admit women to higher education and some to theological studies. Charles Grandison Finney opened Oberlin College to women and African Americans. While seldom admitted to degree programs, increasing numbers of women did attend the lectures of the theological schools and prepared themselves to do pastoral work. More established denominations were less likely to encourage women's preaching, but the growing needs of the population in its westward expansion, created opportunities for women. In denominations with congregational types of organization, the Baptists, the Congregationalists, the Universalists and Unitarian, individual congregations could and did ordain women to be their pastors. Other denominations such as the Methodists, had licensed women among their lay preachers. According to a study done by Frances Willard, by the turn of the century a handful of denominations had together ordained some two hundred women in the United States.[7] These women in effect made the church their household and expanded their venue for building the public conscience.

B. Women and the Church in the Progressive Era

Edith Steinmetz was part of this generation of women who were beginning to be ordained to ministry, usually for mission work. The ordination of women within American Protestant Christianity signaled a change in the way Protestants regarded the Scriptures and other traditional teachings about women. Denominations began to signal their alliance with other like-minded churches by their official policies regarding the ordination of women. These denominational policies did not always correlate with the actual practice regarding women's ordination, but the expansion of women's roles thus signaled a modernizing move within Christianity.[8]

Steinmetz, reportedly ordained by the Baptists in 1912, worked with her husband in the Philippines and exemplified the role of female missionaries. Though tracing official records of Baptist ordinations is not always easy, we do know that the Northern Baptist Convention, to which Steinmetz belonged, granted ordination to women at its founding in 1907.[9] Historian Mark Chaves noted, "Among both northern Presbyterians and Baptists, women's mission societies became associated with women's ordination, and both of these were seen by fundamentalists as part of a "liberal conspiracy" to realize a modernist agenda."[10]

Steinmetz used her ordination as authorization to teach. While her husband, a physician, built and ran medical clinics, she taught in a day school and served as housemother for nursing students living in dormitories.[11] She does not seem to have claimed her ordained status or practiced a particular ministry requiring ordination during her time in Seattle. Among the ironies of the American missionary movement was the freedom and authority granted to women in the mission field, unavailable to them at home among the churches which sent them as missionaries.

By World War I, in several American denominations, notably the Northern and Southern Baptist, Methodist, Episcopal, Congregational, Christian, Disciples and Presbyterian Churches, the barriers to women's role in local congregational governance were already weakening. In some more conservative congregations and denominations, women did not achieve the right to local congregational roles of authority until later in the twentieth century and in some congregations and denominations, they do not have it to this day. One or two denomination[12] have rescinded earlier decisions to allow women to be ordained or to serve in congregational leadership.

Despite the lack of access to local church or denominational leadership positions in the nineteenth century, women created numerous female-led societies within the denominations and para-church organizations that functioned apart from denominational structures. Often these worked in parallel with male-led organizations of the same kind. One particular example is the YMCA and the YWCA. In other cases women organized auxiliaries to the larger male-led organization as was the case in most of the women's fellowship groups, mission and aid societies within the various churches.

The Christian Friends for Racial Equality in Seattle was not of this kind. It was a para-church organization, but did not function exclusively as a female-led body. It had some male presidents and always contained male members on the governing board. Male and female sponsors appeared on its letterhead. Nor was it a body within which the males took the lead and the women assisted. Rather it was a genuine collaboration across gender lines. It is unclear whether her collaboration across racial lines with Victor Carreon in the formation of the CFRE signaled a similar shift in understanding of the nature of race in society. It does suggest the growing ease with which Protestant laymen and women cooperated.

The generation of women who participated in the formation and the active years of the CFRE were not always working from an explicitly feminist foundation. Feminism as an ideology has a complicated history. The female members of the CFRE were most likely to support women's right to vote, their right to a good education, and their right to participate in public life, all classic feminist goals. But they did not tend to question traditional institutions such as marriage or the churches and the constraints these institutions often placed on women's lives, nor did they record any awareness of the parallels between racial and gender prejudice. In this sense, they were not particularly feminist in their approach. While they took a cultural rather than biological approach to understanding race, they did not similarly think self-consciously about gender in a cultural sense. Although some of their members, such as Bertha Pitts Campbell, had been active in the woman suffrage movement, gender relations were not their primary concern.

After the achievement of women's right to vote in the 1920s, there was a lull in popular feminist consciousness, at least among white women in the United States. For black women, the social pressure on African Americans in many places not to exercise their right to vote complicated a woman's sense of her right to exercise her right once she had it. Perhaps the Great Depression and the coming Second World War presented enough problems. In spite of these complications, Seattle had women civil rights activists in the early twentieth century. Emma Ray and Amanda Berry Smith, preachers and activists from the holiness and Pentecostal churches of the urban poor in the city, reached across racial lines to their white sisters to advocate for whites in prison, in soup lines, and who otherwise shared in the plight of the African American poor.[13] The women of the CFRE were consciously or unconsciously building on these earlier efforts. After the generation of women, professionals whose careers spanned the Progressive Era a retrenchment of male dominance took hold in these professions and women's presence in professional work declined.[14] Women of the CFRE such as Edith Steinmetz and Bertha Pitts Campbell fit this moderate picture. They also fit the pattern of women of the Progressive generation consumed with the tasks of their professional lives, who did not manage to mentor the next generation of women to take their places.

Ernest Barth and Baha Abū Laban noted in their study of power structures in the black community in Seattle, that the most influential organizations in the community were of two kinds, social and civic or professional. Influential women tended to be the majority of the leaders in social organizations and made up

44 percent of all the influential leaders, of which the CFRE was the most influential; men tended to be the majority of leaders in the civic or professional organizations such as the NAACP or the Urban League.[15] In addition, Barth and Abū Laban note that the influential leadership tended to have a liberal perspective. They worked hard for liberal legislation, better education better housing, and an open market. As more people moved to Seattle from the South and brought segregationist assumptions of social order with them, this leadership cohort tended to resist segregation efforts because they risked moving backward on these causes. Despite their activism, these authors noted that the influential leaders were not necessarily the ones with the most power to make actual decisions, but that their influence worked behind the scenes. This is often true for women with influence.[16]

While the CFRE was most definitely a group influenced by women's leadership and a general feminist approval of women's public role in society, I would argue that it would not be appropriate to classify it as a feminist project. The CFRE is, though, a piece of women's history and gender was a factor in shaping its project. As an organization, it illustrates the role of Christian women in the effort to achieve racial equality. The female leadership of the CFRE resulted, I argue, in a characteristically female approach to public problems. Recent research by Mara Mather of University of Southern California, into the differences in brain activity between women and men under stress, shows that women faced with stressful situations, as racism certainly produces, react with increased empathy, whereas men reacted with decreased empathy.[17] Mather and her group sought to understand the observation that under stress, men tend to withdraw socially and women tend to seek nurturing and social bonding.[18] Whether one argues these different tendencies are somehow biologically essential or whether culture produces them (the subjects in Mather's study were all college students), such differences exist in the ways that men and women approach situations that cause them stress.

C. Feminism and Civil Rights in the work of the CFRE

Those involved in the CFRE approached the stress of racism by working to create bonds between people and social networks among those who shared a desire for social change. The founders of the CFRE did not give as a reason for their method, their socially assigned female role as primary nurturers of relationship among people, nor did they press for specific women's rights. Because the major leaders of the CFRE were women, it makes sense to understand their method as derived from a female cultural practice. Since the specific social problems they chose to address grew out of the relationships they built across racial lines, they paid more attention to women's issues than did other civil rights organizations.

The problem of Filipino and African American nurses turned away from jobs at the Harborview Hospital[19] was one of the first such issues addressed by the CFRE at its initial meeting. Helen Harris introduced the problem of the County Harborview Hospital not accepting minority nurses. Dr. Penick, the minister of the People's Institutional Baptist Church, offered to locate a young black woman who would be willing to apply to the nursing school. This would "test whether the race issue enters into the qualifications of a new student."[20] The CFRE pursued the issue through a personal visit to the hospital administrator who assured them that there was no discrimination. The next year the hospital began to hire minority nurses. The extant records do not indicate what the influences were that resulted in the hospital change of policy.

Bertha Pitts Campbell, in her memories of the CFRE, gave more attention to the effort of the group to change the Red Cross policy of not allowing racial minority nurses to serve. Campbell noted, "As a result of some if it [CFRE efforts], for instance, the Red Cross trained three Negroes and one Chinese, as Nurses

Aids. They were trained by the Red Cross. [Before this the] Red Cross refused to have Negroes in their thing."[21]

The refusal of a cemetery to bury a bi-racial daughter of a Caucasian mother in the family plot and the refusal of burial of an African American baby in the children's section of a cemetery that had, apparently, various segregated sections for different parts of the population was another issue touching women closely. Cemetery segregation hit a nerve with the CFRE people because there seemed to be no end to racial discrimination; it lasted beyond death. Because of women's long history of association with care of the dying and rituals of burial and grief, the effort to end racial segregation in the Seattle cemeteries was one of the longest running efforts of the group. Among the women involved in the CFRE, this struggle to integrate the cemeteries was a particularly important one. Ethelyn Miller Hartwich, active in the CFRE at the end of its active years remembered the effort in this way. In an article for the *Seattle Post Intelligencer* she wrote,

> Many who remember Mrs. Steinmetz recall the dynamic little woman who stood on the platform at a meeting called to raise $700 to carry up a court case concerning the refusal of cemetery to bury a Negro child in one of our city cemeteries. Her closing words were "dedicated indignation" and they struck home. That $700 was raised in 15 minutes, and it was in 1961 that the Washington legislature obliterated cemetery discrimination.[22]

The effort to integrate the Seattle cemeteries had been a primary effort of the CFRE for over a decade.

Other issues the CFRE tackled were also rooted in women's experience and related to places women frequented. The lack of jobs in the department stores for women of color in the sales force and the concern for housing (rather than simply home ownership) particularly attracted the attention of the CFRE because of its women members. The group was willing to entertain a more activist approach to cemetery and housing integration that it was ordinarily comfortable with, possibly because these were issues that touched women closely. An article in the *Racial Equality Bulletin* April 1952 articulated the relationship of social acquaintance to the social problems the group addressed.

> The other organizations, both in Seattle and elsewhere, are doing a necessary and professional job in stopping discriminations in business practices, in housing, in education, and other fields where the minority groups are given unequal treatment. It is done largely by statute, by such pieces of legislation as the Fair Employment Practices Act, by the adoption of fair rulings in labor unions, and such things. These matters are very important and when they begin to function effectively they add to the desirable take-it-for-granted attitude of the whole population.
>
> But there is still — an untouched field – that of prejudice. We are all influenced – and more than we realize or intend, by our prejudices. These arise from the prevailing attitudes around us. Prejudices come out of feelings – not out of intelligent consideration.
>
> It is here that our organization does its most vital work – promoting understanding by social acquaintance. Numbers of us have found satisfaction in friendships made, in the sometimes surprising [discovery]that folks are folks and that color or creed actually ceases to be a dividing line when we get acquainted with individuals.[23]

The women of the CFRE were more like the "womanist" described by Alice Walker.[24] They were concerned with women's rights but primarily within the context of race relations. Layli Phillips in her introduction to *The Womanist Reader* describes the womanist approach in this way:

> Womanism is a social change perspective rooted in Black women's and other women of color's everyday experiences and everyday methods of problem solving in everyday spaces, extended to the problem of ending all forms of oppression for all people, restoring the balance between people and the environment/nature, and reconciling human life with the spiritual dimension.[25]

As a group working in a womanist way, long before Alice Walker coined the term, the CFRE did not place gender issues or sexism in the center of their concerns. They defined their project in terms of people's everyday experiences and they preferred everyday methods of problem solving based on face-to-face relationships among members of the community. They sought to integrate their experience as women and as Christians into the more complex problem of understanding and moving their society to change. They were not simply interested in outward change, but sought to end prejudice through cultivation of a public conscience. They thought that personal relationship, where strangers became a Beloved Community, would most deeply shape this conscience.

Another reason why they did not place gender issues at the center of their work for racial equality, was the particular crisis in women's self understanding that emerged as the second World War ended. The women who had found themselves empowered as "Rosie the Riveter" or as those who had taken over male leadership roles in their churches because so many men were away fighting the war, suddenly found that people assumed they should step down. Society immediately granted privilege to the returning male veteran in the search for scarce jobs. The economy underwent a sudden large shift from a wartime economy to an economy no longer pressed by immediate and overwhelming military demands. There was no place for women even though the Seattle economy continued to depend on the burgeoning post-war defense industry. In Seattle, as in other West Coast cities, this sudden change disproportionately affected women of color. While women temporarily enjoyed economic freedoms during the war, the generation as a whole did not protest the call for women to go back home, though they often suffered from the sudden restrictions on their economic possibilities.

The CFRE relied on the volunteer labor of women who were for the most part retired. While many of the women leaders of the CFRE were white women, retired and well enough off to spend considerable volunteer time on the cause, the active black women members such as Mrs. Albert Chaney, Arlene Yarbrough, Bertha Pitts Campbell, Lola Day and Dorothy Hollingsworth knew much more clearly the dilemma faced by families where neither the men nor the women could find good jobs because of their skin color. The women of Bertha Pitts Campbell and Edith Steinmetz' generation had experienced the first wave of feminism, and had lived to see the hopes of that movement realized in the right to vote. It had only been twenty years since then, and the wars and the Great Depression had taken their toll on society's willingness to grant women economic equality. Christian women such as Steinmetz had not succeeded in mentoring a second generation of women ready to push on against the tide of wartime necessity.[26] Not until the economic boom of the 1960s would women again be able to make a place for themselves in the largely male industries and professions. As we will see below, this was not simply a characteristic of the women of this generation.

One can trace the beginning of decline of explicitly Christian organizations such as the YMCA, YWCA, the Student Christian Movement, and even in the churches themselves, to the retirement of the Progressive generation in the post-World War II period. That generation was not able to pass on their commitment to the next generation, the generation some call

"The Greatest Generation" came of age during the Depression.[27] The ambition to change the world surfaced again in their grandchildren during the 1960s, but by then the issues had changed dramatically and the gradual, relational, integration approach of the Progressive era CFRE women did not fit the new day. Perhaps the Greatest Generation was simply too overwhelmed by the next wave of crises in the twentieth century to plan careers that would build on those of their mothers.

The premise of the Christian Friends for Racial Equality, that people will be more inclined to work for policy changes to alleviate injustice if they know each other was in many ways a female approach.[28] The CFRE undertook to foster and nurture relationships. They did not immediately analyze the problem of racial equality systemically, though they did think about the overarching structures of society that made their work particularly difficult. They did not understand their task as the creation of fair rules of the game within a context of competition as their "brothers"[29] in the NAACP, Urban League or CORE might have done.

II. The Progressive Generation

A generation after the Civil War, political movements emerged in the United States aimed at addressing the perennial concerns of the economic cycles of boom and bust, depression and inflation, driven by the massive transition of the industrial, manufacturing economy and free market capitalism into a global system. Many of the problems ordinary people faced were not new; the powerful have always tried to gain more wealth at the expense of the small landowners and working class. But the rapid industrialization of the first part of the nineteenth century, the creation of mass transportation, rapid communications networks, and the exploitation of fossil fuel energy sources, and after the war, the advent of new electronic and space technologies, made traditional ways of working life not only difficult but increasingly impossible.

Beginning in the 19th century, movements started in rural areas of the Mid West. The Grangers and the Populists in the Post Civil War decades sought to address the growing difficulties of farmers, as their way of working and doing business changed rapidly with mechanization and the peculiar circumstances created by land speculation in the West. Farmers found themselves squeezed by the railroads' rising shipping rates and low prices resulting from abundance of produce generated by the mechanization of farm labor. Former farmers flocked to the cities along with the immigrants in search of waged labor. Ordinary working people suffered from low wages, long hours, uncertain job future, and the fluctuations of the money supply. Often the whole family had to work to make ends meet, meaning that children left school earlier and earlier to help support their families. Few people had pensions and almost none had the capacity to endure for very long the financial strain of serious illness. It was a period of increased immigration, immigrants outnumbering native-born citizens in many American cities. Workers born in the United States perceived immigrant labor as a threat, keeping their wages low. The Populist movements ran their course by the 1890s. Historians generally date the Progressive movement in the period from 1890 to World War I, though it remained influential through the period of the New Deal.[30]

The Protestant Christianity characteristic of the Christian Friends for Racial Equality and the Seattle Council of Churches had not been able to address this rapid economic change. The majority of American mainline Protestants retained a basically evangelical approach to Christian life emphasizing individual conversion and relationship to Jesus Christ, and personal piety and morality as sufficient to produce a good society. The revivalists of the Progressive Era, such as Dwight L. Moody, saw the problems of poverty in terms of individual work ethic. The temperance movement in its more radical branches called for the Prohibition of the sale of alcoholic beverages as the primary solution to the problems of the cities. The inability of the white Protestant middle class to find a supportive stance toward workers opened the way for the rise of Pentecostalism and for the continuing influence of the Roman Catholic Church among the new immigrants.[31]

African American Protestant churches shared the generally evangelical character of most mainline Protestantism of the era. African American congregations were present in most of the major Protestant denominations but were in the minority. Protestant denominations founded by African Americans, the African Methodist Episcopal Church or the National Baptist Convention for example, were more successful in helping their congregants deal with the rapid economic changes of the time. These churches also became centers of civil rights work in ways that the white Protestant churches have never been. Class differences appeared in these churches also, which also contributed to the dramatic rise of Pentecostalism in the black communities as well as new religious movements such as those centered on Father Devine and Daddy Grace. These new religious movements gave practical and spiritual support to those who did not have any hope of achieving middle class status.[32] Neither the Roman Catholics nor the Pentecostal churches in Seattle were a strong presence in the ecumenical circles of the city. They appeared with groups that strove to address the problems of racial justice, particularly neighborhood associations, for example the Jackson Street Neighborhood Council. The Progressive Era produced a parallel theological movement, the Social Gospel, which I will discuss in more depth below since it was influential among Seattle churches.

A Progressive Politics at the Turn of the Century

Several features became characteristic of what is now recognized as the Progressive Movement: support for the right of labor to organize and engage in collective bargaining, limits set to working hours, an end to child labor, regulations to stabilize the economic cycles and to make the workplace and its products safer, the institution of pension plans and health insurance, and changes in the nature of city government for the benefit of the general population. Journalists such as Lincoln Steffens and Ida Tarbell (the muckrakers) identified corrupt connections between companies and government and exposed systems of political patronage that compromised the integrity of government. Their revelations caused Progressives to add to their movement support for political reforms, the referendum, and the ability of the voters to legislate directly by means of propositions, the recall of corrupt officials, and the direct primary.[33] Many cities, though not Seattle, changed their government from that of an elected Mayor to a city manager plan.[34] Finally, Progressives were often advocates for a new sense of the value of conserving natural resources for future use.

By the turn of the century, the Republican Party had taken on many of the Progressive causes. Theodore Roosevelt became their champion. Through as series of political changes within both parties, at mid-century, Progressivism was associated more with the Democrats and Franklin Delano Roosevelt's New Deal. With the New Deal, the Progressives had achieved much of what they had worked for during the first half of the twentieth century. It remained for the benefits of the Progressive policies to extend to racial minorities and women. While a few Southern Progressive leaders tried to work across racial lines, Progressives in general did not overcome the common racial prejudices of the day, nor were they entirely sympathetic to feminism. Mark Matthews, the Progressive Social Gospel pastor of First Presbyterian Church of Seattle was clearly anti-feminist. The Progressives also inherited the Populist hostility to immigrants. Mary Lease, one of those who articulated the Populist mind, suggested, in 1895, that Caucasians should be the landowners and "Orientals and Negroes" be the "tillers of the soil."[35] Echoing particular constructions of race based in a narrow interpretation of Genesis and Social Darwinism, Lease's widely read book reflected the underlying assumptions of the Progressives regarding race relations.

B. Progressive Republicans

The Progressive Republicans included many of the people involved in Seattle's Christian Friends for Racial Equality, Council of Churches, and particularly the African American bodies such as the NAACP and Urban League. The association among the African American community of the Republicans with Abraham Lincoln persisted long after the party began to work actively against what many black people perceived as their best interests. Mainline Protestants tended to remember the Republicans as the party that supported their desire to shape the social norms of the country to fit Protestant values, Prohibition being the foremost example. The historian Richard Hofstadter, argues that Progressivism was characterized by Yankee Protestant religious values and ideals.[36]

Except in the South, white middle class Protestants generally believed that the Republicans had served them well, even though the party increasingly served the interests of wealth and big business. These Protestants were never completely comfortable with the labor union, and by the end of the Second World War, often associated labor movements with Communism. Mainline Protestants focused on personal behavior. Restricting consumption of alcohol and regulation of vice seemed to them to be the most effective ways to address the problems of poverty and corruption in the cities. The problems of racial equality, integration, equal protection under the law were not high priorities in the movement. The white Progressives tended to assume that the white race fared better in society because they worked harder, were more virtuous, and thus had earned their position. American Protestants often saw one's lot in life as an indication of the state of one's soul.[37] Early Progressives tended to frame the race issues, as they did poverty, in terms of Social Darwinism. They saw society as a collection of competing peoples and those more fit or more virtuous improved their lot over time. Later Progressives began to have a more complicated view of race and framed the question in terms of assimilation, and treated immigrant identity as changeable, but racial identity as fixed. The Progressives expected the individual, acting with virtue and industry to be able to rise above circumstances. While they assumed people could overcome the artificial barrier of prejudice, and went on persuading people to change their views, by the end of the era, people such as those in the CFRE and the Council of Churches in Seattle knew enough to suspect that individual change, while necessary, would not be enough.

C. The Social Gospel and Liberal Theology

During the Progressive Era, two theological movements were influencing the thinking of mainline Protestants: the Social Gospel and liberal theology. The Social Gospel was more particularly associated with the Progressive political movements, but also had its roots in Christian socialism. Social Gospel theologians drew inspiration from the Hebrew prophets, particularly where they addressed the treatment of workers, the poor, the weaker and the oppressed. The movement conceived the Christian life as building the Kingdom of God in this world, transforming the social order to conform to the teachings of Jesus. Early Christianity had its roots in a society of vast discrepancies between the few wealthy and powerful and the masses of poor people. The Gospels present Jesus' teachings in this context, drawing upon the tradition of the Hebrew prophets. While the Gospels do not present a specific plan of political or economic reform, they envision a community of cooperation, equality, and social justice. Some Social Gospelers understood the process of change as gradual, others were more politically radical.

Liberal theology emerged from the Enlightenment of the eighteenth century and was popular with those who desired to maintain a Christian dialogue with science and with people of different religions. While liberal theology often undergirded social gospel proposals, it was primarily an intellectual movement working to articulate Christian theological concepts without appeal to the supernatural or to a special revelation, but by using human reason and experience. This allowed liberal theologians to remain open to conversations with science and modern intellectual movements. The liberal theologians shared with the Social Gospel an emphasis on Christianity as a way of life rather than a creed to be defended.[38] Many church leaders were interested in both streams of thought and both liberal theology and the social gospel influenced the twentieth century civil rights movements.

For women and racial minorities the influence was ambiguous. Male theologians in both camps assumed traditional roles for women. Both movements, when they addressed race, acknowledged racial equality in theory, but neither adequately addressed practical race questions. The Social Gospel originated in northern cities before the Great Migration. As a movement, it never addressed the question of racism as a central problem, though some black theologians such as Benjamin Mays, Mordecai Johnson and Howard Thurman built on the Social Gospel tradition and liberal theology's call to Christian society to take its own teachings seriously.[39] Asian American Christians left little record of their theological thinking during the Progressive era. Their later contributions to liberation theologies show connections with the social Gospel. Paul Nagano, in a sermon to the Japanese Baptist Church in Seattle while he served as pastor there, affirmed Jesus solidarity with the poor and the church's responsibility to address power structures in society.[40] Filipino theologian A. C. Ubalde Jr. articulated a Social gospel based liberation theology from a Pacific immigrant experience in an undated essay, "Church and Society." "The worker became alienated because he was deprived of the human features of his labor. . . . The author suggests that the messianic theology implies the category of responsibility."[41] This responsibility included freedom, power and accountability for those economically exploited by this society. The prophetic gospel liberates the oppressed; a salvation of the type envisioned by those who see Christianity as a way of life.

Christianity in this period, whether the observer was liberal or conservative, had two basic interpretations. The first understood Christianity as a spiritual matter, focused on the salvation of the soul. It emphasized Jesus death and resurrection, and the work of the Holy Spirit. The moral life can be either a means to or a sign of salvation. The second understood Christianity primarily as a way of life, while this way tends to be more characteristic of liberals; various holiness movements have this emphasis. The moral life in this view is the means of salvation, not only for the individual but also for all of society, since by means of following the way of Jesus Christ, the Christian helps to make the Kingdom of God real in this world. The Social Gospel had in common with the Christian Friends for Racial Equality, an emphasis on Christianity as a way of life. The CFRE people almost never referred to the resurrection, or salvation, or the soul, but kept their focus on living so as to manifest the Kingdom of God on earth. This difference in approach to the Christian life is discernable in almost all periods of Christian history.

The Social Gospel was not always associated with liberal theology nor was liberal theology always associated with social reform or Progressive political views. In addition to formal identification with a theological school of thought, more characteristic of the clergy than the laity, Protestant Christians participated in both movements informally in their attempt to apply Christian teachings to their lives whether or not any particular pastor or theologian influenced them. Despite the complexity of theological thinking in the twentieth century, clearly the ecumenical civil rights work of the CFRE and the Seattle Council of Churches rested on a shared set of basic theological sources and the deeply held understanding that the Christian life was important not only for the individual but for the salvation of society lay behind their belief that they could shape a public conscience. This foundation rested on previous Christian public witness before the 1940s.

Seattle had a history of a strong Social Gospel voice in the early twentieth century in the person of Rev. Mark Matthews, pastor of the First Presbyterian Church of Seattle. He was an influential voice for labor rights and other Social Gospel causes, but was increasingly a Fundamentalist in his theology.[42] He shared the desire for civic righteousness with the majority of mainline evangelical Christians of the time, opposing gambling, the sale of alcoholic beverages, and prostitution. He clearly set out to shape a public conscience in the city through preaching to his congregation. In 1909, he preached a series of sermons in Seattle with this aim. "The Friendless Man" pointed out the need of everyone for a purpose outside of him or herself, a common revival theme in American Christianity but also echoing the loneliness of the economically isolated individual. "The Penniless Man" exposed the problems of laziness and extravagance that contribute to poverty, a common theme among American Protestants. But the next sermons, "The Heartless Man" and "The Conscienceless Man" focused on the greed of capital, the abuse of women and animals [most people still used horses in 1909], and the exploitation of labor.

> Do you suppose landlords who are systematically and persistently raising rents on office buildings, stores, restaurants,

> bakeries, barber shops, hotels, flats and residences are controlled by the dictates of a righteous conscience? No.[43]

First Presbyterian was a church filled with those who owned the office buildings, stores, apartments and businesses. The sermons were a direct challenge to them. Matthews used even stronger language in support of workers. "Capital has no right to accumulate wealth until it crushes to death those who seek the right to live and the right to toil."[44] He referred to those who became rich by taking advantage of workers as parasites in society. Matthews urged his congregation to apply Christian principles to their business practice, and to assume leadership in changing public policy to prevent the abuse of workers. As did other Progressives, Matthews focused attention on particular personal behavior he believed led to poverty, such as consumption of alcohol and gambling, and wanted those things regulated as much as he advocated that business change its ways.[45] In keeping with his Progressive and Social Gospel approach, Matthews seemed blind to the relationship of racial injustice and women's subordination to the exploitive practices he decried. Matthews was a well known and influential figure in Seattle until he died in 1942, at about the same time the Christian Friends for Racial Equality organized themselves. They were building on the foundation of the conscience he tried to raise among the city's prosperous business people.

Rev. Fred Shorter, an active member of the CFRE and pastor of the Church of the People is another example. He had come to Seattle to be pastor of the Pilgrim Congregational Church in the 1920s, but his support for union labor, particularly the International Workers of the World (or the Wobblies as they were known), his preaching against lynching, his indignation about the plight of farmers who could not afford to harvest their crops for the little money they would make and his response to other issues of economic justice did not please his congregation and they voted him out of office in the mid-1930s. With several members of the Pilgrim Congregational Church, who left because of that vote, Shorter formed the Church of the People located near the University of Washington [46]

The Social Gospel premise of the Church of the People also showed the influence of the Social Gospel in the Federal Council of Churches, particularly in the department responsible for issues of church and society. In its newsletter, The New Religious Frontier, the Church of the People reprinted the "Social Principles" from the Methodist Church.[47] In general the Methodist Church's rhetoric followed the larger ecumenical consensus on race relations, "A non-segregated church in a non-segregated society."[48] Soon after the Methodist Church put forward its list of social principles, the Federal Council of Churches issued a statement that followed is format and content, using the same phrase to articulate its vision of racial equality.

Where the Social Gospel emphasis on labor issues did not always lead white churches to see the link between these and issues of race, the black churches were clear about this problem. "The Church and Race Relations," an official statement approved by the Federal Council of Churches at a special meeting in March 1946, detailed the presence of segregation in Protestant churches and society. "The pattern of racial segregation in America is given moral sanction by the fact that churches and church institutions, as a result of social pressure, have so largely accepted the pattern of racial segregation in their own life and practice."[49] The statement noted that "Negro membership is less than 1% in predominantly white churches." The statement went on to note that segregation was more prevalent in church than in public school. It was especially prevalent in hospitals. White church-controlled hospitals largely excluded Negro doctors, Negro nurses, and Negro patients. Church schools were less segregated than hospitals, but theological seminaries frequently denied admission to black students. The statement proposed integration at all levels - especially urging the opening of white churches to minority groups. The Federal Council invited responses from the member churches and others. In its response, the National Baptist Convention's statement on race relations was explicit about economic policy issues that were largely missing from the Federal Council statement the listed several issues that needed to be addressed:

> Establish Permanent Fair Employment Practices Commission; eliminate the poll tax; oppose restrictive covenants; improve economic lot of non-whites in Asia, Africa, and the US; support movements toward self-government; affirmed the right of collective bargaining; government has the obligation to open public works in times of depression when industry cannot provide jobs; and employers and workers obligation to create Christian relations.[50]

This list represented a Social Gospel approach to the issues of race relations, refusing to simplify the problem of race relations to one of segregation alone, and urging instead that the churches take seriously the economic structures that granted privilege to white workers at the expense of others. The difference between the National Baptist Convention approach and the Federal Council of Churches illustrates the failure of the Social Gospel to address racial injustice. Walter Rauschenbusch, the central theologian of the Social Gospel and a white man, stated near the end of his life that the racial situation was so tragic he did not know what to say.[51] He argued that true Christianity is not prejudiced toward those of other races, but he failed in his career to protest the blatant racial inequalities of his day.

III. The Limits of Seattle Progressivism and Social Gospel Protestantism

In the 1930s and 1940s, most of the Seattle congregations were content to celebrate Race Relations Sunday and did not take the more radical approach of the Church of the People which tried to create a deliberately integrated church.[52] Nonetheless, the Church of the People, as the First Presbyterian Church before it, provided a public articulation of the Social Gospel. Unlike Mark Matthews, Fred Shorter lost his first pastorate because of his stance, but both pastors were influential voices, especially in white Seattle, creating an awareness of the economic implications of their reading of the Christian Gospel.

The Social Gospel, particularly through the connection of their denomination to the Federal Council of Churches and more locally their own connection to the Seattle Council of Churches and Christian Education, influenced a few other Protestant pastors in Seattle. The lay people in their congregations were likely to hear sermons containing Social Gospel themes, and most churches were involved in some effort to relieve the plight of the poor. The voluntary nature of church membership tended to have a dampening effect on the minister's ability to be prophetic and call for significant social change.

As we have noted, churches were in many ways braver in groups. The Federal council of Churches, the social justice branches of denominational organizations, and ecumenical groups such as the CFRE were much more able to speak with a radical voice. They were able to a point. They too depended on the voluntary contributions of the members of the churches they served and laity had little mind to support groups they thought strayed from the path of appropriate religious activity. The Council of Churches was particularly vulnerable to this limit, in part because it had a significant budget and need for contributions, but also because it represented churches rather than individuals. The Council had to be more careful that whatever position it took, the denominations it represented would support it. The CFRE was much freer, having almost no budget and therefore little worried about losing funds. In addition, it represented individuals who did not have to be careful to represent a sense of the group. In its newsletter, *The Racial Equality Bulletin* and it its community activities it could say things more explicitly about the contradictions between church teaching and practice with regard to racial equality.

The Seattle Council of Churches was first of all a body formed to foster the welfare and growth of the member churches.[53] Attention to social justice issues was secondary to that main goal. The Council's primary commitment to the well being of member congregations hampered in its civil rights work, because those congregations, most of them white, did not often understand civil rights to be an issue vital to their survival. The Christian Friends for Racial Equality were also concerned about the well-being of the Council's member churches, but they realized that promoting this well-being required them to engage actively in political efforts their local churches might have been reluctant to undertake.

The Council of Churches, in its affiliation with the Federal Council of Churches worked within another limit as well. The Federal Council of Churches tended to frame race relations in terms of black and white, focusing their historical analysis of the racial justice problems on slavery, reconstruction, and Jim Crow style segregation. The Seattle African American population was relatively small in relationship to the Asian and Pacific Islander immigrant population, and thus the concerns of Pacific region immigrants of color were not part of Federal Council emphasis. The local Council of Churches in Seattle considered the matter of race relations in a limited way. Due to language barriers, many of the immigrant churches did not participate. In addition, many more immigrants from Asia were not Christian.

Chinese, Japanese and Filipino immigrants often came to the United States recently converted to Protestant Christianity by British or American missionaries; those from the Philippines, who were most often Catholic, represented a settled community of Christians dating to the Spanish colonial days. When the United States annexed the Philippines, Protestant missionary efforts began immediately afterward. Filipino Protestant immigrants, through the missionary efforts, had come to believe that the United States was a Christian nation where its ideals of political equality of all people would apply to them. This was the concern Carreon and Baaoa raised that helped to start the CFRE. Once in the United States, Filipinos found that Americans applied their common ideas of race to them due to their darker skin color in addition to their accents. The debate in American society during the early Twentieth Century about whether Filipinos were eligible for citizenship because of the status of the Philippines as a United States protectorate took these immigrants by surprise. The Chinese and Japanese communities had a longer history of similar experiences.

The Progressive era people retained the racial assumptions made by white people about black people and assigned those assumptions to others based on their perceptions of skin color.[54] For the Filipino immigrant it was a complex negotiation between the identity given by family and community and the identity assigned by a society that did not know them. While Filipinos were associated with blacks in the popular American media, Chinese and Japanese immigrants, unlike the Filipinos who were more often already Christian, faced additional prejudices since they did not come from cultures Americans recognized as Christian.

Public opinion in Seattle tended to regard immigrants from China and Japan with less anxiety than those from the Philippines because restrictions in immigration had been in place for some time for people from East Asia. The Philippines, recently acquired as a colony, had a closer relationship to the United States and Filipinos came to the United States fairly easily in search of new economic opportunities. Seattle was one of the centers of Filipino migration. The salmon canneries employed hundreds of Filipino immigrants, as did the farms of Eastern Washington. Most Roman Catholic Filipinos belonged to the Maryknoll Church, Our Lady Queen of the Martyrs, in Seattle's Central District. The Filipinos associated with the Christian Friends for Racial Equality were Methodists, active also in the Filipino Christian Fellowship Association, along with Baptists and others. The YMCA was another important link between them and the greater Seattle society. The generation of Filipinos active in Seattle civil rights movements was part of a generational transatlantic migration that formed extended families across the Pacific. The churches served as centers for social organization and provided alternative families for those who pioneered the move to the United States. Because the Filipinos were mostly Christians the churches, both Protestant and Catholic, served as a location of interface between the Filipino immigrant community and the larger American society. Dorothy Fujita-Rony also points out the class issue that complicated Victor Carreon's life in the United States. He was already a teacher when he came to the U. S. with the hopes of getting a university education, but ended up as a laborer, though he played an important leadership role within the Filipino Christian Fellowship Association.[55] When the Filipino immigrants experienced exclusion from the white churches, it not only called into question their idealized picture of the United States but also their sense of identity as Christian people.

The difficulty of crossing class lines in the black church community and among the white mainline Christians also complicated the work for racial justice in Seattle on the part of the churches. Not only were most members of the CFRE and the Council of Churches from the progressive generation who tended to be less radical in their approach to social change. The majority were female in an era when women were not encouraged to be outspoken. They were also largely middle class. Though the CFRE occasionally met in a Pentecostal

Church, its sphere of influence remained among the mainline churches at a time when their influence in society was on the wane.

In the end one could argue that the Christian Friends for Racial Equality was simply naive and ineffective in how they set about to accomplish racial equality in Seattle. This 1948 survey suggests that there was some evidence of the very public conscience they wished to develop. Similarly, the Seattle Council of Churches, while it often stood up for racial equality, also did not succeed in shaping a just society in the city. On the other hand, the more activist and confrontational methods of CORE and the Black Panthers in the following generation, while they accomplished much, in the end did not succeed in completely eradicating prejudice. Each generation begins again to work on this complicated problem in American society.

Both the CFRE and the Council of Churches, now the Church Council of Greater Seattle, worked on issues of racial justice from a particularly Christian religious perspective. To them the Beloved Community was something related to the work of God to save humanity from its own selfishness and evil. They drew on millennia of prophetic traditions calling for justice for the alien and the poor. They also drew upon the preaching of Jesus and his followers who urged a community built first in love for each other. They had also the example of the prophets and Jesus who did not work comfortably within the state structures, but tended to favor human community over social control. This primarily theological understanding of their call to create a public conscience resisted the countervailing attempts to create a public sense of support for rapid economic growth for the relatively wealthy without regard for those they exploited in this effort. The loyalty called forth by the public conscience the CFRE had worked to develop was a loyalty to humanity and its flourishing. The members of the Christian Friends for Racial Equality understood their spiritual task to be always engaged in a public struggle to form relationships across lines of race and also class, and to look out for each other.

Conclusion

The Christian Friends have disappeared; the last trace of them appeared in a newspaper ad alerting people to unclaimed property deposited at a bank. The Church Council remains, and carries on the same kind of task, seeking to shape a public conscience for racial justice, even in an increasingly secular society. Mary Sawyer, in her study of black ecumenism, concluded that local ecumenical movements such as the CFRE face the challenge of direct involvement with individual people and their immediate needs, rather than having the luxury of time to consider principles and policy. They can be highly influential, but require a high level of energy and commitment from their constituents.[1] The churches and neighborhoods where the CFRE was active are still there and people in Seattle still struggle with issues of racial equality.

The CFRE and the Race Relations Department of the Seattle Council of Churches represent historical examples of people who out of loyalty to each other and to an ideal of Beloved Community, as Josiah Royce articulated it in the early twentieth century and as Martin Luther King Jr. articulated it in the 1960s, worked for racial equality and a just society in their city. Their story forms a piece of people's history. Stories such as theirs do not appear in conventional histories of Christianity because they focus on denominations, institutions, famous people and theological ideas. What the lay people and the many local church pastors accomplish by living out their beliefs does not fit the conventional criteria for importance. Often historians have considered local history to be only of interest or importance to local people. Recent historical trends suggest that these people's histories are important to everyone. They do not simply illuminate a local interest, but they serve as lenses for understanding a deeper presence of a religious tradition as complex as

Christianity in its relationships with the social movements of a particular time and place. The CFRE and the Council of Churches illustrate how Christianity can function and has functioned in society.

These two ecumenical organizations, working for civil rights, were self-consciously living out particular theological ideas, forming, not a systematic theology, but a systemic application of Christian ideals in the larger society. They encountered serious difficulties in doing this, modified their practice as time went on, and in the end left the quest for the Beloved Community unfinished for another generation to take up. Gender roles and relationships were changing rapidly in their day. The Social Gospel progressive project was proving to be too optimistic. The liberal advocacy of freedom of thought and action failed to take account of systemic privilege and disempowerment. The CFRE and the Council of Churches faced a rapidly changing society, and though they were flexible creative people, they were not able to work effectively in every situation. This is not unlike the perpetually unfinished nature of Christian theology in its quest to talk coherently about God.

The most effective thing they did, and one most characteristic of their loyalty to the Beloved Community, was to help to create and strengthen the network of civil rights organizations in Seattle. A theologian, working during this period of the 1940s and 50s, echoed Royce's estimation that the heart of Christianity, at least if not other religious as well, is human relationship of love. Reinhold Niebuhr wrote:

> The mechanically contrived togetherness of our great urban centers is inimical to genuine community. For community is grounded in personal relations. In these the individual becomes most completely himself as his life enters organically into the lives of others.[2]

It was the network rather than the individual institutional members that was able to accomplish the advances in civil rights that occurred in the city during the 1940s, 50s and laid the ground for the work of the 1960s. In this network, they were able to provide a visible and embodied example of the Christian ideal of love for the neighbor. They certainly did not enjoy perfection. There were power struggles even with this network of people focused on civil rights. Not everyone was included in the main organizations. The network drew some people in for particular causes, as when the Lutherans joined the cemetery integration struggle; others chose not to participate for some reason of creed or class. For the most part, though, according to the limitations of their views and knowledge, they succeeded in increasing the integration and possibility for inter-racial friendship in Seattle. They participated in creating more just social structures and raising awareness of issues that continued to make life difficult for people of color in the city. Archie Smith Jr. describes this legacy.

> The neighborhood in which I grew up reflected a multiracial, ethnic minority population which included the indigenous people, Afro, Asian, Jewish, and Italian Americans. A few Anglo-Americans also lived in our neighborhood and were among the first to leave. During the late forties and fifties my neighborhood became increasingly black, yet the ethnic mix was maintained. I came to believe that that early experience of growing up in an ethnically mixed community later contributed to my ability, in my community ministry to relate to others across ethnic and social-economic groupings.[3]

The ideal always exceeded their grasp. That is not to say that the CFRE did not accomplish anything. The Black Panthers found a foundation already built upon which they were able to work. There remains in the atmosphere of the city, an ideal, a memory, of a call to conscience that makes the city perpetually unhappy with its progress on the issue. Cultural anthropologists sometimes speak of fragments or memories of cultural practices, images or worldviews that persist for a long time and shape the character of society over several millennia. The idea of a racial equality remaining in Seattle from the work of the CFRE is such a fragment of cultural memory and still calls forth a public conscience in support of racial equality, though the CFRE itself is forgotten and the work needed to achieve it is hardly over.[4]

Endnotes

Introduction

1. "Minutes of Seattle Council of Churches and Christian Education," Monday June 1, 1942. Church Council of Greater Seattle Records, Accession number 13558-007, Box 1, 1941 ff. 18. University of Washington Libraries, Special Collections.
2. Edith Steinmetz and Ethelyn Hartwich, "Twenty Years History of the Christian Friends for Racial Equality - Seattle, WA 1942-1962, Or What Were Seattle People Doing?" (1962) Christian Friends for Racial Equality Records, Accession Number 4040-3 Box 1 ff1. University of Washington Library, Special Collections. This potluck took place while the pressing concern of both the Seattle Council of Churches and the CFRE was the internment of the Japanese.
3. People in this period considered social acquaintance across racial lines to be dangerous. When people met for social occasions, they were inclined to form friendships and even marry. The prejudices of the day created sometimes sever social penalties for such social relationships. One of my colleagues, Archie Smith Jr. was a student at Garfield High School at this time and reports that in that multi-racial school, students related across racial lines as a matter of course, whereas, students at more exclusively white schools did not have that opportunity. We will note below several instances of concern about public schools – an important venue for such relationships among young people.
4. The phrase "Beloved Community" is often associated with the thought of Martin Luther King, Jr. and is widely used in religiously based civil rights discourse. It is older than this; one can find it in the philosophy of Josiah Royce who was writing in the early twentieth century. Later I will discuss Royce's use of the term.

5. Ralph L. Moellering, *Christian Conscience and Negro Emancipation* (Philadelphia: Fortress Press, 1965) p. 101
6. Patricia O'Connell Killen, "Patterns of the Past, Prospects for the Future: Religion in the None Zone," in Patricia O'Connell Killen and Mark Silk, eds. *Religion and Public Life in the Pacific Northwest: The None Zone*. (Walnut Creek, CA: Altamira Press, 2004) 9-19. In contrast to this picture of secularization, some students of religion have suggested recently that religion is of growing importance, citing the growth of Christianity and Islam in the world and the movement of population from Asia, Latin America and Africa where these religions are growing particularly strongly to areas of the world that have been regarded as highly secularized.
7. Killen, p. 15.
8. I am borrowing the phrase from Killen and Silk's book title.
9. These figures are from the 1936 U. S. Department of the Census survey of religious bodies, a notoriously difficult statistical collection to use for trying to draw an accurate picture of the religious landscape of a given community. The census did not completely count non Christian religions, and the Christian denominations each have different understandings of what counts as a member leading to incomparable reported numbers. U. S. Department of Commerce, Bureau of the Census, *Religious Bodies, 1936* (Washington, D. C.: U. S. Government Printing Office, 1941) vol. 1 p. 636 ff.
10. Mark A. Shibley, "Secular but Spiritual in the Pacific Northwest," in Patricia O'Connell Killen and Mark Silk, eds. *Religion and Public Life in the Pacific Northwest: The None Zone.* (Walnut Creek, CA: Altamira Press, 2004) 139-167.
11. I am grateful for a short conversation with Joseph Driskill which clarified his thinking about this.
12. Shibley, p. 139. He is using Wade Clark Roof's definition of spirituality and religion found in *Spiritual Marketplace: Baby*

Boomers and the Remaking of American Religion (Princeton, NJ: Princeton University Press, 1999) 33-35.

13. Patricia O'Connell Killen and Mark Silk eds., *Religion and Public Life in the Pacific Northwest: The None Zone* (Walnut Creek, CA: Altamira Press, 2004) considers this phenomena in several of the essays using data from the Gallup Polls about religion in public life and the Glenmary Research Center's data on religious demographics from the 2000 census year.
14. Sources of religious demographic data include the U. S. Census of Religious Bodies which the Bureau of the Census took every decade until the 1940s. After that the National Council of Churches of Christ in the U. S. gathered data, but frustratingly left out data from the black churches. After the 1970s the Glenmary Research Center, a Roman Catholic related institution, took over the problem of gathering the data, based both on the self reports of religious organizations and public opinion surveys. Each of these organizations used somewhat different methods of gaining information, and we have to exercise care with all of them.
15. Nancy Tatom Ammerman, *Pillars of Faith: American Congregations and their Partners*. (Berkeley: University of California Press, 2005). Ammerman discusses each of these factors at length in her study of congregations. She included churches in Seattle in this study and she has this to say about congregations in the region. "Seattle, Washington shares none of the nostalgia for nineteenth-century rural America. Reinventing traditions is what Seattle is all about, and often that means leaving organized religious life entirely. . . . But many of them do join congregations, and often they start new ones. Seattle is too new to have many really old congregations. Indeed, well over half of today's groups have been created since World War II. Three-quarters of them told us that most of their members grew up in a different denomi-

nation, and most congregations described their members as mostly newcomers to the community. Very little about this city seems to be nailed down. It sits on the edge of the continent facing west, and that means it has more Asian than African American or Hispanic residents. That is reflected in Asian Christian congregations, centers for Buddhists and Hindus, and congregations in which Asian, Hispanic, Anglo and African American members mix in nearly equal numbers."

16. Patricia O'Connell Killen, "Patterns of the Past, Prospects for the Future: Religion in the None Zone," in Patricia O'Connell Killen and Mark Silk eds., *Religion and Public Life in the Pacific Northwest: The None Zone* p. 12.

    ". . . The ambiguity of the larger religious environment propels them [those who choose affiliation with a particular religion] toward commitment that is clearly defined, emotionally significant, and often inflexible because it has been hard won, and thus is in need of protection."

17. Matthew's Gospel, portrays Jesus saying these words during his trial. He quoted from the Hebrew Scripture Deuteronomy 6:5 and Leviticus 19:18.
18. Archie Smith, Jr. *The Relational Self: Ethics and Therapy from a Black Church Perspective,* Nashville: Abingdon, 1982) p. 32.
19. Peter Brown, *The World Of Late Antiquity AD 150-750* (New York: W. W. Norton, 1971)49-57. Brown, a historian of late antiquity, gives a succinct discussion of why Christianity appealed to people in its early years, even though it was not a legal religion. These characteristics of Christianity continue to draw people. Also William Herzog, "Why Peasants Responded to Jesus," Richard Horsley, Ed. *Christian Origins, A People's History of Christianity* Vol. 1 (Minneapolis: Fortress Press, 2005) 47-69 also develops this theme.

20. I say this early on, in case the reader agrees with the modern, secular stance and finds no contradiction between religion, specifically Christianity, and the modern economic systems. In this case, the rest of the book will make little sense and I can save the reader valuable time. I find the picture troublesome and the perennial need of a public conscience seems clear.
21. Edwin Gaustad and Philip Barlow, *A New Historical Atlas of American Religion* (New York: Oxford University Press, 2001)319.
22. The essays in Russell Richey and Donald Jones, *American Civil Religion* (New York: Harper and Row, 1974) lay out the parameters of this common set of values.
23. Charles H. Long, "Civil Rights – Civil Rights: Visible People and Invisible Religion," in Russell E. Richie and Donald G. Jones, *American Civil Religion* (New York: Harper and Row, 1974) p.214-215. "The religion of the American people centers in the telling and retelling of the mighty deeds of the white conquerors. This hermeneutic mask thus conceals the true experience of Americans from their very eyes. Matching the invisibility of Indians and blacks is a void or a deeper invisibility within the consciousness of white Americans. The inordinate fear they have of minorities is the expression of the fear they have when they contemplate the possibility of seeing themselves as they really are." (p. 214) Long's argument here depends on the existence of a public conscience no matter how repressed it has become.
24. An example relevant to our case in Seattle is the decision made in the 1990s by the U. S. Congress to acknowledge the internment of the Japanese in World War II as wrong and to pay reparation to each person who had suffered internment.
25. The political scientist Daniel Elazar expands on this biblically derived sense of covenant in Puritan thought in Daniel Elazar, *Covenant and Constitution: The Great Frontier and the*

Matrix of Federal Democracy (New Brunswick, NJ: Transaction Publishers, 1998). The character of the covenant as it came to be expressed in American politics is shaped by acknowledgment of God's sovereignty and justice as foundations for the moral order, the freedom of human beings to act within the bounds of the moral order, the enjoyment of liberty but with responsibility, and the highest ideals expressed in the Constitution and rule of law (p. 261). My thanks go to Joe Zikmund for introducing me to the work of Elazar.

26. Daniel Elazar, *The Constitutional Matrix and Modern Democracy,* (New Brunswick, NJ: Transaction Publishers, 1998) p. 245.
27. Archie Smith Jr., *The Relational Self,* p. 21.
28. Janet Parachin *Engaged Spirituality: Ten Lives of Contemplation and Action.* (St. Louis: Chalice Press, 1999)
29. The formulation of this rule in the Christian Gospels is in the gospels of Matthew and Luke. Matthew 7:12 reads, "Whatsoever ye would that men should do to you, do ye even so to them." King James Version (KJV). Luke 6:31 reads, "As ye would that men should do to you, do ye also to them likewise."(KJV) I quote the King James Version here because the people of the CFRE most likely were familiar with the King James Version of the Bible. The Revised Standard Version and other newer English translations did not appear until after the war.
30. "The Creed of the Golden Rule," Christian Friends for Racial Equality *Racial Equality Bulletin,* vol. IX no. 10 (March 1955), 3. The information was quoted from Oveta Culp Hobby's address to the National Conference of Christians and Jews, February 1955 as reprinted in *New Outlook* (February, 1955).
31. Seattle Council of Churches Records Acc. no. 13558-007 Box 1 of 50, ff 16, Minutes of Executive Committee Meeting, November 20,1939. University of Washington Library, Special Collections. The Council decided at this meeting on

the wording of the statement of purpose for their membership form.

> "The Purpose of this organization, expressed briefly, is to promote and extend the Christian religion in Seattle through cooperative action on behalf of member bodies in such fields of effort as Christian Education, evangelism, temperance, comity, and public affairs."

Seattle Council of Churches and Christian Education Membership Application Form included with the minutes for the November 20, 1939 meeting.

32. I will say more about this as the CFRE and Seattle Council of Churches' stories unfold. Kenneth Smith and Ira Zepp, *Search for the Beloved Community: The Thinking of Martin Luther King, Jr.* (Valley Forge: Judson Press, 1998) discusses the development of this idea in King's thought.
33. "If your brother sins against you go and tell him his fault, between you and him alone. If he listens to you, you have gained your brother. But if he does not listen, take one or two others along with you, that every word may be confirmed by the evidence of two or three witnesses. If he refuses to listen to them, tell it to the church; and if he refuses to listen even to the church, let him be to you as a Gentile and a tax collector." Matthew 18:15-17 Revised Standard Version.
34. Cynthia Taylor, *A. Philip Randolph: The Religious Journey of an African American Labor Leader* (New York: New York University Press, 2006). Taylor noted the scholarly tradition about Randolph for fifty years characterized him as a "doubter of Christianity," and as one who "stood against all religion." She argues that Randolph had a generally positive relationship to religious institutions and "never strayed far from his African Methodist roots." (p. 2).
35. Some of the most important of these critiques are in James Baldwin, *The Fire Next Time* (1962); Martin Luther King Jr., *Why We Can't Wait* (1963); James Forbes, *Black Manifesto*

(1969); Charles H. Long, "Civil Rights – Civil Religion: Visible People and Invisible Religion," in Richey and Jones eds., *American Civil Religion*, p.211-221; Roy Sano, *The Theologies of Asian Americans and Pacific Peoples* (Berkeley: Asian Center for Theology and Strategies, Pacific School of Religion, 1976) contains such critiques from the Asian American perspective.

36. Mark Chavez, *Ordaining Women: Culture and Conflict in Religious Organizations.* (Cambridge, MA: Harvard University Press, 1997) makes this clear using the example of women's ordination.
37. Two issues of the *American Historical Review* have lately been devoted to the topic of the "long sixties." "AHA Forum: The International 1968, Part I," *American Historical Review* (February 2009) 42-135 and "AHA Forum: The International 1968, Part II," *American Historical Review* (April, 2009) 329-404.
38. Such hero stories have been a common part of American national narratives. White Protestants had long shaped the national history in their own theological frame. The Puritans came to represent all Americans. Civil religion canonized George Washington and Abraham Lincoln as national saints, complete with mythological narratives of their youth and deeds. The phenomena was pointed out by Robert Bellah, "Civil Religion in America," in Richey and Jones, *American Civil Religion* pp. 21-41, though he did not note the assumption that white people could also stand for all Americans. African Americans had done the same, writing histories of the country that placed them within a version of the national story and within a larger context of world history, which gave their experience transcendent meaning. The heroes of the majority come out differently in these stories. Laurie Maffly-Kipp has collected some of these narratives in her recent book. Laurie F. Maffly-Kipp, *Setting*

Down the Sacred Past: African American Race Histories (Cambridge, MA: Belknap Press, 2010).

39. This point was Prof. Maffly-Kipp's response to a question put to her in a discussion of her book. Regarding the importance of the narratives she had studies; she noted that their importance lay in the power to keep people alive. The historians had written and published them because of the need for a memory to undergird the will to live. Conversation at which the author was present, Bay Area American Religion Group meeting at Santa Clara University, May 24, 2010.
40. Deborah Lee explains this delineation of the spiritual problem of forgiveness in telling stories and hearing stories. Deborah Lee, "Faith Practices for Racial Healing and Reconciliation," in Fumitaka Matsuoka and Eleazar S. Fernandez, eds., *Realizing the America of Our Hearts: Theological Voices of Asian Americans*. (St. Louis, Missouri: Chalice Press, 2003) 147-156.
41. Deborah Lee, "Faith Practices for Racial Healing and Reconciliation," p. 153.
42. Another thinker who has addressed this difficult problem of forgiveness, though from the point of view of feminism, is Helen Luke, "The Revenge of the Repressed Feminine," *Woman Earth and Spirit: The Feminine in Symbol and Myth* (New York: Crossroad Press, 1985) 93-100. Luke also argues for understanding the difficulty of reconciliation and forgiveness, and the necessity of both parties to "accept the necessary death within ourselves, which is the only way to prevent its infliction on someone else, whether consciously or unconsciously." (p. 99). She argues that the other person's guilt is also in a deep sense one's own because of our shared human condition. This is not easy to accept.
43. This does not mean that Seattle did not have demonstrations, bombs and tense times, see Quintard Taylor, *The Forging of a Black Community: Seattle's Central District form 1870 through*

the Civil Rights Era, (Seattle: University of Seattle Press, 1994).

44. *Report of the National Advisory commission on Civil Disorders* (Washington D. C.: U. S. Government Printing Office, 1968) pp. 65 (note 4) , 66 (note 8), and 324.
45. The civil rights movements often used the concept of "beloved community" in discussing their goals. The idea is rooted in Christian theology and refers the relationship among human beings by virtue of their being each individually loved by God. The community of the beloved in turn comes to love one another. As we noted above, the idea shows up as early as the turn of the century in the philosophical work of Josiah Royce, particularly in *The Problem of Christianity*. I will discuss the ways in which the CFRE and the Council of Churches framed their work out of a similar understanding.
46. Dale E. Soden, *The Reverend Mark Matthews: An Activist in the Progressive Era.* (Seattle: University of Washington Press, 2001).

Chapter 1: Setting the Stage: The Ideal and the Reality in Seattle and The Problem of Integration

1. Quote from Edith Steinmetz in [Rev.] Edith Steinmetz and Ethelyn Hartwich, "Twenty Years History of the Christian Friends for Racial Equality - Seattle, WA 1942-1962, Or What Were Seattle People Doing?" (1962) Christian Friends for Racial Equality Records, Accession Number 4040-3, Box 1, ff. 1. University of Washington Library Libraries, Special Collections.
2. Edith Steinmetz, in her remarks after she was presented with the Seattle Civic Unity Committee award for her contribution to bettering race relations in the city, said, "First, it is the dedicated Filipino Victor Carreon who urged the formation of the Christian Friends for Racial Equality,"

quoted in "Former Missionary in the Philippines Honored for Race Relations Activity," *Filipino Forum* (February 13, 1959) 2.

3. Several accounts of the founding of the CFRE are available. The earliest is probably a profile done in *The Christian Century,* April 1946. This account credits Carreon with founding the group, but connects it to the Council of Churches as an affiliate branch possibly because several of the CFRE members were also active in the Council of Churches race relations work. The next was written by CFRE Executive Secretary, Mary Lund, "'Christian Friends' Tackle the Problem of Race Discrimination," prepared for the *Filipino Forum,* April 1950. Edith Steinmetz and Ethelyn Hartwich, "Twenty Years History of the Christian Friends for Racial Equality - Seattle, WA 1942-1962, Or What Were Seattle People Doing?" (1962) is their distillation of the early years of the organization. A Senior Thesis at the University of Washington gave the first analytical picture of the group's history. Johanna McClees, "Christian Friends for Racial Equality: A Unique Approach to Race and Religious Relations in Seattle, 1942-1970" (University of Washington, Senior Thesis, Winter 2000). She subsequently published this thesis on line as Johanna Phillips, "The Christian Friends for Racial Equality 1942-1970," through the Seattle Civil Rights and Labor History Project link http://www.blackpast.org. (Accessed March 2011) An article about the CFRE newsletter, *The Racial Equality Bulletin,* by Brooklynn Gregorich, "Racial Equality Bulletin and the Christian Friends for Racial Equality, 1951-1953: A Seattle Ethnic Press Report" http://depts.washington.edu/civilr/news-racialequality.htm 2009, is also posted at the site. These articles accessed most recently March 2011. This site contains oral history interviews with several people involved in the CFRE and Council of Churches, but many do not contain much information

about the organizations themselves. One interview with information about the CFRE not available in other sources is Esther Mumford's interview, "Bertha Pitts Campbell: An Oral History," interview April 23, 1975, Washington Oral History Project. www.historylink.org Essay number 2427. (Accessed March 2011)

4. "Bertha Pitts Campbell: An Oral History," interview April 23, 1975 by Esther Mumford, Washington Oral History Project www.historylink.org contains four files about Campbell of which this is one, (Accessed March 2011).
5. This is Johanna McKlees Phillips conclusion. "The Christian Friends for Racial Equality 1942-1970," http://depts.washington.edu/civilr/Christian_Friends.htm 2007 (Accessed March 2011).
6. *Racial Equality Bulletin*, (January-February 1966).
7. Membership Application Form, Minutes of the Executive Committee, Seattle council of Churches and Christian Education, Nov. 29, 1939. Church Council of Greater Seattle Records, Box 1 ff. 16. Special Collections, University of Washington Library Accession Number 1358-007. Comity refers to agreements between denominations not to form competing congregations in the same locations.
8. Jessie Kinnear Kenton, "Changing Values in Educational Strategy in the Greater Seattle Area, 1919-1984" (San Francisco Theological Seminary, M.A. Thesis, 1985) p. 114. This thesis is the primary history for the Seattle Council of Churches.
9. Kenton, "Changing Values in Educational Strategy in Greater Seattle," p. 24.
10. Jeffrey Zane and Judson L. Jeffries, "A Panther Sighting in the Pacific Northwest: The Seattle Chapter of the Black Panther Party," in Judson L. Jeffries, ed. *On the Ground: The Black Panther Party in Communities Across America*. (Jackson: University of Mississippi Press, 2010) pp. 44-46.

11. Zane and Jeffries, "A Panther Sighting in the Pacific Northwest," p. 45
12. The concept of race is fluid. While central to understanding American society, no single definition of race exists. I attempt to understand both what the various people in Seattle might have meant by the term and to discern in hindsight some of the background meanings that were in play.
13. Quintard Taylor, *The Forging of a Black Community: Seattle's Central District from 1870 through the Civil Rights Era.* (Seattle: University of Washington Press, 1994) 31.
14. As late as 1947, Senator Allen Joseph Ellender, Democrat from Louisiana, put the matter this way during testimony in Congress related to the bill to forbid racial discrimination in employment. "Let your little white children play with little Chinese children; let your children and Negro children go to the same schools, theaters, churches. If they don't intermarry within a few years then I don't know the first rudiments of this issue." "Antidiscrimination in Employment," Extract from U. S. Senate hearings on S. 984, June 11- July 18, 1947 (Washington D. C.: US Government Printing Office, 1947) p. 80. In the National Council of Churches Records Record Group 18, Federal Council of Churches, Department of Race Relations Box 56, Presbyterian Historical Society, Philadelphia, PA. Ellender's concern appears to have been, that allowing integrated employment opportunities would lead to all these other cases of non-discrimination and integration and would ultimately result in mixed marriages.
15. Michael Omi and Howard Winant, *Racial Formation in the United States from the 1960s to the 1990s*, 2nd ed. (New York: Routledge, 1994) p. 10, gives a more detailed presentation of this development.
16. Fay Botham, *Almighty God Created the Races: Christianity, Interracial Marriage, and American Law* (Chapel Hill: University of North Carolina Press, 2009) shows the secular

and religious theories in relationship to each other.

17. Omi and Winant, p. 14-23. The Chicago School of sociologists developed this theory during the Progressive Era; Horace Kallen, who studied cultural pluralism and Robert Park who argued for assimilationism. Omi and Winant also point out several on-going difficulties with the ethnicity paradigm for understanding race.
18. Servando Halili Jr., "Visualizing the New Empire: Race and Gender Images and the American Colonization of the Philippines." (Bowling Green State University, Ph. D. Dissertation, 2003). Using political cartoons taken from *Harpers, New York Herald, Chicago Tribune,* and *Puck* , Halili traces the way the Philippines were construed as black, savage, childlike, and feminized and how opponents of McKinley's policies were also characterized as childlike (rebelliously so) and feminized.
19. Erika Lee, "The 'Yellow Peril' and Asian Exclusion in the Americas," *Pacific Historical Review* (2007 no. 4) 537-562 and Omi and Winant p. 23.
20. Michael Omi and Howard Winant, *Race Formation in The United States from the 1960s to the 1990s,* Second Edition. (New York: Routledge, 1994). Omi and Winant discuss three paradigms used during the 20th century to explain race and give a critique of each one. The three paradigms are ethnicity, class and nationality. These replaced the nineteenth century paradigm based in evolutionary theory. The authors see these as inadequate because none of them take account of the way in which society assigns race based on categories that have little to do with ethnicity, class or nationality, but rather skin color and other subjectively judged physical features. These categories also do not account adequately for the ways in which racial identity can shift; a single person can experience the assignment of different racial identities in different times and different

settings. In the authors' view, race is a "fundamental axis of social organization in the United States." (p. 13). In the following discussion we will see how these critiques apply to the development of racial ideologies and patterns in Seattle.

21. Lee cites a letter written by Theodore Roosevelt in 1908 to Canada, Great Britain and Australia to promote what he apparently called a "white Pacific." This was to promote collectively an English speaking hegemony to counter the expansion of the Japanese.
22. Peggy Pascoe, What Comes Naturally: Miscegenation Law and the Making of Race in America. (New York: Oxford University Press, 2009) pp. 192 and 243.
23. The issue of racial mixing is not simple. American white people treated African Americans differently from other groups, notably Native Americans. In the nineteenth century, as the United States expanded its territory westward, and at the same time was sustaining the slave economy in the South, and difference in treatment of the two races with regard to intermarriage took place. It was in the interests of the white population of the United States to decrease the claim the Native Americans had on the territory they wished to occupy. They did this in two ways. One was of course outright war. The other was more subtle, involving a tacit permission to intermarry. The children of these Native American and White intermarriages became progressively whiter as the generations passed and thus the children lost their sense of tribal belonging and attachment to the land. As treaty enforcement became a problem later in the century, it was easier to decrease the numbers of tribal members by limiting the percentage of Native blood that would make one a tribal member. In contrast, in the slave society, it was important to increase the African population and so people counted any child with any African blood as black. Patrick Wolfe, "Land, Labor, and Difference: Elementary Structures

of Race," *American Historical Review* (June, 2001) 866-905 contains a comparative discussion of this phenomena in a study of Australian treatment of aboriginal people and American treatment of slaves and Indians. These historical racial definitions based on heredity, that one is black if one has even one drop of African blood, whereas one has to be at least one eighth Native American to claim any tribal rights, also shaped miscegeny laws in many states continuing to make marriage between Whites and people of Native American ancestry possible where marriage between whites and blacks was strictly forbidden, even to the point of annulment of marriages where one party was found later to have some African ancestor in his or her past.

Cultural stereotypes also shaped racial identity. Scholars Michael Omi and Howard Winant note that ethnicity is a common twentieth century paradigm for explaining racial difference. Ethnicity refers to a person or community's cultural origins and practices. This paradigm places the characteristics of race primarily in cultural upbringing and thus explains economic differences for instance as effects of cultural practice embedded in individual behavior. The Protestant work ethic would thus be a cultural characteristic many identified as part of the white race. Omi and Winant give an example of this attitude. "If Chicanos don't do well in school, this cannot, even hypothetically, be due to low quality education; it has instead to do with Chicano values. After all, Jews and Japanese Americans did well in inferior schools, so why can't other groups?" (Omi and Winant, p. 21). According to this paradigm, individual effort could overcome ethnicity as well as class. This seemed to explain how so many European immigrants managed to become mainstream white Americans regardless of their ethnic origins.

24. Robert E. Park, "Our Racial Frontier on the Pacific," *Survey*

Graphic (May 1926) p. 192.

25. Omi and Winant pp. 165-166, note 7.
26. Tadeo Kimura, "Some of My Experiences," 1924 Major Document #163, Survey of Race Relations 1924-1927, Box 27. Hoover Institute Special Collections.
27. Ruth H. Greiner, "Seattle's Japanese George Washington," interview with Harrison School principal Eugenia Pariseau. 1924. Major Document #164, Survey of Race Relations 1924-1927, Box 27. Hoover Institute Special Collections.
28. Robert Marks, *The Origins of the Modern World: A Global and Ecological Narrative from the Fifteenth to the Twenty-first Century*, second edition, (New York: Rowman and Littlefield Publishers, Inc., 2007) points out the luck involved in this development due to circumstances rather than to the ingenuity of a particular people.
29. Max Weber, *The Protestant Ethic and the Spirit of Capitalism*, Trans. by Talcott Parsons, (New York: Charles Scribner's Sons, 1958). "The Puritan wanted to work in a calling; we are forced to do so. For when asceticism was carried out of the monastic cells into everyday life, and began to dominate worldly morality, it did its part in building the tremendous cosmos of the modern economic order. This order is now bound to the technical and economic conditions of machine production which to-day determine the lives of all the individuals who are born into this mechanism, not only those directly concerned with economic acquisition, with irresistible force. Perhaps it will so determine them until the last ton of fossilized coal is burnt. In Baxter's view the care for external goods should only lie on the shoulders of the 'saint like a light cloak, which can be thrown aside at any moment.' [Richard Baxter was a Puritan pastor] But fate decreed that the cloak should become an iron cage." (p. 181).
30. Thus when we describe the racial and cultural demographics of Seattle during the mid-twentieth century, we must be

careful to note upon what criteria we base our information, and how changes in understanding of racial identity affected the possibilities of race relations.

31. In 1922 the United States Supreme Court heard a case, Ozawa v. United States in which it denied a Japanese man citizenship based on the judgment that he was not of the white race, meaning he was not Caucasian, rather than with reference to his skin color. The next year 1923, the Supreme Court heard another case United States v. Bhagat Singh Thind, who argued that he was a Caucasian since he was from Punjab, India. The Supreme Court denied him citizenship because he was not "white" based on his skin color. These cases have been discussed in several places, one of the most concise summary of the dilemmas they raise for understanding race is in Natalia Molina, ""In a Race All Their Own": The Quest to Make Mexicans Ineligible for U. S. Citizenship," *Pacific Historical Review*, (May 2010) 176-177.
32. Jennifer C. Snow, *Protestant Missionaries, Asian Immigrants, and Ideologies of Race in America, 1850-1924*. (New York: Routledge, 2007). Snow discusses this theological development in detail and its relationships to missionary experience in Asia as well as in efforts to advocate particular immigration policies in the United States.
33. These African American histories are discussed at length in Laurie Maffly-Kipp, *Setting Down the Sacred Past: African-American Race Histories* (Cambridge, MA: Belknap Press, 2010).
34. Maffly-Kipp, p. 224. Some of these views can also be found in Mia Bay, *The White Image in the Black Mind: African-American Ideas about White People, 1830-1925*. (New York: Oxford University Press, 2000).
35. W. E. B. Du Bois, "The Souls of Black Folk," (1903) in Nathan Huggins, ed. *W. E. B. Du Bois Writings* (New York: Literary Classics of the United States, 1986) See especially Chapter

IX, "Of the Sons of Master and Man."

36. Tat-Siong Benny Liew, *What Is Asian-American Biblical Hermeneutics?* (Honolulu: University of Hawaii Press, 2008) Chapter 2 "Reading with Yin-Yang Eyes: Negotiating the Ideological Dilemma of a Chinese American Biblical Hermeneutics," pp. 18-34.
37. Paul Nagano, "Identity, Identification, and Initiative," in Roy Sano ed. *The Theologies of Asian American and Pacific Peoples* (Berkeley: [Pacific]Asian Center for Theologies and Strategies, 1976) p. 220.
38. Lamin Sanneh, *West African Christianity: The Religious Impact.* (Maryknoll, N. Y.: Orbis Books, 1983). Throughout this book Sanneh discusses the complex nature of African American missionary belief about race and culture.
39. Snow, *Protestant Missionaries,* p. xv. Compare this paradigm of pluralism to that offered by Kallen and the Chicago School during the same period.
40. G. Spiller, ed. *Inter-Racial Problems* (Boston: U. S. A. World's Peace Foundation, 1911) reviewed in *International Review of Missions* Vol 1, 1912, pp 168-169.
41. Snow, *Protestant Missionaries,* xvi. Here Snow quotes the missionary Sidney Gulick in testimony to the U. S. Congress arguing against the exclusion of the Japanese. This is essentially his argument, though it was not unique to religious people. The concern for the foreign policy consequences of American discriminatory policies was also a matter of secular concern. An example is the instance, in 1952 in San Francisco, of a Chinese American family trying to buy a house in a suburb of the city. The neighborhood had not, until that time, had an exclusionary covenant. But, as a result of this family's offer to buy a house, the neighborhood voted in such an exclusion clause. Many Americans, hearing of the decision, worried that it would influence Asian nations away from democracy. It was the period of the Cold War and

relations with Asian nations were often tense. Similarly there had been concerns about the effect of the Japanese Internment on U. S. relationships with allies during World War II. See Charlotte Brooks, "Sing Sheng vs. Southwood: Residential Integration in Cold War California," *Pacific Historical Review* Vol. 73, No. 3, (September, 2004) 463-494. The CFRE watched this case with interest.

42. Some people of color regarded it as the frontier or the community of last resort in their quest to find a place where they could live free of prejudice. Both Quintard Taylor and Jeffrey Zane quote Rev. John Adams as saying that Seattle was one of the few cities that could still solve its race problems before they "became unsolvable." Taylor, p. 158; Zane and Jeffries, p. 41. John Adams arrived in Seattle in 1958, the same year as Rev. Samuel McKinney. He was pastor of the First AME Church. Like McKinney, he was active in several civil rights organizations and in the Church Council of Greater Seattle (as the Seattle Council of Churches was called by that time), but unlike McKinney, he was not part of the CFRE.

43. Quintard Taylor notes that in the mid 1940s "Whites Only" signs suddenly began to appear all over town. (Taylor p. 168) This discrimination steadily increased through the forties becoming worse by the sixties. "Seattle's Racial Gap: 1968," a report prepared in the Spring of 1968 coinciding with the release of the Report of the President's Commission on Civil Disorder, and was updated in 1974 and 1977. The pattern of lack of good jobs, deteriorating housing, substandard schools and poor health described in the report persisted through the decade. "Progress has been made but in a familiar pattern of mildly accelerated, highly publicized "gradualism." Seattle Urban League, "Seattle's Racial Gap: 1968," updated 1974 and 1977. Seattle Public Library, Seattle Room Special Collections.

44. Seattle Council of Churches Executive Committee minutes Nov 20, 1939. University of Washington, Special Collections, Church council of Greater Seattle Records, Accession number 13558-007, Box 1 of 50, ff 16.
45. Seattle Urban league, "A Survey of Racial Attitudes in the Broadview District," November 1948. Mimeograph of typescript. p. 8. Seattle Public Library, Special Collections. Stuart C. Dodd and Robert W. O'Brian, faculty of the University of Washington conducted this survey.
46. Stuart C. Dodd, Ruth A Inglis, Robert W. O'Brian, "Interracial and Other Tensions in a Public Housing Project." Mimeograph of typescript, 1948. Seattle Public Library Special Collections.
47. Hyung-Chan Kim and Cynthia C. Mejia, eds. *The Filipinos in America 1898-1974*. (Dobbs Ferry, NY: Oceana Publications, Inc., 1976) 77-78.
48. Quintard Taylor discussed the relationship of the Tydings-McDuffie Act on Filipinos in Seattle and their relationships to the black community in the city. Taylor, p. 124-5.
49. Eric T. L. Love, *Race Over Empire: Racism and U. S. Imperialism, 1895-1900* (Chapel Hill: University of North Carolina Press, 2004). Love argues that the abrupt decision of the United States not to annex the Philippines as U. S. territory after winning the Spanish American War rested in large part on the popular American concern about race. "The United States had the best of both worlds: hegemony in its hemisphere without the more daunting or politically hazardous responsibilities over their "new caught sullen peoples, half Devil and half child" (p. 200). The exclusion from land ownership is another example of the pattern of exclusion. Denial of land ownership focused on the Chinese, Japanese and other immigrants from Asia. "Even the Negro, who has suffered all kinds of injustices and discriminations and Jim-Crow customs, has never had the land Jim-Crowed,

for he has always had the right to own the land and thereby feel he has much at stake in the success or failure of America." George L. Cady, "An Oriental Survey," *American Missionary* (February 1924) 615.

50. Eric T. L. Love, *Race Over Empire,* pp. 159-161.
51. The CFRE minutes record Carreon's resignation letter. Stenographer's Notebook, September 15, 1942. Christian Friends for Racial Equality Records, Accession Number 4040-3 Box 1 of 1, ff 5.
52. Stenographers Notebook, July 21, 1942. Christian Friends for Racial Equality Records Accession Number 4040-3 Box 1 of 1, ff 5.
53. My colleague Archie Smith Jr. who was a high school student in Seattle during the period pointed this out to me.
54. Quintard Taylor, *The Forging a of A Black Community* p. 188-189.
55. Elliott R. Barkan, "American in the Hand, Homeland in the Heart: Transnational and Translocal Immigrant Experience in the American West," *Western Historical Quarterly* (Autumn 2004) 348.
56. Barkan, "American in the Hand" p. 348. Barkan made extensive use of oral history archives in the Washington State Archives from which he derived this quote. "Filipino Pioneer: Reflections on His Life in the United States," interview with Mariano Angeles, 6 November 1975. Oral History Collection, FILIPINO-KING Project, FIL-KING 75 - 32 cm. Washington State Archives, Olympia.
57. Dr. Walter W. Van Kirk of the Federal Council of Churches of Christ, "Ten Commandments of Good Will" quoted in The New Religious Frontier June 23, 1938 vol. 1 #43 Church of the People, Seattle, records, ff. 12. University of Washington, Special Collections.

    "1. I will respect all men and women regardless of their race or religion.

2. I will protect and defend my neighbor and my neighbor's children from the ravages of racial or religious bigotry.
3. I will exemplify in my own life the spirit of good will and understanding.
4. I will challenge the philosophy of racial superiority by whomsoever it may be proclaimed, whether by kings, dictators, or demagogues.
5. I will not be misled by the lying propaganda of those who would set race against race or nation against nation.
6. I will refuse to support any organization that has for its [purpose?] the spreading of anti-Semitism, anti-Catholicism, or anti-Protestantism.
7. I will establish comradeship with all those who seek to exalt the spirit of love and reconciliation throughout the world.
8. I will attribute to those who differ from me the same degree of sincerity I claim for myself.
9. I will uphold the civil rights and religious liberties of all citizens and groups whether I agree with them or not.
10. I will do more than live and let live; I will live and help live."

58. "The Church and Race Relations" An official statement approved by the FCC at a special meeting in Columbus, Ohio, March 5-7, 1946. National Council of Churches Records, Federal Council of Churches [previous body] Record Group 18, Box 56 Department of Race Relations, ff. 14. Presbyterian Historical Society, Philadelphia, PA.
59. "The Church and Race Relations" 1946, p. 3.
60. For instance in 1959, Garfield High School in the Central District was 33% black, 15% Asian (Japanese and Chinese), 48% white. People who attended the school in that era remembered interacting with peers of other races in positive ways. Of the 1959 graduating class, the majority went on to

college. By 1962, Garfield High School had become mostly black and the school suffered from the deterioration of the financial stability of the neighborhood following years of rising racial segregation in housing and business practices. Taylor, pp. 182 and 210.

61. The Seattle Civil Rights and Labor History Project transcribed the interviews and published them on their website, http://depts.washington.edu/civilr/interviews.htm. The interview with Walter Hubbard, a member of the Catholic Interracial Council, he remembered that in the 1950s as a World War II veteran, he was not able to buy a house in the Madrona neighborhood of Seattle due to racially restricted covenants.
62. Centuries of Christian stereotyping had developed in Europe as the Jews became more and more an identified outsider group. From time to time waves of persecution against the Jews coincided with times of rapid social change or economic crisis. The legacy of these times of persecution in the past and the dire situation of the Jews in central Europe under the Nazis in the mid-twentieth century complicated the relationship of the Jewish community in Seattle to the rest of the population.
63. The idea originated from a speech given by Martin Luther King Jr. in 1963 at western Michigan University. There are various versions of this speech available, but most probably he said "At 11:00 on Sunday morning we stand and sing "In Christ there is no East or West," we stand at the most segregated hour in this nation." http://www.wmich.edu/library/archives/mlk/q-a.html (Accessed March 2011).
64. "Race Prejudices in San Jose, CA," ca 1948. GTU Archives, GTU 2000-6-02, Small Collections Box 11, ff 2 2/I/1. A college class in Race Relations at San Jose State College conducted this survey in March 1947 (p. 30). In an interview one pastor specifically stated that he would be reluctant to admit a

black person to his church because of the danger of young people meeting and falling in love with people of other races.

65. Quoted and discussed in Daniel C. Dennett, *Darwin's Dangerous Idea: Evolution and the Meanings of Life* (New York: Simon and Schuster Paperbacks, 1995) 467.
66. Here I am using the typology of church and sect developed by the sociologist Ernst Treoltsch, *The Social Teaching of the Christian Churches* volume 1 (New York: The Macmillan Company, 1931) p. 331, and used widely in the twentieth century to describe varieties of Christianity.
67. Leonard Sweet, "The Modernization of Protestant Religion in America," in David Lotz ed. *Altered Landscapes: Christianity in the United States, 1935-1985*. (Grand Rapids: William B. Eerdmans Publishing Company, 1989) pp. 19-41.
68. Killen and Silk, *Religion and Public Life in the Pacific Northwest*, p. 12. ". . . . The ambiguity of the larger religious environment propels them toward commitment that is clearly defined, emotionally significant, and often inflexible because it has been hard won, and thus is in need of protection."
69. Mary E. Hopper and E. Harriet Gibson, "A Frontier of the Spirit," (1953). A pamphlet reprinted in 1963 with a eulogy of Fred Shorter. Church of the People, Seattle Records 1206-7 Box 1 1937-1953. University of Washington Library, Special Collections.
70. The connection between labor and civil rights movements is a theme in the historical materials available on the Seattle Civil Rights and Labor History Project website http://depts.washington.edu/civilr/.htm (Accessed March 2011).
71. The Statement of Faith of the Church of the People summarized his approach. "We are a fellowship dedicated to the consummation of the new society as portrayed in the teachings of Jesus. We believe in the principles of that society,

namely reverence for personality, and the unity of the human family, cannot be fulfilled in a social order based on profit, but only in a cooperative democracy organized for the common good and in which production is for the common need. We pledge ourselves to strive for the realization of that ideal.

As guides to life and conduct we accept and assert the supremacy of conscience; intellectual integrity; freedom of speech and assemblage; and the equality of all men irrespective of race, color, or creed. For inspiration we look to Jesus of Nazareth and all great prophets of Love and justice." Hopper and Gibson, "A Frontier of the Spirit," (1953). Church of the People Records, University of Washington Libraries Special Collections.

72. The Congregational Council for Christian Social Action grew out of Congregational involvement in the Social Gospel movement and favored policies that were in line with his own.
73. "The Church and Race Relations," March 1946. National Council of Churches Records FC 18 (FCC) Box 56 ff 14. Presbyterian Historical Society, Philadelphia, Pa.
74. "The Church and Race Relations," p. 3.
75. "Antidiscrimination in Employment: Extract from hearings on S. 984 bill to prohibit discrimination in employment. June 11, 12, 13, 18, 19, 20, July 16, 17, 18, 1947." (Washington, D. C.: U. S. Government Printing Office, 1947) 80. NCC Records RG 18 FCC Department of Race Relations Box 56 . Presbyterian Historical Society, Philadelphia, PA.
76. In 1942 Buell Gallagher became the first professor to teach in the area of Christian social ethics at a mainline Protestant seminary. He took his commitment to Christian involvement in the betterment of society to the point of running for political office while serving as a professor of a theological seminary. The Pacific School of Religion Board of Trustees

took exception to this and he resigned his position shortly afterward. Gene Zubovich, "Buell G. Gallagher and White Liberalism, 1930s to 1970s: A Career Inspired and Destroyed by the Challenge of Anti-Racism," Manuscript essay in the author's possession p 40.

77. Colin B. Goodykoontz, *Home Missions on the American Frontier*. (Caldwell, ID: Caxton Press, 1939) p. 425. Goodykoontz noted the conservative tendency in the home missionary movement that transplanted a specific kind of religiosity in the West, which put its emphasis on individual salvation rather than on community righteousness.

78. R. I. Moore. *The Formation of a Persecuting Society: Authority and Deviance in Western Europe 950-1250*, second edition. (Malden, MA: Blackwell Publishing, 2007) points out the correlation of economic and political change and uncertainty and the dissemination of stereotypes of people, arranging for their social isolation, and then framing them as villains or somehow to blame for current troubles developed in European society during the late Middle Ages and continues to this day in areas dominated by European culture. These patterns are evident in the social history of the city of Seattle.

79. The debate on this question depends upon the debaters' relationships with those Christian people they considered to be in some way "other." In the context of the Americas the earliest such debate over the question of whether the American Indians had souls was that between Juan de Sepulveda, who argued they did not, and Bartolomé de las Casas, who argued they did. Though technically Las Casas won the argument and persuaded the king that the Indians had a right to respect as human beings, especially if they converted to Christianity, it did little good in the end, since he was not able to achieve an enforceable justice for them.

80. Gary Dorrien characterizes American liberal theology in this way in his book, *The Making of American Liberal Theology:*

Idealism, Realism, and Modernity. (Louisville: Westminster/ John Knox Press, 2003) p. 3.

81. See Gabriel Kolko, *The Triumph of Conservatism*. (New York: Free Press 1977).
82. Leonard Sweet, "The Modernization of Protestant Religion in America," p. 30
83. Eugene Borowitz, *Modern Jewish Thought: A Partisan Guide* (New York: Behrman House Inc., 1983) provides a good overview of these developments.
84. Fred Rosenbaum, *Visions of Reform: Congregation Emanu-El and the Jews of San Francisco 1949-1999*. (Berkeley: Judah L. Magnes Museum, 2000) pp. 233-237.
85. Taigen Dan Leighton, The World as Arena of Transformation: Applications for a Modern Zen Social Ethic," *Religion East and West* (October 2006) 61-71.
86. Letter from [Judas] Hughes, President of the Seattle Branch of the NAACP to Rev. Wendell L, Fifield, chair of the Church Council Public Affairs Committee, March, 31, 1939. Church Council of Greater Seattle Records, Box 1 ff. 16. University of Washington Libraries Special Collections.
87. Letter from the Japanese Congregational Christian Endeavor Society President Rose Soyejima to Rev. C. M. Ridenour, President of the Seattle Council of Churches, March 5, 1939. Church Council of Greater Seattle Records, Box 1 ff. 16. University of Washington Libraries Special Collections.
88. Minutes of the Council Meeting, Monday Nov. 3, 1941, Church Council of Greater Seattle Records, Box 1 ff 16. University of Washington Libraries, Special Collections.
89. Minutes of Special Called Meeting of the Executive Council Thurs. Dec. 11, 1941. Church Council of Greater Seattle Records, Box 1 ff 16. University of Washington Libraries, Special Collections.
90. Statement of the Executive Committee of the Seattle Council of Churches and Christian Education, May 4, 1942. Church

Council of Greater Seattle Records, Box 1 ff. 16. University of Washington Libraries, Special Collections.

91. Minutes of the Executive Committee, Nov. 17, 1941, and Report to the Interracial committee by Mrs. Nella Carter, Nov. 13, 1941. Church Council of Greater Seattle Records, Box 1 ff. 16. University of Washington Libraries, Special Collections. Cassandra Tate, "YMCA East Madison Branch," www.historylink.org (Accessed March 2011). The East Madison YMCA became a center of African American social life and an important venue for popular music in the city during the 1940s. The major expansion of the facility, including installation of a swimming pool, did not occur until 1965.
92. United Good Neighbors, Annual Report 1948. Jackson Street Community Council Papers, Seattle Room, Seattle Public Library.
93. Department of Social Relations, Seattle Council of Churches, "Report of Interracial Clinic September 24-25, 1945." Mimeograph of Typescript. Seattle Public Library Special Collections.
94. "Statement of Purpose," *Racial Equality Bulletin*. University of Washington Library, Microfilm A 7176 2 rolls. The CFRE printed the Statement of Purpose on page 2 of every issue.
95. Edith Steinmetz and Ethelyn Hartwich, "Twenty Years History of the Christian Friends for Racial Equality - Seattle, WA 1942-1962, Or What Were Seattle People Doing?" Christian Friends for Racial Equality Papers, ff 1. Chapter 5 1946-1947. University of Washington Library, Special Collections.
96. Guy Emery Shipler, Jr., "A Dangerous Inconsistency: Fighting for Democracy Abroad, but Violating the Rights of Negroes at Home," *Zion's Herald* (February 4, 1942)98 and 115.
97. Edith Steinmetz and Ethelyn Hartwich, "Twenty Years

History of the Christian Friends for Racial Equality - Seattle, WA 1942-1962, Or What Were Seattle People Doing?" 1962 Christian Friends for Racial Equality Records, box 1. University of Washington Libraries, Special Collections.

98. Steinmetz and Hartwich summarize the story in "Twenty-Years History."
99. Interviews with Dorothy Hollingsworth, Seattle Civil Rights and Labor History Project website http://depts.washington.edu/civilr/ and Bertha Pitts Campbell, www.historylink.org Biographies (Accessed, March 2011).
100. In the 1950s and 1960s several denominations discontinued racially identified judicatories and other organizations designed to establish separate institutional structures. An exception was the continuance of the Spanish language Rio Grande Conference within the United Methodist Church. While rooted in the ideal of countering racism by integration, this integration served to dilute the voice and rob these communities of autonomy and the ability to manage their own affairs. The highest leadership in these denominations tended to remain in the hands of white people until very recently. Roy Sano, "This Matter of Integration," in The Theologies of Asian American and Pacific Peoples p. 262. Originally published in Methodist Layman (February 1963). The United Methodist Church eventually elected Roy Sano as a Bishop. He shared his memories of this time during a panel discussion August 2001 sponsored by the PANA Institute at Pacific School of Religion, "Religion and Public Life in Pacific Asian America." The Asian American communities in the churches still feel the effects of this integration project in the 21st century.

Chapter 2: Development of a Public Conscience in Seattle

1. Esther Mumford interview with Bertha Pitts Campbell,

April 23, 1975, Washington State Oral History Project, Washington State Archives, Olympia, WA. Stacy Carlson, ed. "Campbell, Bertha Pitts: An Oral History," www.historylink.org Biographies. (Accessed March 11, 2011).

2. Shelby Scates, "Seattle Racial Climate: A Study in View Points White and Black," *The Seattle Post Intelligencer*, Tuesday August 8, 1967. p. D-1.
3. Quintard Taylor, *The Forging of a Black Community in Seattle's Central District from 1870 through the Civil Rights Era* (Seattle: University of Washington Press, 1994) pp 3-4.
4. Robert W. O'Brian, "The Changing Cast Position of the Negro in the Northwest," Research Studies of the State College of Washington March 1942 p. 67. O'Brian cited an article by Robert Park, "Our Racial Frontiers on the Pacific," *Survey Graphic* XIV (1926) p. 192, describing a race relations cycle, where on the frontier in newly opened territory, lower caste individuals may gain social position, but as the frontier disappears, the "former horizontal caste lines reappear." Taylor and O'Brian both argue that this was happening in Seattle during the 1940s and 1950s.
5. Ibid.
6. Taylor, *The Forging of a Black Community*, pp 7-10. I want to also acknowledge a conversation with Joanne Braxton about the role of white hegemony in Seattle affirming Taylor's observations.
7. *The Seattle Republican*, June 17, 1898.
8. *The Seattle Republican* April 19, 1907.
9. Ruth H. Greiner interview with Eugenie Parriseau, Principle of Harrison School. "Seattle's Japanese George Washington," Race Relations Survey Records, Document 164, Box 27. Hoover Institute Archives, Stanford University.
10. Tadeo Kimura, "Some of My Experiences," and "The Power of Education," Race Relations Survey Records, Document 163, Box 27. Hoover Institute Archives, Stanford University.

11. Don Greiner, "What the General Public Knows and Does not Know about the Japanese Question," (Ballard High School, Seattle, WA, Modern History Term Paper, 1924) Race Relations Survey Records, Document 146, Box 34. Hoover Institute Archives, Stanford University. The reader may wonder if the high school student Don Greiner and the Survey interviewer Ruth Greiner had any relationship. I was unable to find the answer to this interesting question.
12. Douglas Mark Dye, "The Soul of the City: The Work of the Seattle Council of Churches during World War Two," (Washington State University, Ph.D. Dissertation, 1997) 7.
13. Japanese American Citizens' League Seattle, "Report Submitted to the Tolan Congressional Committee," February 28, 1942. Copy of Typescript. Seattle Public Library, Seattle Room collection.
14. Arthur G. Barnett to President, Representatives, Chiefs of Armed Forces, Director of Social Security and Attorney General, February 18, 1942. Church Council of Greater Seattle Records, Box 15, ff 27. University of Washington Libraries Special Collections.
15. Seattle Council of Churches, "Statement Regarding Minority Groups and the Bill of Rights." December 6, 1943. Church Council of Greater Seattle, Accession Number 1358-7, Box 1 ff. 20.
16. Seattle Civic Unity Committee, "History of the Civic Unity Committee, February 14, 1944 - January 15, 1948," Mimeograph of typescript, Seattle Public Library, Seattle Room Collections. The Committee noted cooperation with a large number of other agencies, most of which were religious: American Friends Service Committee, American Veterans Race Relations Committee, Anti-Defamation League, The China Club, the CFRE, Council of Social Agencies, East Madison YMCA, Jackson Street Community Council, University and Central YWCAs, NAACP, Japanese

American Citizens League, National Conference of Christians and Jews, Neighborhood House, Phyllis Wheatley YWCA, the Race Relations Department of the Council of Churches and the Urban League.

17. Report of Law Enforcement Conference on Human Relations, January 17, 24, and 31, Mt. Zion Baptist Church, 1924, and Seattle Human Rights Commission, Report on Community and Police Relations, Feb. 20, 1997. Seattle Public Library, Seattle Room Collections.
18. Quintard Taylor, *The Forging of a Black Community: Seattle's Central District from 1870 through the Civil Rights Era* (Seattle: University of Washington Press, 1994) p. 3-4.
19. Jeffrey Zane and Judson L. Jeffries, "A Panther Sighting in the Pacific Northwest: The Seattle Chapter of the Black Panther Party," in Judson L. Jeffries, ed. *On the Ground: The Black Panther Party in Communities Across America* (Jackson, University of Mississippi Press, 2010) 42-43.
20. Isaiah Berlin, "The Originality of Machiavelli," in Henry Hardy and Roger Hausheer, *The Proper Study of Mankind*, (London: Chatto and Windus, 1997) p. 289. Pericles, Livy, and later Tacitus articulated these values in the Greco-Roman world and lamented their decline. The perceptive critic will note that Christianity shares many of these same concerns.
21. This thought is also characteristic of the theology of Reinhold Niebuhr, a Neo-Orthodox theologian who was nationally known during this period, particularly among American mainline Protestants.
22. Sigmund Freud, *Group Psychology and the Analysis of the Ego*, translated by James Strachey, (New York: Liveright Publishing Corporation, 1951) 28-29.
23. Charles Long, *Significations: Signs, Symbols and Images in the Interpretation of Religion* (Philadelphia: Fortress Press, 1986) 59-61.

24. Roger Burlingame, *The American Conscience,* (New York: Alfred A. Knopf, 1957) 405.
25. Austin Darcey, *The Secular Conscience: Why Belief Belongs in Public Life*. (New York Prometheus Books, 2008) 18-19.
26. Masumi Izumi, "Prohibiting 'American Concentration Camps': Repeal of the Emergency Detention Act and the Public Historical Memory of the Japanese American Internment," *Pacific Historical Review* 74 (May 2005) 193.
27. Michelle Brattain, "Race, Racism, and Antiracism: UNESCO and the Politics of Presenting Science to the Postwar Public," *American Historical Review* 112 (December 2007) p. 1413.
28. One of the earliest of these is the movement begun by Bartolomé de las Casas in the seventeenth century to change the laws of the Indies to bring about justice for the Native Americans. One of the more recent is the Liberation Theology movement begun in the 1950s and 1960s working toward the same end. In both cases the imperial authorities immediately recognized a religious threat to the wealth they gained by exploiting the labor of the people and worked to discredit and suppress the movement.
29. James Calvin Davis, *The Moral Theology of Roger Williams: Christian Conviction and Public Ethics*. (Louisville: Westminster John Knox Press, 2004) 72-78.
30. Rev. Hayes, "President's Annual Address," Rev. Hayes papers M53355A Box 1 ff. 2, California Historical Society Collections. Hayes drew the line at civil disobedience as a way of expressing and shaping public conscience. In this he was not like Roger Williams.
31. Timothy Tseng, "Trans-Pacific Transpositions: Continuities and Discontinuities in Chinese North American Protestantism Since 1965," Jane Naomi Iwamura and Paul Spickard eds. *Revealing the Sacred in Asian and Pacific America*. (New York: Routledge, 2003).
32. Rev. John G. Fee, "Prayer for John Brown," *New York Herald*,

November 15, quoted in *The American Missionary* December 1959, p. 283. The quote is a reference to 1 Corinthians 13. In the nineteenth century, Congregational missionaries were active among all racial minority groups in the United States. Most notably the American Missionary Association, a Congregationally based voluntary society, initially developed as an anti-slavery organization, started important schools and churches for the education of Freedmen in the South after the Civil War and expanded its work to Native Americans, the Hispanic population of the American Southwest after the Mexican War, and to the Chinese in the West Coast cities and Hawaii.

33. *The American Missionary* April 1870.
34. *The American Missionary*, December 1920, p. 458.
35. *The Advance*, April 1947.
36. Sydney Strong, "How the Gospel Worked," *A Seattle Pulpit* (September-December 1919) pp. 6-7. Congregational Library, Boston, MA Seattle Collection 17.11.1 Se 1.38.
37. The Board of Home Missions and Church Extension of the Methodist Episcopal Church, "A Million for Home Missions and Church Extension: to Entrench Christianity and Patriotism," *The Christian Republic: America for Christ* 1 (January 1907) p. 2.
38. Herbert Johnson, "Report," *Official Journal for the Pacific Japanese Mission of the Methodist Episcopal Church* (October, 1907) p. 8.
39. Guy Emery Shipler, Jr., "A Dangerous Inconsistency: Fighting for Democracy Abroad, but Violating the Rights of Negroes at Home," *Zion's Herald*, February 4, 1942, p. 115.
40. G. Bromley Oxnam, "Tongue-Tied," *Zion's Herald,* April 1, 1942, pp 295-296.
41. David W. Henry, in a letter to the editor replying to "Tongue-Tied," contributed the first Negro voice in an exchange of letters on the subject that went on for several issues. *Zion's*

Herald, July 8, 1942 p. 656.

42. Board of Christian Social Relations, Southern California-Arizona Annual Conference, "Conference on Human Relations, February 11-13, 1958," in Methodist Church (U. S.)Board of Social and Economic Relations, "Interracial Conference Reports 1957-1959," p. 1.
43. "Conscience," from *The Philosophy of Loyalty* (New York: The Macmillan Company 1908) excerpted in John K. Roth, ed. *The Philosophy of Josiah Royce*, (Indianapolis: Hackett Publishing Company, 1982).
44. Josiah Royce, "Race Questions and Prejudice," in *Race Questions and Other American Problems* (Freeport, NY: Books for Libraries Press, 1976 reprint of the original 1902 edition) p. 8.
45. Royce, "Race Questions and Prejudice," p. 43.
46. Royce, "Race Questions," p. 53.
47. Josiah Royce, *The Problem of Christianity: The Real World and the Christian Ideas*.vol. II, (New York: The Macmillan Company, 1913) p. 5. Those wanting further insight into his thought on the relationship of the individual to the community might refer to his later work, *The World and the Individual*.
48. Ibid.
49. Royce, *The Problem of Christianity*, vol. II, p. 44-67. The virtual community of the internet website is possible under Royce's rubric since the ability to communicate is the essential constituent necessary for its presence.
50. Royce, *The Problem of Christianity*, vol. II, p. 426-428.
51. R. I. Moore, *The Formation of A Persecuting Society: Authority and Deviance in Western Europe 950-1250*, 2nd Edition. (Malden, MA: Blackwell Publishing, 2007) p. 4-5.
52. Deborah Plummer, *Racing Across the Lines: Changing Race Relations through Friendship*. (Cleveland: Pilgrim Press, 2004). Plummer recovers the idea that personal relationships can

serve as a powerful means of shaping a public conscience. Joanne Braxton, in a conversation with me about this chapter, noted that in her youth, parents warned children against desiring or cultivating relationships across racial lines. In my own youth, elders exhibited discomfort when my peers and I became friends with the diverse children in our neighborhood and their discomfort grew greater as we grew older.

Chapter 3: Network of Civil Rights Work in Seattle

1. Steinmetz and Hartwich, "Twenty Years History of the Christian Friends for Racial Equality," p. 13.
2. S. Frank Miyamoto, *Social Solidarity among the Japanese in Seattle*, (Seattle: University of Washington Press, 1984) 8-10.
3. R. I. Moore, *The Formation of a Persecuting Society* 2nd edition. (Malden, MA: Blackwell Publishing, 2007) 184-187 describes this process as it arises in times of social tension and rapid change.
4. The Labor and Civil Rights Project interviews with a variety of community activists confirms this sense that cooperation among these groups and the interrelated nature of civil rights groups in Seattle was an important aspect of civil rights efforts. The project webpage, http://depts.washington.edu/civilr/ (Accessed March 2011) contains these interviews. Quintard Taylor noted that the African American community was small, as were all the racial groups in the city and with their diluted voting strength, it was essential that they join forces across racial and cultural lines to achieve racial equality and equal opportunity. (Taylor, p. 168).
5. Ernest A. T. Barth and Baha Abū Laban, "Power Structure and the Negro Sub-Community," American *Sociological Review* (February 1959) pp. 69-76.
6. Mary Sawyer, *Black Ecumenism: Implementing the Demands of Justice* (Valley Forge: Trinity Press International, 1994) p. 91.
7. Johanna Phillips, "Christian Friends for Racial Equality 1942-

1970," Seattle Civil Rights and Labor History Project. http://depts.washington.edu/civilr/Christian_Friends.htm (Accessed March 2011).

8. Johanna Phillips, "The Christian Friends for Racial Equality," p. 6
9. Charter Members of the CFRE – a list left by Mrs. Steinmetz, dated 1965. Rev. Paul Fong, Rev. and Mrs. Penick, Mrs. J. J. Chan, Mrs. Emma Chaney, Mrs. Lew Soun, Mrs. Judson Grant, Mrs. Nella Carter, Mrs. Bertha Campbell, Mrs. Betty Flohr, Dr. and Mrs. Fred Ring, Mr. Victor Carreon, Mr. Grandino Baaoa, Mrs. Helen Harris, Mrs. Hester Miller, Mrs. Edith Steinmetz. CFRE Records, University of Washington Libraries, Special Collections, Box 1, ff. 3. The discussions toward the formation of the CFRE began earlier with twenty-five people in the late fall of 1939. Steinmetz and Hartwich describe them as "Negroes, Chinese, Japanese, Filipinos, Caucasians, and Mr. Lamkin, an American Indian (Chief Yellow Lark)" in "Twenty Years History." By the time they officially founded the organization, the Japanese members were caught up in the Internment.
10. First Baptist Church reports her and her husband as members beginning in 1912 until Edith transferred her membership to the Chinese Baptist Church in 1939 and her husband died in 1941. Email from Diana James of First Baptist Church in Seattle. April 4, 2011.
11. American Baptist Convention, *Annual of the Northern Baptist Convention 1912* (Philadelphia: American Baptist Publishing Society, 1912) p. 143. The reports for 1909, 1911, 1912, and 1915 contain brief amounts of information about H. H. and Edith Steinmetz.
12. Some sources state that the Baptists ordained Edith Steinmetz in 1912, but I have been unable to confirm this. This would be quite early for a woman to be ordained though about two hundred women were ordained by the

turn of the century. Congregationally organized denominations such as the American Baptist Churches were more likely to be the site of women's ordination because individual congregations could make the decision to ordain the person the wanted for their pastor independently from the policies of the denomination. This tended to be a local phenomenon, rather than one encouraged on a national scale.

13. Virginia Lee Hjertstedt, "A History of American Baptist Missions in the Philippines," (Berkeley Baptist Divinity School, M. A. Thesis, 1952).
14. Minutes, March 29, 1942. CFRE Records Box 1, University of Washington Libraries, Special Collections.
15. Obituary for Vivienne Penick, *Seattle Times*, April 8, 1980.
16. William Gough, "Bertha Pitts Campbell, A Founder of Delta Sigma Theta Sorority," *Seattle Times* April 6, 1990.
17. Stacy Carlson, ed. Esther Mumford Interview with Bertha Pitts Campbell, April 23, 1975, Washington State Oral History Project, Washington State Archives, Olympia, WA, "Campbell, Bertha Pitts: An Oral History," March 19, 2000, (Seattle: www.historylink.org Biographies Accessed March, 2011).
18. Stephanie Y. Evans, "Black Greek-Lettered Organizations and Civic Responsibility," *Black Issues in Higher Education*, October 7, 2004.
19. William Gough, "Bertha Pitts Campbell."
20. Minutes of the Christian Friends for Racial Equality, 8th Meeting, Oct. 20, 1942. CFRE Papers, Accession Number 4040-3. University of Washington Library Special Collections.
21. Esther Mumford, Interview with Bertha Pitts Campbell, April 23, 1975. Washington State Oral History Project, Washington State Archives, Olympia, Washington. Edited by Stacy Carlson, March 19, 2000. (Seattle: www.historylink.org Biographies Accessed March 2011).

22. Ibid.
23. Campbell, Bertha Pitts (1889-1990) (Seattle: History Link, www.historylink.org Biographies Accessed July 22, 2010).
24. Stephanie Y. Evans, "Black Greek-Lettered Organizations and Civic Responsibility," *Black Issues in Higher Education* (October 7, 2004) 17 and 21.
25. "Yarbrough Service Set," *Seattle Post-Intelligencer* (October 22, 1992) p. B 6.
26. Sherry Stripling, "Letcher L. Yarbrough, 83, Was Former Head of City, State NAACP," *Seattle Times* (Oct. 21, 1992). p. F 12.
27. Carole Beers, "Equal Rights Drove Arline Yarbrough," *Seattle Times*. (Nov. 10, 1999) p. 4; Sherry Stripling, "Letcher L. Yarbrough, 83, was Former Head of City, State NAACP." *Seattle Times* (October, 21, 1992); "Yarbrough Service Set," *Seattle Post-Intelligencer* (October 22, 1992).
28. Carole Beers, "Equal Rights Drove Arline Yarbrough," *Seattle Times* (November 1999) p. B-4.
29. Alan S. Wong, "Indigenization - Liberation of the Chinese American Churches," Roy Sano ed. *The Theologies of Asian American and Pacific Peoples*, p. 99-108. Unlike the European immigrant communities which put a premium on learning English and becoming American, the Chinese faced obstacles in doing this because once they learned English they were not as assured that society would accept them as American. "As long as the difficulty of language exists, we have the need of a Chinese Church. When this difficulty disappears, all Christian Chinese should be privileged to take part in the larger fellowship. Besides language, there are needs to be met that are unique only in the Chinese Church." Wong, p. 101.
30. David Ng, "The Chinaman's Chances are Improving," Roy Sano, *The Theologies of Asian American and Pacific Peoples* pp. 153-155.

31. Frank G. Mar, "A New Wind is Blowing," Roy Sano, *The Theologies of Asian American and Pacific Peoples*, p. 431.
32. Timothy Tseng, "Chinese Protestant Nationalism in the United States, 1880-1927," in David K. Yoo, ed. *New Spiritual Homes: Religion and Asian Americans*," 18-51. Particularly in his footnotes, Tseng clarifies this complexity.
33. We discussed Carreon's life and situation earlier in Chapter 1.
34. Dorothy B. Fujita-Rony, *American Workers, Colonial Power: Philippine Seattle and the Transpacific West, 1919-1941* (Berkeley: University of California Press, 2003) p. 156.
35. "Levine, Rabbi Raphael Harry (1901-1985)" (Seattle: History Link, www.historylink.org Biographies Accessed May 11, 2010).
36. The conversation about the group's name began as early as 1953 and continued into the 1960s.
37. Sometimes the only information available about who was involved in the CFRE comes from the annual listing of the officers, committees, and volunteers in the *Racial Equality Bulletin*.
38. Church of the People, New *Religious Frontier* (Thursday Sept. 2, 1937).
39. Mary E. Hopper and E. Harriet Gibson, "A Frontier of the Spirit," a pamphlet printed with a eulogy of Fred Shorter, 1963. *Time Magazine*, April 30, 1934 covered the controversy provoked by the murals. Church of the People Records, University of Washington Libraries, Special Collections. Box 1, ff. 1.
40. Hopper and Gibson, "A Frontier of the Spirit."
41. "The Jensen Years according to Number Two Son Jensen" a statement written in memory of Harold Jensen by his second son. Seattle First Baptist Church Papers, Box 9, University of Washington Libraries, Special Collections.
42. Harold Jensen, (untitled article), *Racial Equality Bulletin*,

(December 1951) p. 3. The CFRE became aware that the readers of the *Racial Equality Bulletin* might not be able to tell the religious nature of the group from the material in the bulletin alone. They decided that it would be useful for the active pastors in the group to write columns about the religious basis of their work. *Racial Equality Bulletin* (October 1951).

43. First Baptist Church of Seattle, Minutes of the Christian Citizenship Committee April 25, 1956. First Baptist Church of Seattle Records, University of Washington Libraries, Special Collections.
44. Catalogue for the LeEtta King collection, University of Washington Libraries, Special Collections, Accession Number 1178-001.
45. Margaret Boddie, "Honoring Seattle Heroes," Mayor's Council on African American Elders webpage, (Seattle: http://www.seattle.gov/mcaae/messages/messagesBoddie.ht m Accessed March, 2011).
46. Hollingsworth, Dorothy (b. 1920), (Seattle: History Link, www.historylink.org Biographies. Accessed March, 2011).
47. Ferdinand M. De Leon, "When King Was in Town – The Young Minister was Already the Undisputed Leader in the Civil-Rights Struggle when He Made His Only Visit to Seattle More than Three Decades Ago," *Seattle Times* (January 16, 1994) p. L 1.
48. Lola Day Papers, Box 3, ff 38 Inter-racial Home visits 1964-1965, Accession number 2746 - 001, University of Washington Libraries, Special Collections.
49. Johanna Phillips, "Christian Friends for Racial Equality 1942-1970," (Seattle Civil Rights and Labor History Project, http://depts.washington.edu/civilr/Christian_Friends.htm March, 2008) 6. (Accessed March 2011) Sponsors of the CFRE were members who were also prominent people in the community. They agreed to have their names listed on the

CFRE letterhead in order to attract interest in membership.

50. Johanna Phillips, "The Christian Friends for Racial Equality," p. 7. She notes one item from the *Seattle Times* that presents this impression. "Racial Equality Group Decides to Continue," *Seattle Times* 14 March 1966: 29.
51. Christian Friends for Racial Equality Minutes, July 21, 1942. Christian Friends for Racial Equality Papers, Accession Number 4040-3 ff. 5. University of Washington Library Special Collections.
52. A few historians have pointed out the failure of the Progressive generation to mentor the younger people, and thus several Progressive era organizations struggled or did not survive after World War II. Chapter 4 will discuss this more fully.
53. The CFRE members used mid-twentieth century categories for classifying various religious groups when they thought about the religious diversity of Seattle. In a survey of religious bodies in Seattle, the creators of the survey used the following: Protestants, Non-Protestants (including Roman Catholics, Eastern Orthodox, and Hebrew [which seems to have meant the Jews]), Cults (including Christian Science, Mormons, Spiritualists, and Others), Emotional Sects (including Pentecostal, Rescue Missions, Volunteers of America, and the Salvation Army, and Non-Christian (Buddhist and Shinto, but not Jews). Minutes of the May 18, 1942 Seattle Council of Churches Executive Committee Meeting. Church Council of Greater Seattle Records, Accession Number 13558-007 Box 1, ff. 18. University of Washington Libraries, Special collections.
54. Quintard Taylor, *The Forging of a Black Community*, pp. 238-239.
55. I use the term *middle class* in a general way in this work to indicate people of a particular income bracket. I do not use the term in the classic sense of bourgeoisie. Included are

certainly business owners, but also professionals such as teachers, doctors, lawyers, or dentists, but also blue-color people with considerable education or skill employed for relatively high wages. These were individuals with sufficient income to educate their children and to have leisure time for volunteer for organizations such as the CFRE.

56. See the discussion of Royce's philosophy in Chapter 2.
57. Josiah Royce, *The Problem of Christianity* (New York: Harper and Brothers, 1913) Vol. I, pp. 182-183. Royce was not optimistic about the possibilities of this kind of Beloved Community arising frequently. "One moves thus in a circle [The Beloved Community depends upon the love of its members for the community, but that love is inspired first by the love of the community for them.] Only some miracle of grace (as it would seem) can initiate the new life, either in the individuals who are to love communities, or in the communities that are to be worthy of their love."
58. The "Golden Rule" was the primary principle of the CFRE. In the King James Version of the Bible, probably most well known among CFRE members, the concept is stated this way: "Therefore all things whatsoever ye would that men should do to you, do ye even so to them: for this is the law and the prophets." Matthew 7:12.
59. Phillips, p. 18.
60. Edith Steinmetz, "To Speed up Brotherhood," *Racial Equality Bulletin* (September, 1958) p. 2.
61. "The 9 Most Common Queries and Very Brief Answers," *Racial Equality Bulletin* (November 1963) p. 3.
62. Phillips, p. 16-17. Also "Twenty Years History, p. 18.
63. Mary Lund to Chester Kingsbury, December 30. 1948. In Chester Kingsbury Papers, ACC #3259-1 University of Washington Special Collections, Box 1 ff.7.
64. Reported by Steinmetz and Hartwich in "Twenty Years' History," CFRE Papers, Accession Number 4040-3 Box 1.

University of Washington Library Special Collections.

65. *Racial Equality Bulletin,* special edition, 1951.
66. *Racial Equality Bulletin* April, 1952.
67. "Mount Pleasant Cemetery," (Seattle: www.historylink.org Cyberpedia Library. (Accessed March 2011).
68. "Cemetery Discrimination," *Racial Equality Bulletin,* April 1952. Several short histories of the Christian Friends for Racial Equality note a series of four articles written, supposedly in the *Seattle Times* by the columnist Byron Fish which picked up the CFRE concern and proved influential in the Washington State decision to outlaw cemetery discrimination. I have unfortunately been unable to locate any of these articles. A search of the very new digitized edition of the *Seattle Times* proved negative. To have a well known columnist for a major paper pick up their story, especially if it was at their request, may indicate the failure of their more private face-to-face contact with the cemetery owners in 1952.
69. "Easter-Service Ban Asked in Cemetery Race-Policy Dispute," *Seattle Times* February 1, 1958 p. 1.
70. Evergreen-Washelli Cemetery, (Seattle: History Link www.historylink.org/index.cfm. Accessed March 2011) and "Mount Pleasant Cemetery," (Accessed March 2011).
71. This series of articles is reported in "Twenty Year History," p. 25, "This year the Seattle Times carried 4 excellent articles on the subject by Byron Fish, and these we had mimeographed and distributed. We have been encouraged by a conference with the Assistant to the State Attorney General, and plan further interviews with cemetery owners." As I noted above in note 66, I have not been able to locate this series of articles in the *Seattle Times* or the *Seattle Post Intelligencer* nor did the CFRE archive contain the mimeographed copies.

Chapter 4: Ambiguous and Limited Success: Issues of Gender and Generation in the Life of the CFRE and the Seattle Council of Churches

1. "Former Missionary in the Philippines Honored for Race Relations Activity," *Filipino Forum*, (February 18, 1959) p. 3.
2. *The Racial Equality Bulletin* (April 17, 1959 p. 4 quoting *The Seattle Times* Feb 25, 1959) notes that he was 63 when he began a term on the state Board of Prison Terms and Paroles.
3. Anne Braude, "Women's History Is American Religious History," Thomas Tweed, ed. *Retelling U. S. Religious History*. (Berkeley, University of California Press, 1997) pp. 93-95.
4. Katherine Kish Sklar, *Catherine Beecher: A Study in American Domesticity*. (New York: W. W. Norton and Company, 1973) in the introduction to this book Sklar outlines this process in American women's history.
5. Sklar, p. xiv. The identification of women's self identity with self-sacrifice contributed to the entrance of women into an enlarged public role, but also created problematic consequences that lasted throughout the both the nineteenth and twentieth centuries as women negotiated the rapid social changes affecting them.
6. Catherine A. Breckus, *Strangers and Pilgrims: Female Preaching in America 1740-1845*. (Chapel Hill: University of North Carolina Press, 1998).
7. Frances Willard, *A Woman's Pulpit*. (Boston: D. Lothrop Company, 1888).
8. Mark Chaves, *Ordaining Women: Culture and Conflict in Religious Organizations*. (New York: Harvard University Press, 1997)
9. Chaves, p. 16.
10. Chaves p. 105.
11. Northern Baptist Convention, *Annual of the Northern Baptist Convention*, (American Baptist Publication Society, 1910) p. 148.

12. For instance the Seventh Day Adventists and the Southern Baptist Convention have done so as denominations.
13. Priscilla Pope-Levison, "Interracial Cooperation in the Progressive Era," unpublished paper delivered at the American Historical Association meeting in San Diego, CA, January 8, 2010.
14. Penina Migdal Glazer and Miriam Slater, *Unequal Colleagues: The Entrance of Women into the Professions, 1890-1940* (New Brunswick, N. J.: Rutgers University Press, 1987) discusses this phenomenon at length.
15. Barth and Abū Laban, "Power Structure and the Negro Sub-Community," p. 72.
16. Barth and Abū Laban, p. 76.
17. Mara Mather, Nichole R. Lighthall, Lin Nga, and Marissa A. Gorlick, "Sex Differences in How Stress Affects Brain Activity During Face Viewing," forthcoming in *NeuroReport* (July 2010). http://www.usc.edu/projects/matherlab/pdfs/MatheretalNRinpress.pdf. (AccessedMarch 2011).
18. Ingrid Wickelgren, "Under Threat, Women Bond and Men Withdraw," *Scientific American* (July 2010) p. 20.
19. "Mary Mahoney Professional Nurses Organization (Seattle)," www.historylink.org Cyberpedias (Accessed March 2011). "Each of these founding members of the Mary Mahoney Professional Nurses Organization were employed in Seattle between 1943 and 1947. When they called about nursing positions, they were interviewed on the phone and hired on the spot. In 1941 when Mary Martyn applied (after moving to Seattle), she was denied employment. In 1943, Ida Gordon became the first African American nurse to be employed at Harborview."
20. Christian Friends for Racial Equality Minutes, Tuesday May 19, 1942. Christian Friends for Racial Equality Papers, Box 1, ff 5. University of Washington Library, Special Collections.

21. Esther Mumford, Interview with Bertha Pitts Campbell, April 23, 1975, Washington State Oral History Project, Washington State Archives, Olympia, WA. Printed excerpts from this interview at www.historylink.org Biographies (Accessed March 2011).
22. Ethelyn Miller Hartwich, "Race Freedom Had An Early Start in Seattle," *Seattle Post Intelligencer*, April 25th, 1965.
23. "Are We Different," *Racial Equality Bulletin* (April, 1952).
24. Alice Walker, *In Search of Our Mother's Gardens: Womanist Prose*, (San Diego: Harcourt, Brace, Jovanovich, 1983).
25. Layli Phillips, *The Womanist Reader* (New York: Routledge, 2009) xx-xxi.
26. Glazer and Slater, *Unequal Colleagues*, p. 242.
27. Tom Brokaw, *The Greatest Generation* (New York: Random House, 1998).
28. Carol Gilligan, "In a Different Voice: Women's Conceptions of Self and of Morality," *Harvard Educational Review* 47 (November 1977) 481-517.
29. Just as the CFRE had some male members; some women participated in these organizations as well. The difference lies in the proportions and leadership. The CFRE had a female majority both in its membership and in its core leadership.
30. Richard Hofstadter, *The Age of Reform: From Bryan to F. D. R.* (New York: Vintage Books, 1955). This is an early classic historical work on the Progressive Era and Hofstadter's framing of the Progressive issues and the periods of its active influence are shared widely among historians though they may differ on the success and character of the movement.
31. Leonard Sweet, "The Modernization of Protestant Religion in America," in David Lotz ed. *Altered Landscapes: Christianity in America 1935-1985*. (Grand Rapids: Eerdmans, 1989) 19-41.

32. Albert J. Raboteau, "The Black Church: Continuity within Change, in David Lotz ed. *Altered Landscapes: Christianity in America 1935-1985.* (Grand Rapids: Eerdmans, 1989) 77-91. Anthony Pinn, *Varieties of African American Religion* (Minneapolis: Fortress Press, 1998) also discusses these developments in depth.
33. Hofstadter, in *The Age of Reform* argues that none of these really changed the way local government worked because the political machines soon learned to manipulate these tools for their own benefit. p. 247.
34. Hofstadter, p. 248. This was not only a more business-like model, but one regarded as fair and impartial, and making use of people with expertise in city problems rather than people working for particular personal interests.
35. Mary Lease, The *Problem of Civilization Solved* (Chicago, 1895) p. 17. Quoted in Hofstadter, p. 83.
36. Hofstadter, *The Age of Reform,* p. 8-10.
37. Biblical expressions of this theology can be most clearly seen in the book of Proverbs in the Hebrew Scriptures. The Reformation theologian John Calvin had more complicated views than those usually attributed to him, and would have warned them to be suspicious of this interpretation, but his more well-to-do followers found this simplistic view comforting. It assured them that they must deserve their wealth.
38. Gary Dorrien, *The Making of American Liberal Theology: Idealism, Realism, and Modernity,* 1900-1950. (Philadelphia: Westminster John Knox Press, 2003) p. 5-6.
39. Gary Dorrien, *The Making of American Liberal Theology: Idealism, Realism and Modernity* discusses both Mays and Thurman's thought in the context of the Social Gospel.
40. Paul Nagano, "Identity, Identification, and Initiative: Hebrews 11:23-28." in Roy Sano ed. *The Theologies of Asian Americans and Pacific Peoples: A Reader* (Berkeley: Asian

Center for Theology and Strategies, 1976) p. 223-4

41. A. C. Ubalde, Jr., "Church and Society," in Roy Sano ed. *The Theologies of Asian Americans and Pacific Peoples: A Reader* (Berkeley: Asian Center for Theology and Strategies, 1976) p. 177.
42. Dale E. Soden, *The Reverend Mark Matthews: An Activist in the Progressive Era*. (Seattle: University of Washington Press, 2001).
43. Mark Matthews, "The Conscienceless Man," *Sermonettes* Jan.-July 1909. Quoted in Soden, p. 59.
44. Matthews Scrapbook #8, quoted in Soden p. 75.
45. Soden p. 91-92
46. Mary E. Hopper and E. Harriet Gibson, "A Frontier of the Spirit" [a 1953 pamphlet Printed with a 1963 eulogy of Fred Shorter Church of the People], Seattle Records 1206-7 Box 1 1937-1953, University of Washington Library Special Collections.

    The Church of the People's Statement of Faith read as follows:

    "We are a fellowship dedicated to the consummation of the new society as portrayed in the teachings of Jesus. We believe in the principles of that society, namely reverence for personality, and the unity of the human family, cannot be fulfilled in a social order based on profit, but only in a cooperative democracy organized for the common good and in which production is for the common need. We pledge ourselves to strive for the realization of that ideal.

    As guides to life and conduct we accept and assert the supremacy of conscience; intellectual integrity; freedom of speech and assemblage; and the equality of all men irrespective of race, color, or creed. For inspiration we look to Jesus of Nazareth and all great prophets of Love and justice."

    The Church of the People espoused an active, engaged

Christian spirituality, and while they had a specific set of beliefs, were more inclined to understand Christianity as a way of life rather than simply a creed.

47. *The New Religious Frontier*, February 8, 1940. Church of the People Records, University of Washington Library, Special Collections. The *New Religious Frontier* also reprinted the Roman Catholic Bishops' statement, "The Church and the Social Order," February 15, 1940.
48. Federal Council of Churches of Christ, "The Church and Race Relations," March 1946. FCC Department of Race Relations, Record Group 18 Box 56 ff 14. Presbyterian Historical Society, Philadelphia, PA.
49. Federal Council of Churches of Christ, "The Church and Race Relations," p. 3
50. National Baptist Denominational response to the Federal Council of Churches statement "The Church and Race Relations," March 1946. FCC Department of Race Relations, Record Group 18 Box 56 ff 14. Presbyterian Historical Society, Philadelphia, PA.
51. "Interview with Walter Rauschenbusch," *Methodist Review* (April 1914) p. 258.
52. Only a few West Coast examples of these attempts exist. The Pentecostal revivals in Azusa Street in Los Angeles in 1906 were front-page news because they were integrated. The racial integration of the Pentecostal movement did not last long and the movement divided by race in the 1920s. Howard Thurman's Church for All People in San Francisco, and the South Berkeley Community Church started by the Congregationalists in Berkeley near Oakland both began in the early 1940s and though both still exist, they had their strongest days in the 1940s and 1950s when integration appealed to a growing number of well educated middle class black and Caucasian professionals.
53. Its membership form stated: "The Purpose of this organi-

zation, expressed briefly, is to promote and extend the Christian religion in Seattle through cooperative action on behalf of member bodies in such fields of effort as Christian Education, evangelism, temperance, comity, and public affairs." Minutes of the Executive Committee, Nov. 1939. Church Council of Greater Seattle Records, University of Washington Library, Special Collections. Acc. no. 13558-007 Box 1 of 50, ff 16.

54. Servando Halili Jr., "Visualizing the New Empire: Race and Gender Images and the American Colonization of the Philippines." The rhetoric of the other as childlike, brown or dark, ignorant, and needing guidance appears in American missionary literature in general. Mexicans, Native Americans, Pacific Islanders, and South Asians as well as Africans and African Americans shared this general attitude on the part of white missionaries.
55. Dorothy B. Fujita-Rony, *American Workers, Colonial Power: Philippine Seattle and the Transpacific West, 1919-1941.* p.156.

Notes for Conclusion

1. Sawyer, *Black Ecumenism*, p. 112.
2. Reinhold Niebuhr, *The Irony of American History* (Chicago: University of Chicago Press, 1952) p. 10.
3. Archie Smith, Jr., *The Relational Self*, p. 33.
4. In thinking about these concluding reflections, I am grateful for two conversations, one with Joanne Braxton, Professor of English and the Humanities at the College of William and Mary and the other with Rev. Gayle "Asali" Dickson, a colleague in the ministry of the United Church of Christ and former Seattle Black Panther Party member.

Index

Circle Books

Circle is a symbol of infinity and unity. It's part of a growing list of imprints, including o-books.net and zero-books.net.

Circle Books aims to publish books in Christian spirituality that are fresh, accessible, and stimulating.

Our books are available in all good English language bookstores worldwide. If you can't find the book on the shelves, then ask your bookstore to order it for you, quoting the ISBN and title. Or, you can order online—all major online retail sites carry our titles.

To see our list of titles, please view www.Circle-Books.com, growing by 80 titles per year.

Authors can learn more about our proposal process by going to our website and clicking on Your Company > Submissions.

We define Christian spirituality as the relationship between the self and its sense of the transcendent or sacred, which issues in literary and artistic expression, community, social activism, and practices. A wide range of disciplines within the field of religious studies can be called upon, including history, narrative studies, philosophy, theology, sociology, and psychology. Interfaith in approach, Circle Books fosters creative dialogue with non-Christian traditions.

And tune into MySpiritRadio.com for our book review radio show, hosted by June-Elleni Laine, where you can listen to authors discussing their books.

MySpiritRadio